Bishop Levi S. Ives confirming students at St. Mary's, Raleigh. Oil portrait by James Hart, 1845. Courtesy of St. Mary's College, Raleigh, N.C.

Ambivalent Churchmen and Evangelical Churchwomen

The Religion of the Episcopal Elite in North Carolina, 1800–1860

Richard Rankin

University of South Carolina Press

Published in Columbia, South Carolina, by the
University of South Carolina Press

Manufactured in the United States of America

Library of Congress Cataloging-in-Publication Data

Rankin, Richard.
    Ambivalent churchmen and Evangelical churchwomen : the religion of
the Episcopal elite in North Carolina, 1800–1860 / Richard Rankin.
        p. cm.
    Includes bibliographical references and index.
    ISBN 0–87249–887–5 (alk. paper)
    1. Episcopal Church. Diocese of North Carolina—History—19th
century. 2. Anglican Communion—North Carolina—History—19th
century. 3. Evangelicalism—Episcopal Church—History—19th
century. 4. Women in the Anglican Communion—North Carolina—
History—19th century. 5. Spirituality—Episcopal Church—
History—19th century. 6. Episcopal Church—North Carolina—
Membership. I. Title.
BX5918.N8R36 1993
283'.756'09034—dc20   93-166

To Deneise and Isaac

In Memory of Julie

Contents

Tables

Preface

This is a study of how one group of North Carolina's upper class, Episcopalians, responded to powerful and alien forces of evangelical change during the years from 1800 to 1860. To speak of evangelicalism as an alien religious culture may seem startling to anyone familiar with the current historiography of religion in the Old South, which plainly demonstrates that evangelicalism was the dominant mode of religious expression in the region. It is true, nevertheless, that many antebellum southerners who came from non-evangelical backgrounds opted for different sorts of value systems, including Episcopalianism.

The Episcopal church actually was part of a religious tradition that antedated evangelicalism in North Carolina. Anglicanism had been established on a weak basis in the colony in the first years of the eighteenth century. Evangelicalism appeared fifty years later with the arrival of Shubal Stearns who initiated the New Light Baptist movement. The tremendous late-eighteenth-century growth of the Baptists and, later, the Methodists was the beginning of the rise of a new evangelical religious culture that would dominate North Carolina by the 1820s. Among certain members of the ruling class, however, another cultural tradition survived that was a lineal descendant of the old Anglican ethos. The traditional ethos of the gentry existed in creative tension with the new evangelical culture. The motive force for the restoration of the Episcopal church in the first two decades of the nineteenth century, and for the development of Episcopal piety for the first forty years of the nineteenth century, would be the interaction of traditional and evangelical culture.

Previous historiographical landmarks in the study of southern culture do not focus on Protestant Christianity within the upper class. Instead they concentrate either on the genteel class's ethic of honor or cult of reason, or on the lower middle class's evangelicalism. Although John C. Boles in his pioneering work *The Great Revival* studies the origins of southern evangelicalism, he pays small attention to questions of class and subculture. Donald G. Mathews in *Religion in the Old South* and Rhys Isaac in *The Transformation of Virginia* are keenly aware of class considerations; both argue that a new, austere, evangelical ethos that began among lower-class whites and blacks stood in contrast and opposition to the dominant culture of a self-aggrandizing, ostentatious gentry. Neither, however, directly examines the reverberations of the evangelical awakening within the upper class. Isaac closes his study in the late eighteenth century with lower-class evangelicals and upper-class squires coexisting uneasily in a culturally bipolarized world. Mathews takes a different scholarly approach as he focuses on the rise of the evangelicals and pays only brief attention to their aristocratic counterparts with his discussion of the evangelical Protestant Episcopal Church in Virginia.

Henry F. May and Bertram Wyatt-Brown devote more attention to nineteenth-century genteel culture than other scholars, but Protestantism is less central to their studies. May in *The Enlightenment in America* maintains that from 1815 to 1830 evangelical Christianity triumphed and converted upper- and middle-class southerners from various shades of rational religious thought that they had espoused earlier. According to him, this process assimilated the old aristocracy to the middle-class values of the evangelical masses. Unfortunately, since May concentrates primarily on the Enlightenment, he naturally presents only a suggestive sketch of the Christian conversion of the southern elite, without much elaboration. In "After the Enlightenment: A Prospectus" in *The Divided Heart: Essays on Protestantism and Enlightenment in America,* May offers a brief overview of the transition from the Age of Reason to the Romantic Age.

Wyatt-Brown in *Southern Honor* identifies a more primitive, nonreligious value system based on notions of honor as the controlling ethic in antebellum Southern society. According to him, "gentility" was a special upper-class variant of the ethic of honor in which "moral uprightness was coupled with high social position."

He argues that the evangelical awakening altered notions of gentility among the elite so that by the late antebellum period "piety" was included with older virtues that defined a Southern gentleman. Although *Southern Honor* does not explain why or how evangelicalism insinuated itself among the elite in the first place, a more recent essay, "Religion and the 'Civilizing Process' in the Early South, 1600–1860," in *Religion and American Politics: From the Colonial Period to the 1980s* does scrutinize the interplay between southern honor and evangelicalism and is interested in many of the same cultural phenomena as this work.

The restoration of the church among North Carolina Episcopalians from 1800 to 1860 provides one model of cultural change in the Old South that offers answers to many of the questions that historical scholarship and curiosity raise concerning the effect of evangelicalism on upper-class culture. This book is a synthesis of the work of the aforementioned scholars at least to the extent that it aims to interrelate important southern values such as evangelicalism, Enlightenment thought, and southern honor as they found expression in the lives of North Carolina Episcopalians. The essay rests upon the assumption that North Carolina Episcopalians were members of an upper class faced with personal decisions concerning whether to adhere to traditional cultural norms or to choose new evangelical ones in the first half of the nineteenth century.

The relationship of this work to the important and growing body of historical literature on the plantation system is far more ambiguous. Only further studies that include both nonchurched planters and those from other Christian denominations will determine whether Eugene Genovese is right in contending that a premodern patriarchy was characteristic of southern planters, or, whether, instead, James Oakes is correct in saying that the slave-holding class was divided into a number of factions which, on the whole, were moving "away from paternalism and toward an acceptance of liberal democracy and free-market commercialism." My own hunch is that the Episcopalians who restored North Carolina's church in the early nineteenth century were part of that most conservative group of planters who reacted against democratic forces and clung to an older world view. Oakes describes them as "Masters of Tradition." I would argue, however, that the original threat to patriarchy was family dynamics—and not radical northern reform. The evangelical revival heightened Episcopal men's concern for domes-

tic patriarchy fifteen years before Nat Turner and New England abolitionism endangered planter patriarchy.

The relationship between masters, slaves, and religion does not
figure prominently in this study because Episcopal slave owners seldom discussed such matters and, when they did, the discussion was
impersonal and detached. A few Episcopal planters established
plantation chapels with missionary work among their slaves, but
they have left no evidence that their slaves' Christianity affected
them personally. Similarly, Steven M. Stowe in *Intimacy and Power
in the Old South* finds planter correspondence almost totally ignor-
ing the lives of slaves. Stowe concludes that his findings support the
work of other students of black history "who have found an essential cultural division between the races." If so, then the notion of
planter patriarchy is seriously weakened. At least with respect to
Episcopalians, however, there is another, equally plausible explanation. The failure to discuss the religious lives of their slaves may
simply reflect Episcopal men's own uneasiness with the subject of
Christianity.

Although it is not necessary at this juncture to discuss the specific characteristics of gentility, it is important to question whether
it is accurate to attribute gentility to Episcopalians as a group. Perhaps the most convincing proof for Episcopal gentility is the fact
that contemporaries of all ranks and classes described Episcopalians as "genteel." It is also significant that Episcopalians participated in activities that nineteenth-century observers and recent
historians have identified as "aristocratic" or "genteel." Finally,
when judged against antebellum North Carolina standards, the
Episcopalians referred to in the text displayed such an obvious
measure of political, economic, social, and educational preemi-
nence that it must be apparent that they formed a genteel elite. Jane
Turner Censer in her study of North Carolina's great antebellum
planter families found that nearly 60 percent of all great planters,
those who owned more than seventy slaves, were attached to the
Episcopal church. The Episcopalians cited in this work appear to
be distinguished representatives of a church whose members were
recognized for their wealth, power, and refinement.

The research on antebellum Episcopalianism comes from a wide
variety of sources that include private papers, journals, newspapers, autobiographies, local church records, diocesan records, and
secondary literature. From this wide canvass, however, two partic-

ular types of records deserve special mention because they figure so prominently in the project: membership lists contained in parish registers and private letters. It is only a slight exaggeration to say that this book is an extended effort to explain why women made up the overwhelming majority of Episcopal communicants as recorded in parish registers. Private letters provided the most effective way to answer that question and to chart the development of Episcopal religious belief over time.

Since this study relies so heavily on private papers, it exhibits all the strengths and weaknesses that characterize most intellectual history. The conclusions reached are based upon a wide and thorough reading of a substantial body of personal papers. These include the vast majority of the great private letter collections from antebellum North Carolina. When the evidence seemed incomplete or problematic, conclusions have been qualified. But when similar patterns of action and belief recurred with frequency and regularity in different sets of private papers, I felt justified in drawing conclusions. A critical audience is left to judge whether the interpretations are credible.

I would like to conclude on a note of gratitude to all those who have helped me with this project. The staffs of the North Carolina Division of Archives and History, the Southern Historical Collection at the University of North Carolina, Perkins Library at Duke University, and Everett Library at Queens College have assisted me in countless ways. The North Caroliniana Society supported me with two generous Archie K. Davis Scholarships. Professor Bill Powell has offered help and encouragement on this and other projects throughout my career. It is impossible to calculate his impact on the historical craft in North Carolina. Many thanks to Professor John K. Nelson and Associate Professor Harry L. Watson who provided valuable criticism and editing of work that was the precursor to this book.

My greatest intellectual debt goes to my adviser and mentor, Professor Donald G. Mathews, who challenged me as a graduate student and whose good influence pervades my scholarship. In addition to the interpretive skills he taught me, Don Mathews contributed keen editing and trenchant criticism of my work. Queens College gave me the opportunity to help support my family, and to teach and to learn the subject that I love. Assistant Professor Michael Eldridge introduced me to Samuel S. Hill, Jr., who gave timely, invaluable advice on potential publishers. Warren Slesinger at the University of South Carolina Press has been a marvelous person with whom to work. Professor Robert Calhoon and another reader for the press gave insightful criticism that was enormously helpful in revising my manuscript. My wife has supported me financially, emotionally, and in every other conceivable way. As a practicing pastoral psychotherapist, her theoretical knowledge, particularly regarding family systems, informs my work.

Finally, as a Protestant Christian in the twentieth century, with all the intellectual comfort and, paradoxically, the intellectual questioning that my faith produces, I thank God for giving me the talent and fortitude to complete this labor. I take full responsibility for the book's scholarship, conclusions, and many shortcomings.

Abbreviations

DUA Manuscript Collections, Perkins Library, Duke University, Durham, N.C.

HMPEC *Historical Magazine of the Protestant Episcopal Church*

LCFHS Lower Cape Fear Historical Society, Wilmington, N.C.

NCC North Carolina Collection, University of North Carolina Library, Chapel Hill, N.C.

NCDAH North Carolina Department of Archives and History, Raleigh, N.C.

NCDJ *North Carolina Diocesan Journal*

NCHR *North Carolina Historical Review*

PECA Protestant Episcopal Church Archives, Austin, Tex.

SHC Southern Historical Collection, Wilson Library, University of North Carolina, Chapel Hill, N.C.

UNCA University of North Carolina Archives, Wilson Library, University of North Carolina, Chapel Hill, N.C.

USoA Special Collections & Archives, Jessie Ball DuPont Library, University of the South, Sewanee, Tenn.

Ambivalent Churchmen and
Evangelical Churchwomen

Introduction:
Episcopal Faith and Feeling in an Age of Reason and Dying Orthodoxy, 1760–1805

The history of the development of Episcopal piety and the restoration of the church in nineteenth-century North Carolina is the story of the Episcopal response to the forces of evangelical change. Because the Episcopal revival, however, brought to life a church and a faith with a colonial heritage, any account of the antebellum Episcopal church must begin with the downfall of its colonial predecessor, the Church of England, at a time well before the evangelical awakening resurrected Episcopalianism.

The most accurate way to think of the Anglican church's presence in colonial North Carolina is not as a pervasive and dominating established church, but as a patchwork of separate local Anglican churches whose spheres of influence were limited to a number of locales. The church was strongest in the coastal plain, and especially in the colony's three richest and most sophisticated societies around the ports of Edenton, Newbern, and Wilmington/Brunswick. In the interior of the colony, the church was feeble and virtually nonexistent in many places, and North Carolina had, as a whole, the weakest Anglican establishment in North America.[1]

Many, if not most, of the colony's well-to-do families, nevertheless, belonged to the established church. Anglican families provided the colony with a cadre of native leaders who controlled local vestries and provincial politics. In 1771 forty-five North Carolina

1

gentlemen sent a recommendation to the royal governor on behalf of a local Anglican minister that indicates the intimate connection between the gentry and the Church of England. Among the signers were ten royal councilors, a future signer of the Declaration of Independence, three future governors of the state, and a constellation of the most powerful politicians and prosperous merchants and planters in the colony. Despite all its weaknesses, the Anglican faith was a significant element in upper-class culture in late colonial North Carolina.[2]

A list of pew renters at St. James's, Wilmington, in 1770 also reveals the wealth and prestige of churchmen in the colony's richest region and suggests the character of Anglican congregations in other strong churches in Newbern, Edenton, and Brunswick. Eight active or former royal councilors rented pews in St. James's. The forty-eight pew renters for whom slave holdings can be determined owned an average of 19.4 slave taxables. George Moore (pew 7), son of "King Roger" of Orton plantation, owned 118. William Dry (pew 3) held 104 black taxables as chattel. Between them the forty-eight pew renters accounted for nearly half of all the slave taxables listed in prosperous New Hanover county's 1767 tax list.

Certain characteristics defined the Anglican elite as members of the gentry and distinguished them from social inferiors. The occupation of the male head of household was one important factor. The gentry included not only the families of planters, but also of prosperous merchants, doctors, lawyers, and some clergymen. Almost without exception, even those members of the upper class whose primary occupation was not planting also owned slaves and plantations. To be a gentleman or a lady meant to have a personal stake in the slave economy. Although there was never a minimum requirement, and other outstanding accomplishments might compensate for a lack of human chattel, most gentlemen owned twenty or more slaves; it was not at all uncommon for an individual to own more than fifty.

The ownership of land and slaves was a fundamental criterion for inclusion in the upper class, but other attributes such as education, sociability, and refinement were also important. Indeed, to ignore some of the more subtle traits of the gentry, such as their dress, manner of conversation, and physical bearing, is to ignore signals obvious to any contemporary observer. When an individual walked into the courthouse in Edenton or rode a horse up to the tavern in a rural hamlet in Warren County, spectators, even strangers, recognized the nuances of attire, style, and demeanor that signaled unmistakably whether an individual was a gentleperson. Gentility was a conspicuous lifestyle. Its basis surely rested in acquired wealth, but it also involved a sophisticated and distinct ethos related to but separate from the pervasive habits and assumptions of the larger culture.

The orthodox faith of the Anglican gentry differed radically from the orthodox faith of lower-class evangelicals, or new lights, who had already become a significant force on the religious scene in North Carolina by the 1760s. New lights anxiously sought a sensible experience of conversion, which they understood to be a spiritual rebirth that indicated that God had rescued them from sin and death. Evangelicals believed that a sudden conversion ensured personal salvation. This shared experience of rebirth became a strong social bond that united evangelicals into tightly knit fellowships. Evangelicals also understood that the spiritual rebirth instantaneously endowed the convert with a new set of holy affections that allowed the individual to lead a life of personal sanctity henceforth.

In contrast, Anglicans believed salvation was a birthright conferred by the church's ceremony of infant baptism. The spiritual status of Anglicans was fixed in infancy, not subject to change in adulthood as a result of evangelical conversion. Anglicans understood the acquisition of personal sanctity, or sanctification, to be a gradual and life-long process, or a "humble walk," to use their own words, not an instantaneous change accompanying the new birth. As a result, while Anglicans did not entirely reject the possibility of a physical experience of conversion, they usually relied on other means, including reason, prayer, and liturgy, to effect salvation.

Anglicans understood religious affections to be a natural endowment that only needed to be cultivated within the church to come to fruition, not a supernatural quality that was transplanted at the moment of conversion as for evangelicals. Churchpeople emphasized the benevolence and providence of God, not God's wrath and judgment. Their fundamental religious attitude was one of implicit trust, not evangelical doubt antecedent to conversion. Anglican orthodoxy reassured the gentry that, despite their natural tendency toward sin, they were forgiven. Evangelical orthodoxy warned

3

sinners that unless they underwent a sensible experience of conversion, they were damned.[3]

The Anglican faith also appealed to the gentry because it refrained from the emotional excesses assumed to be characteristic of the lower classes—and of evangelicalism. Anglican men may well have associated the emotionalism and humility of the evangelicals with effeminacy.[4] One Episcopal minister implied as much when he contrasted evangelicalism with "the manly, mas[c]uline, voice of Orthodoxy."[5] Anglicanism tended to be an emotionally restrained religion in which reason sought to subdue and to transform unruly emotions or "passions." A South Carolina Anglican preacher warned, "Suffer not your *Passions to be moved,* but as your *Minds are instructed;* And run not away with the agreeable Voice of the *Preacher* in your Ears, for the *Soundness of his Doctrine* in your Understandings."[6]

According to one Episcopal minister of the Revolutionary War generation, the Anglican's spiritual heirs had been spared the Presbyterian affinity for placing "Religion in a certain movement of the passions, & some religious affections for a time."[7] Anglicans relied on the head to control the heart in religion. Faith for the adult often simply involved intellectual assent to orthodox doctrine as taught by the church. Anglican faith was genuine, nevertheless. The religious language of their wills and letters was largely formulaic. But their formulas had profound meaning and were the essence, or the distillation, of the entire corpus of beliefs to which they ascribed.

Anglican doctrine and practice buttressed the elite's notions of proper social arrangements. The hierarchical nature of the Anglican church, in fact, paralleled the gentry's assumptions concerning proper social order. For Anglicans, the older world view inherited from feudal Europe remained alive. The upper-class husband was a patriarch who dominated his wife, his children, and his slaves. Gentlemen and ladies were also, by definition, elitists who regarded themselves as socially superior to those of more common estates. And people of the lower ranks, by and large, concurred with these assumptions and expressed an appropriate attitude of deference. Anglican orthodoxy declared that God, in His wisdom and beneficence, had ordained that the gentry would rule this stable, organic society.

Although Anglican orthodoxy was a major source of genteel culture, other non-Christian values also played important roles in de-

4

termining upper-class behavior in the late colonial era. Specifically, ethics of honor and fashion controlled the actions of Anglican gentlemen and ladies. The male elite accepted a special genteel version of the code of honor, a primitive ethical system that operated in all ranks of society. Men of honor were bound together by a shared system of values that recognized personal valor, hospitality, and risk taking as its most respected male attributes. These men sought public approval and esteem through demonstrations of manliness, which included the prescribed use of violence.

The ultimate solution to a dispute between gentlemen of "touchy honor" was the ritualized combat of the code duello.[8] Duels preserved "honor" while still restraining the passions through a system of rules and procedures. Anglican gentlemen were men of honor who would have found the humility and resignation of evangelicals particularly objectionable because it appeared cowardly. In the late colonial era, one Cape Fear Anglican criticized a Wilmington doctor, not because he issued numerous challenges to mortal combat, but because he was too cowardly to consummate the duels.

Genteel women accepted, and by so doing encouraged, the male code of honor, but they did not participate in it themselves. Instead, standards of fashion served as the controlling ethic that not only determined their behavior, but also established strong bonds among ladies. The preeminent qualities of fashionable ladies were stylishness in dress, conversational skills, and polite accomplishments like the ability to dance; balls were a favorite form of entertainment. There they visited with their female friends and flirted and bantered with their male admirers. There they twirled, and laughed, and trysted—all the things they could not do in church or the isolation of their homes. The public life of women consisted of public entertainment in which beauty and social grace were the basis for emotional fulfillment and social approval.

Although the codes of honor and fashion operated on two different sets of values reflecting upper-class gender conventions, public approval was at the heart of both codes. The opinions of other ladies decided whether or not a peer was fashionable. Their smiles of approval or frowns of displeasure rendered a final verdict on acceptable behavior.

Historian Elizabeth Fox-Genovese argues that women of the Old South generally renounced the code of fashion as they matured and became married women in charge of households. Among Anglican wives of the colonial period, however, the code of fashion continued to be influential, to a greater or lesser extent, throughout upper-class women's lives. Certainly, domestic responsibilities required a practicality and a seriousness that competed with the gay life of fashion, but married life seldom completely extinguished the female ethic of fashion anymore than it did the male code of honor. Sociability, attire, and polite accomplishments, such as dancing, remained important to the self-understanding of Anglican ladies even in old age.

In addition to honor and fashion, another principle that exerted a profound influence over genteel behavior during the late colonial era was reason. The exaltation of human reason had begun after the discoveries of Sir Isaac Newton had suggested the fundamental orderliness, regularity, and reasonableness inherent in nature. According to Newton, human beings could understand the beneficent character of the universe and the Creator using the faculty of reason. By 1750 the middle and upper classes in England and America had absorbed many of the ideas of Newton, John Locke, and other theoreticians whose rationalism ushered in the age known as the Enlightenment.

Reason soon assumed such an authority in the lives of Englishmen and colonials that it began to challenge the reliability of traditional religious authority as the reasonableness of Christianity was called into question. In response, hundreds of seventeenth- and eighteenth-century Anglican theologians published natural theologies that sought to reconcile faith and reason. These apologetics relied on the same presuppositions that underlay the scientific method and purported to demonstrate the intellectual soundness of Christianity. In its simplest form, the fundamental argument employed by the natural theologians was a syllogism beginning with the premise that nature everywhere exhibits elements of purpose and design. The second premise was that design must always be the product of a designer. The conclusion was that nature is the product of a grand designer, God. Natural theologies were intended initially not to undermine but to supplement revealed religion and to reassure the orthodox of the reasonableness of their faith by demonstrating the existence of God.

Although appeal to nature began as a Christian apology to bolster orthodoxy, it eventually became a substitute for revealed religion. By the 1760s Anglicans adopted a whole range of differing religious opinions, which included questioning the divinity of Christ. Cornelius Harnett, a vestryman in St. James's, Wilmington, exemplified this enlightened outlook. His purchase of a book on the "Religion of Nature" in 1777 reflected an interest that was expressed in his epitaph, which was borrowed from the English Deist Alexander Pope:

> Slave to no sect he took no private road,
> But looked through nature up to natures' God[.]

Embracing the religion of Enlightenment led individuals like Harnett quietly to reject many of the old doctrines of the church as outmoded in the new age, while they continued to support the church as a valued source of morality and social order. Enlightenment thinkers actually had much in common with the orthodox, even apart from culture and class: they believed in the existence of God; they believed God should be worshipped; and they believed in eternal life. They also shared with other members of the gentry a common revulsion at religious enthusiasm and the emotionalism of the evangelicals. Enlightenment religionists of all varieties believed that the unbridled passions had no place in religion. Religious passion or enthusiasm tended to hinder the operation of right reason, thus preventing the acquisition of an accurate knowledge of the true character of God.

The various values that were interwoven to form the fabric of genteel ethics in late colonial North Carolina, including reason, honor, fashion, and orthodoxy, all tended to emphasize and reinforce the importance of self-control. Charles Pettigrew, an Episcopal minister, gave the following advice to his son some thirty years after the close of the colonial period, but his remarks reflected the Anglican elite's traditional emphasis on self-control: "I must therefore insist on the necessity of your acquiring happy tempors & Dispositions,—& entire self command. In order to do this, keep your passions alway[s] down, & cool; this will give you time for thought & deliberation."[9]

Anglican self-control, of course, did not mean a complete denial of the importance of feeling. Instead, Anglicans distinguished between acceptable emotions, or "affections," and excessive ones, or "passions." They expressed specific feelings through certain culturally sanctioned forms of behavior. Anglican morality was never so strict as to proscribe amusements such as card playing, drinking, horse racing, theatergoing, and dancing, all of which provided permissible emotional outlets. Anglicans, nevertheless, constantly monitored themselves to ensure that their behavior never transgressed the bounds of propriety.

The American Revolution interrupted the colonial routines of Anglican worship and genteel life as attention shifted to the all-consuming demands of politics and war. The Revolution also accelerated social, economic, and ideological change that was undermining the traditional social order and replacing it with one that emphasized individualism as well as social and economic mobility. The war may also have unleashed energies that eventually would create new patterns of religious expression among the elite, but if so, such changes were imperceptible at the outset. The war's effect on the Anglican church, however, was immediate and permanent. From the beginning, the break with England called into question the future of the established church, and the final resolution of the contest dealt a crippling blow to genteel religion.

For Anglicans the most fundamental formal change brought by the Revolution was the abolition of a state-supported church by the new state constitution of 1776. Colonial law had provided for support of established ministers and maintenance of Anglican church property through a county poll tax. The new constitution placed all organized religion on the basis of the voluntary support of believers. All Anglican churches and glebes were turned over to local vestries. Because its popular base had been so weak in colonial North Carolina, the church was not able to support itself after the war.

Old churchpeople displayed a marked inability to adjust to the essential demands of religious voluntarism now that the fervor of piety instead of the force of law was the foundation of the church. The Anglican laity had always been held together as much by social and political considerations as by spiritual bonds. Moreover, when the legal, political, and social adhesive was removed from the old church, attempts to resurrect it risked the imputation of disloyalty to the Revolution.

The Protestant Episcopal church that would succeed the Anglican was almost stillborn. Traditional worship in most old Anglican churches or chapels of ease simply ceased except where Baptists occupied the buildings. Some sporadic efforts to keep the old faith alive were attempted during the 1780s, most notably among what remained of the state's three strongest congregations in the ports of Edenton, Wilmington, and Newbern. The case of Edenton is instructive: there forty townsmen, who had been supporters of St. Paul's church before the war, signed a subscription list on 1 May 1778 and pledged money to support the Rev. Charles Pettigrew in his ongoing work as clergyman to the parish. Characteristically, donations fell far short of pledges.[10]

Despite this disappointment neither Pettigrew nor a number of the churchmen were yet ready to abandon the old Episcopal forms. In 1783 they tried again, but this time only twenty-one men signed the list, which included a preamble that explained the need for a local church.[11] The anonymous author provided two major arguments. The first was an "appeal to consensus," a standard device of natural theologians attempting to prove the rationality of their religion. Since all civilized nations on the face of the globe worshipped God in "social and public Adoration," the people of Edenton should feel the need to conform to the religious practice of Western culture—that is, if they wished to remain "civilized."

Secondly, worship fostered the civic stability necessary to protect civil life and property. The church, through its warning of divine judgment after death, theoretically guaranteed civilization by scaring people into lawfulness. The preamble set forth only these two explanations of the need for St. Paul's; it gave no other apology. God was referred to as "the Supreme Governor of the Universe" with no references to the other members of the trinity.[12] All in all, the preamble was a rather cold, formal, and unexciting rationale for the need for public worship, one that befitted enlightened and reserved men who feared passion in religion and remained aloof from the social bonding of an evangelical faith.

The preamble persuaded few, if any, people. The vast majority of Edenton churchmen, by reneging on their subscriptions a second time, prompted Charles Pettigrew to press them for payment in May 1785. He was unsuccessful. Shortly thereafter, he moved across the Albemarle Sound and settled on his farm at Lake Phelps. If Edenton would not support an Episcopal minister on a full-time basis, he had better things to do and places to be.[13]

Down the coast in Newbern another old Anglican congregation, Christ's Church, also struggled with a new identity. In 1787 the leading men of Newbern petitioned the legislature to permit them to sell the church's rectory and use the proceeds to build a school-house, a proposal that suggested the importance of the Episcopal church in their new order. Two years later, however, Newbern town leaders again appealed to the general assembly to incorporate Christ's Church so that old bequests and donations made to the church could be legally appropriated for the use of the local church. From this action it was obvious that at least a few people were still supporting the Old Church.

Unlike Edenton and Newbern, a portion of the townspeople of Wilmington, including a number from the old ruling elite, were ready to renounce the Episcopal Church entirely and form a Protestant Presbyterian Church. Prejudice against the English-tainted Episcopal church may explain this departure from traditional modes. In 1785 one-fourth of Wilmington's white population asked the general assembly to incorporate a Presbyterian church.

The group proposing a Presbyterian church contained a significant number of the few surviving members of the old colonial church. Archibald MacLaine, a member of St. James's, Episcopal, in Wilmington who introduced the bill of incorporation into the legislature, seemed a natural choice since his father was a Presbyterian divine in Ireland. But further elaboration is needed to explain why other respectable churchpeople sought a new denomination.

The Presbyterian church had long possessed a respectability in North Carolina that had been conceded even by the Anglicans. In colonial times, the royal government had made political concessions to Presbyterians that certainly reflected the growing numerical strength and political power of that group in the western part of the state. These concessions were also tacit recognition that Presbyterians were more socially acceptable to the Anglicans than any of the other denominations, with the exception of the small group of Moravians around Salem.

Despite differences in the Episcopal liturgy and the Presbyterian service, worship in both churches was performed with a sense of decorum and restraint absent in the more expressive evangelical setting. In Wilmington after the war, therefore, there was a certain logic in the choice of the Presbyterian church as the Anglican successor. But the Wilmingtonians never implemented the new scheme outlined in the petition, and a Presbyterian church was not raised in the seaport until 1818. In 1787 it may have been a victim of a general social dislocation affecting all institutions in the wake of

10

the war or of the more narrow problem arising from the new voluntary basis of church support.

Although the Presbyterian church was aborted, the local elite made subsequent attempts to reorganize a church in Wilmington. In 1786 town commissioners petitioned the general assembly for state support for a local church since "the Inhabitants are generally without any solemnization of public Worship, to their great regret and to the reproach of the Town." The commissioners proposed that a tax bill be passed "if it may be done consistently with the Constitution," otherwise a voluntary subscription would be raised.[14]

Townspeople had also experienced difficulty renovating dilapidated St. James's because of a legal complication involving the ownership of pews. A number of the old colonial churchmen, who owned their pews outright instead of renting, refused to assist with repairs. The commissioners implored the legislature to compel the pew owners either to help with the cost of improvements or sell their pews. Unfortunately for those who wanted to revive religion in Wilmington, the legislature tabled the bill along with a similar proposal in 1788. These attempts do indicate, however, that backing for a church, and probably an Episcopal church, was never completely extinguished in the 1780s.

Episcopal worship in the piedmont during the 1780s was just as infrequent as in the coastal plain. In Hillsboro, one signer of the Declaration, two future United States Supreme Court justices, and four other distinguished men formed a board of trustees that was more successful in founding a noted academy than it was in supporting Episcopal worship.[15] In nearby Granville County in 1788, Episcopalians in the vicinity of St. John's, Williamsborough, had a worship service once a month conducted by an Episcopal minister. There was also an Episcopal minister in Lincoln County who pastored a combined Lutheran and Episcopal congregation. Almost everywhere else in North Carolina, the Episcopal church seems to have disappeared completely.

Given the virtual extinction of local Episcopal worship, it is not surprising that the attempt in the 1790s to organize the Diocese of North Carolina was so feeble. The initial impetus for reorganization came from out of state as part of a broader effort by Episcopalians in the Middle Atlantic states to revive the church on a national basis. Bishop William White of Pennsylvania asked Gov. Samuel Johnston of Edenton about prospects for reconstituting the

11

church in North Carolina. Johnston forwarded the inquiry to Pettigrew who contacted the handful of Episcopal ministers about the possibility of a state convention, and these clergymen spearheaded the effort.

The resulting three meetings, two in 1790 and one in 1793, were so sparsely attended that they had to be dismissed before any business could be conducted. Undaunted by these failures, the six delegates who attended the third convention sent a circular letter to each county urging them to choose a vestry and select delegates to yet another meeting in the spring.

In May 1794 nine clergymen and a dozen laymen gathered at another convention in Tarboro. The laymen in attendance resided in various eastern North Carolina locales, although one came from distant Lincoln County in the piedmont. The convention apparently succeeded in accomplishing one major goal by nominating Charles Pettigrew as Bishop, but the Albemarle planter never was moved to claim his consecration by traveling to a general convention of the new Protestant Episcopal church. Even if he had, Pettigrew lacked the ability to create single-handedly an Episcopal diocese where none existed.

Without adequate lay support the church was doomed. Certainly the discouraged Pettigrew and a fellow clergyman blamed the laity for their tepid piety. As Pettigrew commented, "such is the coldness, & such the inattention of those in general, who profess themselves members of our Church, with respect to things of a religious nature, that I am affraid [sic] your so laudible [sic] exertions to draw together a full convention, will not be Crown'd with suitable success. As you very Justly observe, they are not even *Lukewarm.*"[16]

The Episcopal laity had not deserted the old church for one of the newer evangelical sects. They remained nominal Episcopalians in a largely fictional church. In 1792 the leading Episcopalians of Edenton avowed their loyalty to orthodoxy as they assured a worried Charles Pettigrew that they had no intention of letting a Baptist minister preach in St. Paul's. Their pledge of Episcopal allegiance rang hollow, however, as the local church continued to languish. In 1796 Presbyterian missionaries, sent from the western part of the state to survey prospects in the coastal plain, noted that "respectable" Episcopalians still remained aloof from the lower-class Methodists and Baptists. The upper class may have been lukewarm but they were not turncoats.[17]

If the Episcopal clergy's critical comments formed the only basis for assuming that Episcopal lay apathy was responsible for the church's failure in the 1790s, one might suspect that the ministers were guilty of scapegoating. There is other evidence, however, that substantiates lay indifference. By 1790 powerful individuals in North Carolina, who were at least nominal Episcopalians, were capable of reviving the church. During that decade and the next, these same individuals would demonstrate their organizational skills and purpose to found academies and hire schoolmasters for their children in nearly all the important towns of central and eastern North Carolina; they could have reorganized their local churches just as well if they had wanted to do so.[18] In Newbern and Wilmington the local gentry hired Episcopal ministers as schoolmasters. In the absence of any sign of life in these local churches, it would appear that these Episcopal ministers served primarily as teachers of the community's young people, not preachers to their parents.[19]

Many Episcopal parents no longer bothered to have their children baptized, even when an Episcopal minister was available. As Nathaniel Blount, an Episcopal minister in Beaufort County, observed in an 1802 letter to Charles Pettigrew, "Perhaps not any part of the United States, where Infant Baptism was once so generally approved of & used, is at this time in a greater state of indiffirency [*sic*], or rather entire coldness about the matter, than the eastern part of this State." Along the Cape Fear, great planters like United States Supreme Court justice Alfred Moore and Hugh Waddell, men whose families had been attached in the colonial period to St. James's, Wilmington, and St. Philip's, Brunswick, never bothered to have their children baptized. In the Episcopal church these children stood outside the saving grace of the church; no one, however, seemed upset by the thought that they no longer even nominally belonged to the church.[20]

The Episcopal elite was becoming more and more detached from the church of their parents. Young Edward J. Mallett of Fayetteville, whose mother was an Episcopalian, was fourteen years old before he even entered a church. There was no church building in Fayetteville, the state's fourth largest town, until 1815. In later years, Mallett himself reflected on the curious priorities of the people of Fayetteville during his youth: "It is very singular that a prosperous, refined and intelligent people [in Fayetteville] should have provided themselves with a theatre first and churches afterward."[21]

13

Mallett's experience was but one example of the general unconcern toward organized religion among the upper class. For the genteel classes the Sabbath no longer included church. One old churchman described Sundays in Edenton in 1810 not as a time of religious instruction or worship, but as a time when families spent their day "in visits, in feasting or in idle and frivolous amusements," when individuals were "to be seen lounging in sunny piazzas, and loitering about public-rooms of offices and taverns," and when young ladies were busy "traversing the streets, wandering in flocks around the town, or jumbled together in discordant and heterogeneous groups in places of fashionable or customary resort!"[22]

James Iredell, Jr., future governor, and son of a United States Supreme Court justice who was a member of St. Paul's, Edenton, advised a college friend in 1808 to become a lawyer or a doctor, but not a clergyman. The ministry as a profession, according to Iredell, "leads neither to honour nor profit, & is productive of but little advantage to the community—Deplorable as this reflection may appear I believe it to be just & that the cause may be traced to the want of some established religion." For Iredell and most other Anglican descendants, little enthusiasm remained for the Protestant Episcopal Church.[23]

It would be easy to attribute Episcopal lay apathy to a pervasive upper-class irreligiousness, but circumstances in the 1790s suggest that the religious situation among the elite was much more subtle and complex. First of all, it is evident that some North Carolina Episcopalians—even if a minority—still subscribed to the old orthodoxy. A few men, after all, had organized the early conventions. The dozen or so lay delegates to the four conventions, who came from different locales mainly in eastern North Carolina, also represented a kind of proof of enduring Episcopal loyalties. Although in certain cases their presence may have been idiosyncratic, it is more likely that these individuals were representative of a larger body of Episcopalians who resided in the eastern part of the state; and, indeed, the lay participants at the convention may well have been acting as delegates for communities of Episcopalians back at their respective neighborhoods.

Also, in response to the circular sent in preparation for the fourth convention, a group of men in Person County attempted to form an Episcopal vestry as instructed. They also reported that a number of influential citizens in adjoining Warren and Granville counties still considered themselves churchmen.[24]

Other North Carolinians clearly displayed the marks of Episcopal orthodoxy in the 1790s and on into the new century. John S. West, successful Newbern merchant, sent a letter to Edenton in 1808 to inquire if anyone was interested "in the restoration of those admirable principles . . . [of the] Episcopal church." George Davis, member of an illustrious Brunswick County planter family associated during the colonial period with old St. Philip's, Brunswick, advised a grieving friend in 1810 to "take sanctuary from your afflictions in your God—and be certain that whosoever trusteth in him will never be confounded." Samuel Ashe, former governor and great Cape Fear planter, went to his grave in 1812 hoping for God's mercy "through the mediation of my blessed redeemer Jesus Christ."[25]

Even as late as 1818, Frances Roulhac, widow of a prosperous Bertie County planter, expressed herself in a traditional, orthodox way when she spoke of God's providence and of "those benevolent feelings" that it inspired. The religious sentiments of genteel persons like John S. West, George Davis, Frances Roulhac, Samuel Ashe, and others provide proof of survival of an older religious orientation that, though steadily dying off, remained alive among an indefinite number in the ruling class and their offspring. In the absence of an institutional church, orthodoxy's only hope for survival depended on a noninstitutional church composed of parents who might raise their children as an orthodox remnant.[26]

One of the most plausible explanations for the decline of Episcopal orthodoxy among the genteel class was the growing popularity of religious skepticism associated with the more radical Enlightenment thought of the American and French revolutionary eras. Enlightenment thinkers were nothing new in North Carolina's Episcopal church, and many churchmen in the 1790s resembled those who had filled the pews of the colonial church. In 1792 Nathaniel Allen, a prosperous merchant in Edenton who considered himself an Episcopalian, believed that God might still intervene providentially in human affairs under certain circumstances, but that God never did so, even in times of calamity, when man possessed natural means to avert disaster. According to Allen, if mankind failed to discover and to employ the natural means of obviating such disasters, God would not come to the rescue: providence was only available in the absence of all natural solutions. Allen was still orthodox enough not to completely abandon providence, but he had greatly circumscribed the divine will within a more scientific view of natural cause and effect.[27]

Mr. Justice James Iredell of Edenton deviated from orthodoxy in a slightly different direction. In 1796 he listened with great approval to two sermons in Philadelphia given by the eminent English scientist and Unitarian, Joseph Priestley. According to Iredell, Priestley's Unitarian beliefs only disagreed with "prevailing ones, in regard to some unessential doctrines, which may either be believed or disbelieved without prejudice to a sincere faith in the divine authority of the Christian Religion."[28]

While enlightened individuals like Allen and Iredell benignly neglected the church, a new generation of radicals viewed orthodoxy more contemptuously. The orthodox clergy were alarmed over the proliferation of this anti-Christian religious skepticism, which they dubbed "deism." Henry Patillo, a scholarly Presbyterian minister in Caswell County, in a broad definition that probably would have satisfied other orthodox clergymen too, divided deists into three separate groups: those who believed in one God, but denied the divine character of Jesus Christ; those who professed a natural religion, but denied the validity of revealed religion; and those who believed that reason was a sufficient guide to faith and practice and, therefore, denied the place of scripture as divine revelation.

Despite Patillo's tripartite division, however, all deists shared certain fundamental theological assumptions. They rejected special revelation and believed that reason enabled them to comprehend God as He continuously and generally manifests himself in nature. Deism was synonymous with natural theology that excluded special revelation.

If the observations of orthodox clergymen are any indication, deism was widespread among the state's elite. In 1795 Joseph Caldwell, Presbyterian clergyman and newly arrived professor of mathematics at the University of North Carolina, remarked that "in North Carolina, and particularly in the part east of Chapel Hill, every one believes that the way of rising to respectability is to disavow as often and as publicly as possible the leading doctrines of Scriptures. They are bugbears, very well fitted to scare the ignorant and weak into obedience to the laws; but the laws of morality and

16

honor are sufficient to regulate the conduct of men of letters and cultivated reason."[29]

Frederic Beasely, a North Carolina native at the College of New Jersey, and a future Episcopal clergyman, wrote his uncle Charles Pettigrew in 1797, "I now find the most ignorant men are the most positive in expressing their opinions and that thousands ridicule the Scriptures who have not the smallest acquaintance with them. This you know is too frequent in North Carolina—and even among those characters who should set examples to the rest and who are supposed to be the wisest."[30]

Deism took on a particularly menacing aspect for the clergy at this time as a result of the radical philosophies associated with the French Revolution and the publication of Thomas Paine's *Age of Reason*. The natural theology that shaped Paine's book differed not at all from the beliefs of earlier Christian apologists. Paine passionately believed in God and looked forward to an after-life. Where he diverged from his predecessors was in his scathing attack on revealed religion. According to him, the Bible "is a book of lies, wickedness, and blasphemy for what can be more blasphemous than to ascribe the wickedness of man to the orders of the Almighty?"[31]

The impact of Paine's thought on the North Carolina elite is difficult to gauge. According to John Pettigrew in a 1796 letter, which probably sent chills down his father Charles's spine, the students at the University of North Carolina preferred Paine's *Age of Reason* "to all the books that were ever wrote since the creation of the World." He added that the students claimed Paine "was sent into the World to set menkind [*sic*] to liberty." In spite of young Petti-grew's remarks, it seems probable that Paine's work served more as an excuse for student rebellion against authority than as a reli-gious text.[32]

The actions of other prominent North Carolina gentry, however, do suggest an opposition to Christianity that may well reflect the influence of Paine and other radical religious philosophers. In the first decade of the nineteenth century, for example, Alfred Moore, Jr., forbade family prayers at his Brunswick County plantation. Willie Jones, solicitor general and speaker of the house from Halifax and Raleigh, rejected a Christian burial when he specified in 1801 that at his funeral "no priest or any other person is to insult my Corps by uttering any impious observations over it." The radical religious philosophies of Paine and others may well have pushed the most forward members of the elite toward an uncompromising deism that was intolerant of orthodoxy.[33]

Without any churches to indoctrinate the genteel youth of the state, and with Enlightenment creeds like those propagated by Paine drawing attention in the 1790s, it was increasingly likely that the rising generation would refuse to listen to the dying echoes of religious orthodoxy and would instead adopt a more skeptical natural religion. In Edenton one orthodox churchman in 1810 was concerned enough about the spread of deism and the decline of orthodoxy to write two columns in the newspaper warning of the dangers of the former and encouraging the students at the Edenton Academy to seek the latter.

Radical religious thought was gaining an eager audience among the cream of the state's genteel youths. Topics for formal debate at the Dialectic Society of the University of North Carolina in the late 1790s included "Whether religion makes mankind happy" and "Whether the Bible ought to be believed." In the former instance, there is no indication as to how the debate was decided. In the latter, the debate was decided in the affirmative. The fact that such issues were raised at all reveals much about the religious tenor of the times.[34]

Even individuals raised in orthodox homes were perusing Enlightenment literature. As a young man in 1806, Ebenezer Pettigrew, son of bishop-elect Charles, read with interest Volney's *The Ruins; Or A Survey of the Revolutions of Empires,* a book that condemned religion as the source of political injustice.

One graduate of the University of North Carolina, an Episcopalian at least by heritage, delivered an 1801 address to the Dialectic Society on the subject of religious devotion that showed the unmistakable influence of deism. The author, John De Rosset Toomer, graduated with distinction from the University in 1798 and went on to a notable political career. Toomer was the son of a wealthy Wilmington planter and merchant who had married into the powerful DeRosset family. The elder Toomer had rented one of the choicest pews at the front of St. James's, Wilmington, during the late colonial period.

Son John, however, had drifted away from old orthodoxy to embrace deism. Like others who espoused a natural theology, Toomer saw evidence of God in the design of nature. According to him, "religious devotion" consisted of "that veneration and awe for the deity, which is naturally and imperceptibly kindled in our bosoms by looking through all his works, observing their beauties, and withal the harmony existing in every part."[35]

There was no need for Episcopal rites and ceremonies or for revelation in Toomer's theology; all the believer needed was the earth, the sea, and the sky: "When a devout man surveys this vast universe, where beauty and goodness are every where predominant, his heart glows within him, and prompts him to look up to one great first cause as the bestower of all these benefits, for which he is and ought ever to be thankful." Indeed, there was no need even to mention salvation because a benevolent God intended for all humanity to be happy and prosperous; only human ignorance was responsible for human misfortune and failure.[36]

Toomer listed four arguments that attempted to prove that his religion was reasonable: the natural propensity of the human mind to religious worship; the natural tendency for humans to seek divine assistance in times of crisis; the feelings of love and awe that naturally arise from human meditation on the divine; and the universality of religious adoration. Toomer concluded his essay by arguing that religious devotion was the source of "all the most amiable virtues" in this world and the foundation for "immortality and eternal happiness in the next."[37]

John De Rosset Toomer may have been an "infidel" in the eyes of an orthodox minister, or later evangelicals, but his theology was sophisticated and orderly. An Edenton physician, Dr. James Norcom, espoused the same natural theology as Toomer. The examples of Toomer and Norcom are highly suggestive of a religious world view at the turn of the century that may have been increasingly widespread in genteel society and that offers the most likely reason for the elite's indifference to orthodoxy.

The natural theology of a Toomer or a Norcom was not completely devoid of feeling. Some deists could survey nature and be filled with feelings of awe and wonder not altogether unlike the religious experience of a pantheist. Toomer, after all, claimed that when a deist like himself contemplates the creation, "his heart glows within him."[38] Even for the most sensitive and receptive deists, however, the emotional content of their religion was much "cooler" than that of the demonstrative evangelicals. For other Enlightenment thinkers, deism may have been an even more lightly held opinion, one that had minimal impact on the way they led their lives.

The proliferation of Enlightenment thought and the decline of orthodoxy had surprisingly little impact on genteel morality. Although gentlemen at the turn of the century espoused a variety of doctrines, including deism, unitarianism, and Episcopal orthodoxy, there was a broad consensus concerning morality. Anglican orthodoxy had always stressed virtuous living as one of its primary goals, and upper-class ethics in an age of reason continued to support a morality that had not changed significantly since independence.

John De Rosset Toomer's deism, for example, emphasized morality just as strongly as had the old Anglican faith. According to him, "Devotion inculcates temperance, sobriety, justice and every thing that is beneficial to youth, as it assuages the passions, restrains the desires, recommends moderation in all our actions, and teaches a strict adherence to moral rectitude." As the Rev. Joseph Caldwell had so insightfully noted, the elite still possessed "laws of morality and honor" to guide their moral actions even in the absence of orthodoxy.[39]

The moral imperative supplanted the religious impulse even in the few places where upper-class organized religion survived during this period. In Edenton in 1806 local Episcopalians began the first restoration of an Episcopal church in North Carolina since the Revolution. After the by now well-known litany of reasons for the establishment of religion, which were reminiscent of the preamble made by the same congregation twenty years before, the subscribers listed the real reason they were renovating the structure: it was because "the late institution of an Academy in the aforesaid Town promises to increase the number of youth whose Morals fall under our province to attend to."[40]

In Fayetteville during the first years of the nineteenth century, a Presbyterian clergyman served as schoolmaster and community minister; he delivered his sermons in the market house since there was no church. John A. Cameron, an Episcopalian by heritage, lamented the minister's eventual departure in 1808, not because the clergyman was a great preacher or an able pastor, but because his moral rectitude had "contributed to awe licentiousness and to infuse a general spirit of morality and correct deportment through every class of citizens in this place." Even in these last remnants of organized worship among the state's upper class, religion served primarily as a control on community behavior, not as a vehicle for religious expression. Religion for the elite had become almost identical with personal morality or virtuous living.[41]

Although the Episcopal church was nearly extinct, genteel culture among Episcopalians in 1800 was remarkably similar in many respects to its appearance in the late colonial era. Ethics of honor and fashion continued to influence the actions and behavior of unchurched Episcopalians. For gentlemen, the duel was still an acceptable solution to serious disagreements between aggrieved parties. In 1802 two nominal Episcopalians from Newbern, John Stanley and former-Governor Richard Dobbs Spaight, participated in perhaps the most celebrated duel in the state's history. The code of honor was so inextricably bound up with other genteel notions of morality that when Stanley killed Spaight, the Rev. Thomas P. Irving, Episcopal minister and schoolmaster, eulogized Spaight as a man "jealous of his own reputation . . . from the principle of honor."[42]

Public outcry was so strong in the wake of the Stanley-Spaight duel, however, that the legislature outlawed the practice in North Carolina; henceforth, gentlemen of honor in North Carolina slipped across state lines into either Virginia or South Carolina for duels, or participated in them surreptitiously. In 1803 Duncan Cameron, son of a Virginia Episcopal minister, and brother of John A. Cameron of Fayetteville, left his home in Orange County and went across the border into the Old Dominion where he crippled a rival suitor in a duel. Apparently with no sense of irony whatsoever, Cameron remarked afterwards, "God have Mercy on him a Sinner—I could have killed him as easily as I pleased."[43]

As the new century approached, the code of fashion remained the female counterpart to the code of honor. In 1784 Elizabeth Hogg, a member of a family who rented pews in colonial St. James's, Wilmington, wrote a friend about her gay social life at the balls. According to another young female observer in Wilmington two years later, a trendy hair style had become a prerequisite for a lady of fashion: "The Ladies here are very fashionable[.] [E]very body that pretends to be a Ladie must have her hair craped and it is the most troublesome fashion that ever was invented."[44] In 1806 the Edenton ladies became excited over a new fashion, masquerade balls.

21

While so many aspects of genteel culture demonstrated great continuity with the past, however, the Episcopal church seemed headed for oblivion. Even in the three coastal societies of Wilmington, Newbern, and Edenton, the old church had practically expired. In both Wilmington and Newbern, the communities continued to have Episcopal schoolmasters who held only irregular services. In Newbern the church building began to decay. In Edenton churchpeople had begun to restore St. Paul's because of the students at the Edenton Academy, but they never employed a full-time minister.

When Charles Pettigrew died in 1807, the headmaster of the local academy in Edenton, who was also a Presbyterian divine, was pressed into performing the ceremony because the three remaining Episcopal clergymen in the state lived at too great a distance to make the journey. A Presbyterian minister buried the bishop-elect of the Episcopal church in North Carolina! The old church and the people who espoused its precepts and principles were dying a lingering death. It was hard to imagine who or what might make them restore the Episcopal church.

Notes

1. Gary Freeze, "Like a House Built Upon Sand: The Anglican Church and Establishment in North Carolina, 1765–1776," HMPEC 48 (December 1979): 405–32, especially 430; Freeze's article provides an excellent institutional history of North Carolina's Anglican church at the close of the colonial era.
2. Freeze, "Like a House Built Upon Sand," 405–15; Joseph Blount Cheshire, Jr., ed., *Sketches of Church History in North Carolina* (Wilmington: William L. De Rosset, 1892), 91–155; William L. Saunders, ed., *The Colonial Records of North Carolina*, 10 vols. (Raleigh: State of North Carolina, 1886–90), 9:61–62.
3. The primary sources for my discussion of late colonial Anglican theology are colonial North Carolina wills, which contain much religious sentiment, and Sarah McCulloh Lemmon, ed., *The Pettigrew Papers*, vol. 1 (Raleigh: State Department of Archives and History, 1971). Much of the material in the Pettigrew Papers comes from the early republican period but is still revealing, since early Protestant Episcopalianism was theologically continuous with colonial Anglicanism. The Pettigrew Papers are much more than just an ordinary letter collection; Charles Pettigrew's position as bishop-elect of the church makes them a sort of unofficial archives of the Episcopal church in North Carolina for much of the period before 1800. In addition, I have relied on Henry F. May's treatment of southern Anglicanism in *The Enlightenment in America* (New York: Oxford University Press, 1976), 66–75. Robert Bruce Mullin's consideration of the theology of John Henry Hobart in *Episcopal Vision/American Reality: High Church Theology and Social Thought in Evangelical America* (New Haven: Yale University Press, 1986) is also informative since Hobart's thought was derived from earlier Anglican and Episcopal sources.
4. See Philip J. Greven, Jr., *The Protestant Temperament: Patterns of Child-Rearing, Religious Experience, and the Self in Early America* (New York: Knopf, 1977), 243–50.

5. Will of the Rev. John Alexander, quoted in Sarah McCulloh Lemmon, "The Genesis of the Protestant Episcopal Diocese of North Carolina, 1701–1823," *NCHR* 28 (October 1951): 457.

6. Alexander Garden, *Regeneration and the Testimony of the Spirit. Being the Substance of Two Sermons Lately preached in the Parish Church of St. Philip, Charles-Town, South Carolina. Occasioned by some erroneous Notions of certain Men who call themselves Methodist* . . . (Charleston, 1740; Boston, 1741), quoted in Richard Beale Davis, *Intellectual Life in the Colonial South, 1585–1763*, 3 vols. (Knoxville: University of Tennessee Press, 1978), 2:755–56.

7. Charles Pettigrew to [Brother] Ebenezer Pettigrew, 25 May 1789, in Lemmon, *Pettigrew Papers*, 1:69–70.

8. Richard Rankin, " 'Musquetoe' Bites: Caricatures of Lower Cape Fear Whigs and Tories on the Eve of the American Revolution," *NCHR* 65 (April 1988): 173–207; Bertram Wyatt-Brown, *Southern Honor, Ethics and Behavior in the Old South* (New York: Oxford University Press, 1982), 349–61.

9. Charles Pettigrew to Ebenezer Pettigrew, 10 April 1802, in Lemmon, *Pettigrew Papers*, 1:280–81.

10. Subscription list for support of the Rev. Charles Pettigrew, 1 May 1778, Pettigrew Family Papers, SHC; List of Ballances due the Rev. Charles Pettigrew, May 1785 [?], Pettigrew Family Papers, SHC.

11. Subscription list for support of the Rev. Charles Pettigrew, 1783, Pettigrew Family Papers, SHC.

12. Preamble, subscription list for support of the Rev. Charles Pettigrew, 1783, Pettigrew Family Papers, SHC.

13. List of Ballances due the Rev. Charles Pettigrew, May 1785 [?], Pettigrew Family Papers, SHC; Bennet H. Hall, "Charles Pettigrew, First Bishop-Elect of the North Carolina Episcopal Church," *NCHR* 28 (January 1951): 25.

14. Petition, included with "Bill for better ascertaining of property in the town of Wilmington, etc., 29 December 1786, General Assembly, Session Records, November 1786–January 1787, NCDAH.

15. Minutes of the Board of Trustees of the Hillsborough Academy, 1, 12, Hillsborough Academy Papers, NCDAH; Walter Clark, *The State Records of North Carolina*, 16 vols. (Winston: State of North Carolina, 1895–1907), 24:606.

16. Solomon Halling to Charles Pettigrew, 28 October 1793, in Lemmon, *Pettigrew Papers*, 1:121; Charles Pettigrew to Solomon Halling, 2 February 1794, in Lemmon, *Pettigrew Papers*, 1:127.

17. William Lowther, Nathaniel Allen, et al. to Charles Pettigrew, 15 July 1792, in Lemmon, *Pettigrew Papers*, 1:113; William Littlejohn and Joseph Blount to Charles Pettigrew, 15 July 1792, in Lemmon, *Pettigrew Papers*, 1:114; James Hall and John M. Wilson, "Missionary

24

Reports," Minutes of the Seventh Sessions of the Synod of the Carolinas, October 1794, microfilm at Union Theological Seminary in Virginia.

18. The North Carolina General Assembly, Session Records from 1785 to 1815 are full of acts of incorporation for local academies. See also Charles L. Coon, comp., *North Carolina Schools and Academies, 1790–1840* (Raleigh: State of North Carolina, 1915).

19. Leora Hiatt McEachern, assisted by Bill Reeves, *History of St. James Parish, 1729–1979*, (Wilmington, N.C.: n.p., 1985), 53; Gertrude S. Carraway, *Crown of Life: History of Christ Church, New Bern, N.C., 1715–1940* (New Bern: Owen G. Dunn, 1940), 112–17; Coon, *North Carolina Schools and Academies*, 50.

20. Nathaniel Blount to Charles Pettigrew, 23 January 1802, in Lemmon, *Pettigrew Papers*, 1:277–78; Jane Williams to Elizabeth Eagles Haywood, 20 February 1813, Ernest Haywood Papers, SHC; Maria B[urgwyn?] to Frederick Nash, 4 May 1809, Frederick Nash Papers, NCDAH; Ida Brooks Kellam and Elizabeth Francenia McKoy, *St. James Church, Wilmington, North Carolina: Historical Records, 1737–1852* (Wilmington: Mimeographed by Ida B. Kellam, 1965), 25, 27; Clark, *State Records* 23:191.

21. Edward Jones Mallett, *Memoirs of Edward Jones Mallett* (n.p.: by the author [ca. 1885]), 36–37.

22. Letter to the editor from "Lelius," *Edenton Gazette*, 2 March 1810.

23. James Iredell [Jr.] to James Booth, Jr., 24 June 1808, Charles E. Johnson Papers, NCDAH.

24. Charles Moore to Charles Pettigrew, 21 April 1796, in Lemmon, *Pettigrew Papers*, 1:186–88.

25. John S. West to the Wardens of the Episcopal Church at Edenton (if any) or Josiah Collins, Senr. Esqr., 22 October 1808, Robert Brent Drane Papers, SHC; George Davis to Jane Williams, 29 January 1809, Ernest Haywood Papers, SHC; Samuel Ashe will, 1813, New Hanover County Will Book AB, 188, NCDAH.

26. F[rances] Roulhac to Mrs. Margaret Roulhac, 5 September 1818, Ruffin-Roulhac-Hamilton Papers, SHC; for an article that deals with the role women played in a noninstitutional Episcopal church, see Joan R. Gundersen, "The Non-Institutional Church: The Religious Role of Women in Eighteenth-Century Virginia," *HMPEC* 51 (December 1982): 347–58.

27. Lemmon, *Pettigrew Papers*, 1:43n; Nathaniel Allen to Charles Pettigrew, 25 April 1791, Lemmon, *Pettigrew Papers*, 1:98–100; William Lowther, Nathaniel Allen, et al. to Charles Pettigrew, 15 July 1792, Lemmon, *Pettigrew Papers*, 1:113.

28. James Iredell to Hannah Iredell, 25 February 1796, in Griffith J. McRee, ed., *Life and Correspondence of James Iredell, One of the*

Associate Justices of the Supreme Court of the United States, 2 vols. (New York: D. Appleton and Co., 1858), 2:461.

29. Joseph Caldwell to [John H. Hobart], [8 November 1796], in R. D. W. Connor, comp., *A Documentary History of the University of North Carolina*, 2 vols. (Chapel Hill: University of North Carolina Press, 1953), 1:71.

30. Frederic Beasley to Charles Pettigrew, 6 February 1797, in Lemmon, *Pettigrew Papers*, 1:200–202.

31. May, *The Enlightenment in America*, 174.

32. John Pettigrew to Charles Pettigrew, 12 April 1796, in Lemmon, *Pettigrew Papers*, 1:183.

33. Jane Williams to Eliza E. Haywood, 9 July 1813, Ernest Haywood Papers, SHC; Willie Jones will, 1801, Halifax County Will Book 3, 355, microfilm at NCDAH.

34. Connor, *A Documentary History*, 2:130, 135.

35. John De Rosset Toomer, ["Address on Religious Devotion"], 4 October 1801, "Addresses and Debates," Dialectic Society Papers, UNCA.

36. Ibid.

37. Ibid.

38. Ibid.

39. Ibid; Joseph Caldwell to [John H. Hobart], [8 November 1796] in Connor, *A Documentary History*, 2:71.

40. Restoration Documents, 1806–9, St. Paul's, Edenton, microfilm at NCDAH.

41. John Cameron to Duncan Cameron, 10 September 1807, Cameron Family Papers, SHC.

42. Guion Griffis Johnson, *Ante-Bellum North Carolina: A Social History* (Chapel Hill: University of North Carolina Press, 1937) 43–44; *Controversy between Gen. Richard D. Spaight and John Stanley, esq., to which is annexed an abstract from a funeral discourse, intended to have been delivered by the Rev. Thomas P. Irving on the death of the former* (Newbern, N.C.: John S. Pasteur, 1802).

43. Duncan Cameron to Thomas D. Bennehan, 21 April 1803, Cameron Family Papers, SHC.

44. Elizabeth Huske to Nelly [Helen Blair], 30 January 1786, James Iredell Papers, DUA; see also Penelope Swan to Aunt [Hannah Iredell], 25 February 1804, Charles E. Johnson Papers, NCDAH; A[nne] I[sabella] Iredell to James Iredell [Jr.], 30 June 1804, Charles E. Johnson Papers, NCDAH.

CHAPTER ONE

A Ladies' Revival:
Female Religious Enthusiasm and the
Creation of a New Genteel Piety,
1805–1820

The unchurched upper classes drifted into the nineteenth century along the same, uninterrupted course—victims of inertia—with the gradual extinction of orthodox Episcopalianism and the proliferation of deistical religious skepticism. In the first decade of the new century, however, the evangelical movement, for so long active among lower-class whites and blacks, added a new dimension to the religious life of the elite as it finally began to attract individuals, especially women, from upper-class ranks.

The rise of the Baptist and Methodist evangelicals had begun in the mid-eighteenth century outside the privileged class among the economically unimposing and socially demeaned whose emotional religion disturbed genteel sensibilities. In the years before evangelicalism spread to the upper class, the gentry hurled a variety of disparaging epithets at the evangelicals. According to various unchurched Episcopalians, evangelical worship was "fanatical," "enthusiastic," and "hypocritical." Upper-class derision of the evangelicals was testimony to the increasing attention that evangelical societies commanded as their religious societies grew.

Above all it was the "noisy" Methodists with their emotional and at times uproarious religious meetings who initially gained the attention of the elite, especially after the Methodists in North Carolina extended their mission into the towns. Prior to this critical moment in the development of Methodism, the strength of the denomination had lain in the rural areas where lonely and indomitable Methodist preachers rode the circuits connecting the often far-flung meeting houses under their care. Before 1805 townspeople witnessed Methodist worship only as curious onlookers at the occasional conference and camp-meeting revivals held inand near local towns. Only rarely did the Methodist revivalists succeed in converting a lady or gentleman. Every now and then, however, they would convict and convert someone such as the son of the planter and Revolutionary War general, Robert Howe, who wept for his sins at a Methodist revival in the countryside near Wilmington in 1804.[1]

During the first decade of the nineteenth century, however, the Methodists moved into North Carolina's towns, where they began to erect chapels, instead of meeting in houses as they did in the countryside. These new Methodist sanctuaries, often located on the margins of town, superseded the once fine but now decaying Episcopal churches as the center of urban religious activity. The new setting demanded a different style of ministering from the Methodists. By the second decade of the 1800s, a settled, married, Methodist clergy complemented their unmarried, rural counterparts who still traveled the circuits. The Methodist town churches were right under the noses of a substantial portion of the genteel population who lived there and in plain sight of the rest of the gentry who came to town often enough for important political, commercial, and social exchanges. The evangelicals could no longer be ignored.

The Methodist movement into North Carolina towns began in Wilmington and Fayetteville among urban blacks, many of them workers, artisans, and craftsmen whose plantation masters allowed them a degree of autonomy as hired town laborers. In return the masters appropriated the high wages that the often skilled slaves commanded. At first, elite reaction to the evangelicals was violent. Masters considered them a threat to their control of the urban slave force, and local magistrates took steps to prevent Methodists from preaching. But the elite's attitude quickly mellowed when they realized that converted slaves made more obedient workers as the "effect [of the Methodists] on the public morals of the negroes . . . began to be seen, particularly as regarded their habits on Sunday, and drunkenness."[2]

By 1800 Methodists had already surrendered their antislavery appeal, although there was a studied ambiguity in their moral attitudes toward slavery. During the first decade of the nineteenth century, the Methodists in North Carolina towns established segregated seating for worship when the members of the two races met in common; they split into separate white and black societies for class meetings during the week. White Methodist ministers were actually becoming the friends of slave holders, marrying their daughters, adopting their ways, absorbing their values.

African-American Methodists accommodated themselves to the master class as well. Henry Evans, the gifted free black Methodist minister who founded the black Methodist church in Fayetteville, epitomized the deferential attitude by "never speaking to a white man but with his hat under his arm; never allowing himself to be seated in their houses; and even confining himself to the kind and manner of dress proper for negroes in general."[3] Even with these concessions to slave owners, however, Methodism still represented a threat to upper-class notions of social order. According to Donald Mathews, evangelical worship completely confused the traditional social scheme as different races—and soon different classes—worshipped together in ways that redefined social relationships not on status, but on the basis of intimacy, mutual respect, and communal discipline.[4]

The Methodist presence in the two Cape Fear towns was followed quickly by extension into a half-dozen other important towns of the state, and the denomination's growth was impressive among both whites and African-Americans. White Methodists in Newbern had already begun to build a church, and the African Methodists were preparing to build a separate church in 1802.[5] During the final meeting of a Methodist conference held in Newbern five years later, thirty or forty new converts were made, prompting one local gentleman to predict, "I expect in a few years half of Newbern will fall victim to this enthusiastic sect."[6] In January 1810 Methodist bishop Francis Asbury preached in the new chapel at Edenton to twelve white women, six white men, and about one hundred blacks.

A year later a Presbyterian missionary sent out to Halifax as a scout observed that "there are a few red hot Methodists and a great many red hot sinners."[7] Whether they were in touch with each other, he did not say. In February 1811 at another annual conference in North Carolina, Methodists ignited a revival in Raleigh in which, according to a local paper, "many young persons have been awakened to a sense of Religion, and the number of professors in and about this city, will receive a considerable increase."[8] So considerable in fact that shortly afterward the Methodists organized a local church on land donated by Willie W. Jones. Jones had forsaken the freethought of his father Willie Jones, who probably would have rolled over in his unconsecrated grave had he been sensible of his son's change of heart.

As Jones himself noted, his new-found faith was exceptional among gentlemen: "God hath chosen the poor of this world rich in grace, and heirs of his kingdom. . . . the wise of this world . . . sit down in security; the doctrines of self denial war too strongly [against] their evil appetites and they finally drop into hell."[9]

Many of the elite, who would have disputed Jones's prediction of their eternal damnation, nevertheless, would have been the first to admit that they had little time for evangelicals. In 1807 Thomas B. Haughton wrote to his friend (and the future governor) James Iredell, Jr., describing the uncouthness of a recent Methodist conference in Newbern during which "there was a large concourse of people of various colours, classes & sects assembled for various purposes—confusion, shouting, praying, singing, laughing, talking, amorous engagements, falling down, kicking, squealing, & a thousand other ludicrous things prevailed the most of the time & frequently of night, all at once—In short it was the most detestable farsical scene that ever I beheld."[10]

Ebenezer Pettigrew, the bishop-elect's son, who was a friend of Haughton, was less expansive but just as derogatory in his description of a Methodist camp-meeting in the Albemarle region. According to him, the Methodists "are tolerable orderly [while preaching] but immediately after, they get together as they call it to pray & be prayed for; There will be half a dozen praying at a time[,] some singing, some slap[p]ing hands, some laughing, some crying, some falling dead, with what they call the spirit of co[n]viction. They lay in an entire state of insensibility." Gentlemen continued to regard the Methodists with contempt for years to come. In 1831 a gentleman in New Hanover County expressed the same low regard for Methodists' "groaning & grunting" which he likened to "the growls of a surly mastiff" and "the grunting of a bed of pigs."[11]

For Haughton, Pettigrew, and others brought up in genteel homes, Methodist worship seemed to violate the thoughtfulness,

30

deliberation, and self-control expected in genteel religion. The expressiveness of Methodist worship was repugnant to these men because it involved the sort of emotional display that was regarded as inappropriate for a man. It was permissible for a gentleman to exercise his temper through prescribed rituals when his honor was impugned. But to give in to the religious emotions of evangelicalism was to demonstrate a weakness of will associated with individuals of inferior status like slaves and poor whites. Gentlemen, who prized education and the appearance of learning as badges of gentility, also shunned the "enthusiastic" religion of the unlettered evangelicals because it seemed to downplay the role of intellect and rationality.

Although the unbridled emotionalism and the physical exuberance of the Methodists appalled unchurched gentlemen, the evangelical message enthralled others unfettered by genteel reservations and prejudices. The power of evangelical preaching was the main attraction. Methodist ministers delivered sermons with authority and conviction because they knew what it meant to be "born again." In evangelical parlance to be born again meant to have a vivid psychic experience that left the convert certain that he or she had been saved. This experience was so profound that it could sometimes alter personality dramatically.[12]

In theological terms, the transformation of the individual was believed to involve an engrafting of an entirely new set of religious affections by the Holy Spirit, which allowed the believer to begin a life of personal holiness. This engrafting was often described as "regeneration" or "a change of heart." Like all effective evangelical preachers, Methodist ministers had the ability to communicate and make real their own psychologically wrenching religious experiences to their listeners. According to Mathews in *Religion in the Old South,* the evangelical preacher was able "to make the life-death-resurrection of Christ a contemporaneous event, and he did so with such vivid and evocative imagery that many who heard him experienced the meaning of the Christian religion through a familiar, reassuring, psychic ritual: the conviction of pervasive sin, the nausea of just condemnation, the joy of Christ's salvation."[13]

Thomas Haughton's description of a service at the Newbern conference of 1807 captures some of the intensity and excitement of a Methodist service. A typical Methodist sermon began by describing the damned future of the unrepentant sinner in fiery and vivid language. Next the preacher emphasized the listener's sense of

31

utter hopelessness apart from an experience of rebirth accompanying an acceptance of Christ as Saviour. Finally, building to a crescendo of emotion, the preacher invited the unconverted forward to the altar. Then, according to Haughton, "they march up to the pulpit to be prayed for in crowds,—the preachers assemble about them, & all begin to pray at once—then for the yelling, during which scene will be heard the articulate words 'do Lord, come Lord, glory, glory' and each of those favourite words, is accompanied with a clap of the hands."[14]

What followed for some at Newbern that day, and what was definitely happening to increasing numbers of people who came forward in similar circumstances, was a conversion experience of the most profound and transforming nature. When they emerged on the other side of this powerful event, their perceptions of the world were altered and they were convinced that they had joined the ranks of the twice born: they were evangelicals.

As long as the Methodists appeared to bolster slavery, and as long as they drew only from the lower classes, social superiors could dismiss them as a group of the feeble-minded and superstitious, just as Haughton did. But a remarkable thing began to happen in the first decade of the nineteenth century as a small but growing number of upper-class women became drawn to the drab and poorly constructed Methodist meeting houses.

Mr. Justice James Iredell's daughters, for example, went to an evangelical service in Edenton in 1803 to satisfy their curiosity. The young Iredell women returned from their visit to ponder the meaning of the strange, yet wonderful, scenes they had witnessed. Other ladies felt something even more compelling in the direct, personal, almost intimate, invitation to open themselves to the love of Christ and somehow were swept up into the whirlwind of religious experience.

Perhaps these upper-class women were attracted to evangelicalism, in part, for the same reasons as lower-class whites and blacks of both sexes. All were in a position of submission to various authority figures, whether masters, gentry, or husbands. Christ's yoke may have appeared easy to those accustomed to subserving other men. It was, nevertheless, a dramatic step for these first lady converts, who must have felt both "found" and "lost." They had been found by a loving Christ but were somehow lost to their class or station in life.

These female conversions could completely unsettle a town's genteel society. This happened in Wadesboro in 1812. According to one observer, practically everyone there, including the elite, "have become canting Methodists." But "everyone" was primarily the womenfolk, as a contemporary confirmed: "The Miss Jacksons exhort and pray publicly—Miss Wade, pilgrim-like, walks half a dozen miles on foot to meeting, Mrs. Jackson too. Hannah Robinson and her little sister ten years old fancy themselves converted and make much to do about it. And Sherwood Auld's wife has caught the infection to the no small mortification of her husband." The whole cultural aspect of the town had been transformed as "once cheerful little Wadesborough has become the dullest spot upon the globe." Whether the Misses Jackson, Wade, and Robinson would have agreed is doubtful.[15]

One thoughtful Presbyterian minister, a native of North Carolina, offered several explanations why ladies were so much more susceptible to the evangelical appeal than gentlemen. First of all, females had more leisure time than their husbands, with fewer outlets and distractions.[16] Perhaps they were bored and searching for a novelty to give their lives more zest; evangelical worship provided them with a deeply fulfilling personal religious experience and also served as a locus for enjoyable social interaction.

Secondly, since they were used to deferring to their fathers and husbands, women could submit to both the psychological and ethical demands of evangelical Christianity far more easily than their sons and husbands. In contrast, a conversion experience for a proud gentleman involved the emotionally wrenching experience of submission to a greater power, an experience to which self-commanding men were unaccustomed; and gentlemen who did convert were subject to the ostracism of their peers.[17] Moreover, evangelicals had to renounce certain cherished pleasures of the flesh common to masculine society such as gambling, excessive drinking, and carousing—vices in which their female counterparts could not indulge, irreligious or not.

Nancy Cott in *The Bonds of Womanhood* proposes several more reasons why New England women converted during the Second Great Awakening to evangelicalism. First, evangelicalism demanded a certain amount of spiritual self-scrutiny or self-absorption that permitted religious women to take their own thoughts and feelings more seriously than ever before.[18]

33

Cott also argues that evangelical religion provided women simultaneously with both an avenue of self-expression and a new community of peers. As plausible as Cott's explanations are for New England women, however, they do not completely explain the conversions of upper-class women in North Carolina because the old code of fashion had offered the same things: self-absorption, self-expression, and community. The remarkable thing about the ladies' revival is not that it offered completely new opportunities for genteel women but that it was powerful enough to induce the ladies to abandon older practices. For some upper-class women evangelicalism was more satisfying than the meaningless frivolity and boredom of their old way of life. One young evangelical evinced such an attitude when she declared that she looked forward to Bible class "more than I ever did for the night of a party."[19]

Obviously, at an emotional level, ladies found evangelicalism deeply satisfying. Evangelicalism also offered women another extraordinary opportunity: the chance to civilize their husbands and sons. Evangelical fellowship and lifestyle became a new model for domestic relations. Evangelical ladies sought to win their husbands to Christ and away from the traditional rules of masculine behavior, such as gaming, violence, or fornication, that were beyond the bounds of evangelical morality. Evangelical marriages also displayed the same tenderness and emotional intimacy that believers shared in the evangelical worship setting. Perhaps another explanation for ladies' attraction to evangelicalism was the potential to transform their conjugal relations.

The genteel revival among the ladies developed in two distinct but related phases. In every instance, during the first phase the Methodists initiated the revival. In all cases where the evidence is full enough to identify the sexual ratio of the participants, women predominated. In the second phase of the revival, a Presbyterian or an Episcopal minister attempted, sometimes at the behest of the local elite, to capitalize on the initial Methodist efforts.

Most clearly in Edenton and Newbern, and perhaps in Wilmington, the Methodist invasion stimulated unchurched Episcopal men in attempts to revive their languishing Episcopal churches, all of which met with varying degrees of failure. Episcopalians in Edenton actually had begun to restore old St. Paul's church, which had "gone to decay so as to be unfit for the purpose for which it was intended, unless repaired," before the Methodists came to town.

The Episcopal restoration was an extension of the traditional effort to provide the rising generation of students at the Edenton Academy with moral training as a part of their broader education. Townspeople involved in the cause included the foremost gentlemen and ladies of the community.

One indication that the adults were only half-hearted in their support for organized religion was their failure to hire a minister. Edenton Episcopalians also were not serious enough about organized religion to reestablish the church vestry, which had long-since disbanded. Church repairs took four years to complete. They were barely finished in 1809 when the Methodists arrived and constructed a new chapel.[20]

In all likelihood, the Episcopalians had never anticipated either the arrival or the impact of Methodism in Edenton. The Episcopal restoration was intended to exert a moral influence over school children, but the convicting and convincing sermons being delivered in the Methodist chapel began to attract Episcopal adults. The Methodist church's white membership was small, but from the outset its potential appeal to the women of the town was apparent. Bishop Francis Asbury, of the Methodist Episcopal church, preached to forty of them one night in a local home. Although Asbury's sermon topic that evening is unknown, he probably emphasized the same thing that he so often did: the need for sinners to experience personally a spiritual rebirth as a result of the atoning sacrifice of Christ.

Less than a year later, the first of two successive Methodist ministers initiated a revival in town that resulted in a number of converts. Some Edentonians derisively dubbed one of the Methodist preachers "The Babbler" and contended that those townspeople who joined the society "had run mad, were going crazy an[d] the like."[21] Methodist worship may have seemed insane to Enlightenment thinkers. But to some of the members of old St. Paul's it was a divine madness; for them the emotional satisfaction of evangelicalism outweighed any competing social pressures to conform to the dictates of reason and propriety.

The Methodist meeting in Edenton was openly perceived to be prospering at the expense of the Episcopal church as the Methodists received financial encouragement from individuals who had formerly been at least nominal Episcopalians. One pseudonymous Edentonian, "Lelius," probably a member of the old Episcopal elite, was concerned enough by the turn of religious events to write a series of letters to the local newspaper discouraging Episcopalians from supporting the Methodists and encouraging renewed financial support for the old church. Other unchurched Episcopalians were obviously just as worried for they embarked on a momentous course not contemplated since the days of the Revolution: they employed a full-time Episcopal minister. The Rev. Frederick W. Hatch arrived in Edenton in September 1811 and entered upon his office as pastor shortly after.

The genteel folk of Edenton did not stop at just calling a new Episcopal rector for the first time in more than twenty-five years. They also elected five of the wealthiest men in town as church trustees, the same name the Methodists used, apparently having either forgotten or forsaken the old term of vestry. The accumulated impact of these various efforts to strengthen the old church was not without some effect. The superintending Methodist minister for the district in 1813 upbraided some of the Edenton Methodists for returning to the "velvet cushions" of the Episcopal church.

Against a background of Episcopal lethargy for the last thirty-five years, any revival, even a modest one of the sagging fortunes of the Episcopal church in Edenton was significant. The Methodists had stirred the local elite into a noteworthy action; but the old Episcopal church was outmoded in the new evangelical age, and it did not prosper. Perhaps Hatch was a representative of the old church and its passionless orthodoxy, ill-suited to proclaim the new religion of the heart.

In Newbern a single Episcopal layman, John S. West, a merchant, has left a record of his opposition to Methodism and of his related attempt to revive the Episcopal church. West's efforts occurred against the background of local excitement for and interest in Methodism arising from a conference held in Newbern in February 1807. In the last months of 1808, West wrote a critical letter to the local Methodist church. According to John Stanley, a political opponent who had read West's letter himself, the letter sought "to establish the doctrine, that a man has by the law of God such dominion over his Wife that she is bound to become a member of any church he prefers." His comments suggest the irritation that other Episcopal gentlemen were feeling as wives defied their husbands' wishes and attended the Methodist church.[22]

West, according to Stanley, went on to accuse the Methodists of SCHISM and to call for a revival of the Episcopal church. Although Stanley detested West, there is no reason to suspect that he had misrepresented the facts. West himself admitted he wrote a critical letter to the Methodists, although he did not elaborate on its contents. At roughly the same time, he also wrote a letter to a prominent Edenton Episcopalian to explore "the restoration of those admirable principles by which the once amiable, but now degenerate Episcopal Church professes to be governed"; so it is certain that he was trying to revive the Episcopal church just as Stanley claimed.[23]

West's defense of patriarchal religion also seems credible. The Methodist church appealed especially to genteel women, not gentlemen. It would be entirely plausible, even predictable, for a gentleman like John West to lash out at a denomination that threatened to undermine his domestic control. The Methodist SCHISM that he abhorred may well have rent his own family. Unfortunately for West, his attempt to revive the Episcopal church in Newbern failed; in fact, the Episcopalians there displayed even fewer signs of life than those in Edenton and Wilmington. The Methodists continued to prosper, causing one local, anonymous poet in 1818 to pen the following doggerel verse:

> Next comes a house without a name
> To that of church it has no claim,
> And yet the long misshapen pile
> Contains a throng 'twixt either aisle,
> And in the galleries perch'd above,
> To join in prayer and feasts of love;
> Its various worshipers can tell
> Why they reject a spire or bell.[24]

The details surrounding the rise of Methodism among the genteel population in Wilmington, and the initial Episcopal response, are not nearly as full as in Edenton, or even Newbern, but the existing evidence does not rule out similar developments. The Methodist church on Front Street originated in the late 1790s under a white minister, William Meredith, who attracted remarkable numbers of blacks. The exact time at which the Methodist church began to attract white women is uncertain, but it may well have been in November 1808, when the Episcopal church in Wilmington appears to have been in the midst of a revival that may have reflected a genteel response to the threat posed by Methodism.

At this time, a visitor from New England attended the Episcopal church and found about one hundred people at the service. To the visitor the crowd seemed small, but a Wilmington friend remarked "that for Wilmington it was an extraordinary large congregation." The sermon topic was on "the proper choice of companions," and the text was "He that walketh with wise men shall be wise; but the companion of fools shall be destroyed." While warning his listeners of the "imperceptible and therefore more dangerous effects of vicious society," the Episcopal minister advised "that the company of the wise" benefited one's "reputation," "comfort," and "profit."[25] It is impossible to know whether the reference to "vicious society" was a veiled allusion to the Methodists in Wilmington or to some other completely unrelated group or persons. If not the Methodists, however, who or what was responsible for the Episcopal attendance after such a long period of inactivity?

Whether or not Wilmington Episcopalians first responded to the Methodist challenge as early as November 1808, sooner or later some of their wives demonstrated a fascination with the new religious alternative. At least one of the most distinguished women in Wilmington, Catherine DeRosset, wife of Dr. Armand J. DeRosset joined the church, and a number of others hovered on the periphery. A few years earlier, Catherine had declared that "my Idea of Religion is that we are free agents, and will, in different degrees, be rewarded or Punish'd according to Good or Evil actions we may commit in this life."[26] Soon she was persuaded differently. What she would have heard from a Methodist minister was that all were "free agents," but that free agency involved our ability either to accept Christ and salvation or reject Him and be damned; otherwise, no amount of "Good or Evil actions" would satisfy an angry God. Catherine DeRosset's conversion involved a major change in her religious beliefs as evangelical conversion replaced virtuous living as the basis of salvation. She, a respectable lady, became one of the most devoted members of the lowly Methodist church.

Other gentlepeople in Wilmington also explored the spiritual claims of Methodism. According to William Capers, the married Methodist minister who took charge of the African church in 1812, "gentlemen and ladies, of high position in society, were to be found from Sabbath to Sabbath attending our preaching." The psychologically satisfying evangelical experience pulled the ladies to Methodism like a magnet.[27]

Two of the most highly stationed ladies visited Mr. and Mrs. Capers at their home, ostensibly to dispute the Methodist minister's claim that "common people could know their sins forgiven," but probably also to learn more about the intriguing faith. Finally, in exasperation at Mr. Capers's declarations, one of the ladies exclaimed, "Well, Mrs. Capers, it must be a very high state of grace this which your husband talks about, and I dare say some very saintly persons may have experienced it, but as for us, it must be quite above our reach. I am sure you do not profess it, do you?" Mrs. Capers only added to their consternation when she quietly assured them that, "Yes, ma'am, I experienced it at Rembert's camp-meeting, year before last, and by the grace of God I still have the witness of it."[28]

For one of the two ladies, the Methodist message proclaimed by the Capers was persuasive, and she obtained the same experience of forgiveness shortly after the interview.[29] If her conversion was like so many others, it left her with an unmatched certainty of personal forgiveness, a certainty that the old orthodoxy's jaded words could no longer provide. The old orthodoxy only offered promises of forgiveness. Evangelicalism offered an experience of forgiveness.

The old Episcopal church in all three of the port towns had demonstrated only a limited ability to cope with Methodism, and genteel women were defecting to the younger denomination. In other North Carolina towns, where no Episcopal church survived, however, another denomination, the Presbyterian, vied more successfully with the Methodists for upper-class souls.

In Fayetteville in 1810, for example, Henry Evans, a free black, began to attract members of the white elite to his predominantly black Methodist congregation. His first convert was Mrs. Bowen, the schoolmistress of the Fayetteville Academy. Her action opened up a floodgate of conversions as a larger number of mistresses, and even some masters, "were brought to think that the preaching which had proved so beneficial to their servants might be good for them also."[30]

Soon the whites attending Evans's congregation became "large and respectable," and the blacks were segregated to the back of the church as more and more whites crowded into the choice seats in front of the pulpit. Finally, the walls were knocked out and sheds were added to the sides of the building to prevent the blacks from being pushed out entirely as more and more whites came to hear Evans.

The Methodist church would likely have claimed even more upper-class females if it had not been for the activities of three successive local Presbyterian schoolmasters who somehow found the spare time to establish a church that met in the market house in the absence of a sanctuary. The second Presbyterian minister, William L. Turner, felt enough of a kinship with Methodists to hold a joint service with Bishop Asbury when he came to town in 1813.[31] By 1814 the Rev. Jesse H. Turner, who had succeeded his deceased brother as schoolmaster, was pastor of a flock of some seventy women and a dozen men that still met on Sunday at the market house. Turner quite logically developed a special affinity with his female charges and once even preached a sermon on the appropriateness of women workers in the church. At least one gentleman, Paris J. Tillinghast, a prominent local merchant, in what probably was a typical pattern for many others, attended the Presbyterian service but did not join, leaving that to the females in his family.[32]

The Presbyterian ministers in Fayetteville had counterparts in a number of other North Carolina towns where Presbyterianism reaped a harvest, the seeds of which had grown in an evangelical environment first created by Methodist activities. In Raleigh, as in the case of Fayetteville, it was the principal of the local academy, the Rev. William McPheeters, a Presbyterian minister and close associate of some of the most prominent evangelical Presbyterian divines in Virginia, who was the founder of the Presbyterian church. He assumed his duties as principal of the Raleigh Academy in 1810, only a year before the annual Methodist Conference created a general mood of religious fervor in the community.[33]

At first McPheeters preached each Sunday to all comers in services held in the state capitol building, but by 1816 he had succeeded in establishing a Presbyterian church. Two years later the session completed a fine brick sanctuary. Twenty-two of the approximately thirty original members of the church were female.

One of the charter Presbyterian communicants was Eliza Haywood, wife of the state treasurer, John Haywood. After a period of religious uncertainty, Mrs. Haywood had experienced a sure sense of conversion. As an outgrowth of her new found religious conviction, Eliza became president and principal actor in the Raleigh Female Religious Tract Society, founded in 1816. The largest benevolent organization of its kind in the state, the society distributed religious tracts throughout North Carolina under the direction of the first ladies of Raleigh.

In Hillsboro the Methodist church became active in 1807. Eight years later, the Rev. J. Hanks, almost certainly either a Baptist or a Methodist, led a revival that converted so many genteel ladies that it left one prominent local lawyer, Frederick Nash, asking a question that has troubled both contemporary observers and historians since Cotton Mather—why were "female professors of religion . . . more numerous than the male." Hanks set the stage for the Presbyterian minister, John Witherspoon, who had the boldness to describe Hanks as a "weak instrument" just a year before coming to town and stealing his converts.[34]

After Witherspoon arrived in 1816, the ladies of Hillsboro clustered around the young, Princeton-educated minister who was the grandson of his namesake, the Rev. John Witherspoon, president of Princeton and signer of the Declaration of Independence. Young Witherspoon was the son of David Witherspoon, a large slave owner and Newbern lawyer. The Hillsboro minister was also connected to prominent North Carolinians through his mother who was the widow of Gov. Abner Nash. The young Princeton minister's pedigree was impressive, but he also possessed evangelical qualities that suited the tastes of Hillsboro ladies. When Witherspoon attended a young, dying female, he questioned her on whether she was prepared to meet her God, rather than assuring her that salvation had been secured by the merits and mediation of the Saviour, as would have been the case in the old Episcopal church.

During the first five years of Witherspoon's ministry, thirty-nine white women, seventeen white men, and four slaves joined the Hillsboro Presbyterian church. In 1821 Witherspoon's church received another boost from the evangelicals when a Methodist revival led by Peter Doub created an additional wave of converts who joined the Presbyterian church. Among the ladies who belonged to Witherspoon's church were some from the highest echelon of North Carolina society, like Mrs. Paoli Ashe, Mrs. Thomas Ashe, and Mrs. Richard Ashe all of whom had married into a family, originally from Cape Fear, that had produced a number of military heroes and distinguished statesmen. When the Ashe ladies joined the

41

Presbyterian church, they aligned themselves with a minister and members of distinguished heritage, education, and wealth.

Ladies who joined the Presbyterian church in the state's major towns must have preferred refined and cultured ministers and ladies to the company of lower-class evangelicals, otherwise they would have joined the previously established Methodist churches nearby. These ladies, like their husbands, appear to have been self-consciously genteel and drawn to those of like status, but they were also, first and foremost, evangelical. Anyone who joined the Hillsboro Presbyterian church presented evidence of "their knowledge and experimental acquaintance with religion."[35]

The Presbyterian church was better adapted than either the old Episcopal or the new Methodist church to attract genteel women because it combined two essential qualities: gentility and evangelicalism. Presbyterian ministers had an advantage over the Episcopalians in being able to speak the evangelical language of "experimental acquaintance with religion," that is the palpable experience of conversion and redemption, just as the Methodists did. The Presbyterian ministers had an advantage over the Methodists by being educated and possessing the refinement associated with it, just as the old Episcopalians did. If the Presbyterians had not appeared on the scene, it is likely that more evangelical ladies would have joined the Methodist church. As it was, the genteel ladies who joined the Presbyterian churches in Fayetteville, Raleigh, Hillsboro, Newbern, Washington, and Wilmington during the first quarter of the nineteenth century climbed up the social ladder away from Methodism without abandoning their evangelical convictions.

Whether genteel ladies joined the Methodist or the Presbyterian churches, they shared a common set of religious values and beliefs that had arisen in the wake of their often dramatic conversion experience. In fact, denominational affiliations indicated nothing about differences in religious belief: genteel Methodist ladies like Catherine DeRosset shared a common religious outlook with the genteel Presbyterian ladies like Eliza E. Haywood. All had either experienced or were seeking to experience a spiritual rebirth, and a growing number were changed into evangelicals in a conversion process that occurred with the greatest frequency during the per-fervid years from 1810 to 1825. All would undoubtedly agree with Catherine DeRosset's observation that "except a man be born again he cannot see the Kingdom of Heaven."[36]

Before experiencing conversion, individuals typically underwent a period of psychological wrestling as a result of their serious consideration of the evangelical message. This period was defined in the spiritual language of the day as being "under serious religious impression." Often during this time an interested minister supervised the religious seeker and encouraged her to convert as quickly as possible. The Rev. James Hall, a prominent Presbyterian minister from the piedmont, urged Eliza E. Haywood to convert as early as 1812, but it would be more than two years before she experienced a spiritual rebirth.

Once an individual had undergone a conversion, she manifested an unshakable confidence concerning her eternal destiny. Eliza Haywood had experienced it, but her mother, Jane Williams, had not, and she longed for it. After one daughter's death, Williams sought the counsel of Wilmington's Solomon Halling, a representative of the old church. Ten years later she underwent the serious religious impressions prerequisite to an evangelical conversion.

Jane confided to daughter Eliza concerning her deep longing for spiritual rebirth, "I feel lost and alone in the World, such a void, such a want of what I miss so much—I pray constantly my Dear Child for Peace of mind and that Changed and Regenerated Heart that so many have Obtained but I feel no Change of that sort, I am still the unregenerate Sinner, I trust I am not cast off and that our father will not be always Angry with me forever, nor Hide the light of his Countenance from me."[37]

Jane Williams had discarded the hollow promises of old orthodoxy forever as she sought the assurance and wholeness of the evangelical experience. No longer able by a process of ratiocination to trust in Episcopal claims, she and others like her wanted to feel their sins forgiven. Another genteel woman expressed outright suspicion of the old Episcopal service in the following verse:

> No Sacrament, no outward form,
> Can save from endless pain.
> We must be of the Spirit born,
> We must be born again.[38]

The evangelical rebirth became a strong bond uniting spiritual sisters into a new Christian communion. Before this time ladies had been linked socially by their friendship and mutual participation in the world of fashion. But now they shared something much more intimate and internal, an experience that was unworldly, yet fulfilling. Anne Hill, wife of Dr. Frederick J. Hill who was descended from aristocratic Cape Fear planters, wrote to Catherine DeRosset in 1817: "As to the union of sentiment which has in many respects ever subsisted between us, is now added the sweet but powerful tie of christian affection. [I]s it not our privilege to take sweet counsel with each other as we journey to the heavenly Jerusalem? Yes our communion is with God, and with his Son Jesus: and with his saints we have sweet fellowship[,] this holy cement which unites the hearts of believers."[39]

Ann A. Turner, wife of the Rev. William L. Turner, had probably become acquainted with Eliza Haywood before coming to Fayetteville, when she and her husband lived in Raleigh while he was principal of the Raleigh Academy. She demonstrated the same sense of spiritual kinship when she wrote to Eliza, "Why should we not be friends, we are both I hope aspiring after higher enjoyments than this World can bestow[.] we profess to be followers of the same Devine [sic] Saviour." The shared experience of conversion was the common denominator around which groups of women coalesced into evangelical churches and networks.[40]

The new female converts exhibited an extraordinary zealousness to make converts of their lost fellows. Eliza Hasell, a Hillsboro Presbyterian, wrote to a young friend in Wilmington encouraging her to convert: "I trust my dear Elizabeth that while the Lord is manifesting himself to your young friends and companions, your soul is not as the mountain of Gilboa—but that you have been cheered by His presence whom you have so long been seeking—and can say with sincerity, Thou art my portion O Lord in the land of the living."[41]

When Polly Ann Rodman's son died, she sought consolation from her evangelical cousin Ann C. Blount, who used the opportunity to encourage Rodman to convert:

> I will thank God that he has led you to enquire of me as it affords me an opportunity of sending you a book, viz. The Rise and Progress of Religion in the Soul, that has been blessed to the conversion of many: read it, my dear Cousin with attention from beginning to end and pray earnestly to God for Christ's sake to enlighten you by his Holy Spirit and give you an understanding heart to discern the things that belong to your everlasting peace. It is the precious blood of Christ that cleanseth from *all sin:* read

your Bible pray for faith to believe in Christ. [A]nd I beseech you listen not to the cavils of unbelievers for assuredly God has appointed a day in which he will judge the world by that man Christ Jesus.[42]

One reason for the sense of urgency with which these converts approached the unrepentant was the conviction that those who died without an experience of salvation were consigned to eternal damnation. Eliza Hasell worried whether a girl who had died recently "had undergone that change which is necessary to salvation." She had her doubts for although the young women "professed repentance . . . , it was to be feared it was more a dread of punishment than that repentance which is unto life eternal." Hasell hoped that the girl's death at least had left "a solemn warning to the young not to delay preparing to meet their God."[43]

In addition to their concern for the eternal welfare of others, the evangelical ladies also were motivated to share their faith out of present considerations. They sought both to enrich the spiritual lives of their friends and relatives and to regain the society of those with whom they had associated prior to their own conversions. When Eliza Hasell spoke of the "dread of punishment" behind many false conversions, she had her own joyful experience of conversion as a reference, and she wanted to share it with others. Moreover, when Hasell or any other evangelical lady successfully converted a friend, she simultaneously affirmed her own religious lifestyle— and renewed an old friendship on a new evangelical basis.

Catherine DeRosset could not comprehend why others were indifferent to the salvation offered by an evangelical rebirth, especially since she was so certain that any "reasonable" person could know where they stood with God. "[N]ow it is the most astonishing thing in the World to think that reasonable Creatures, who know they are born to die, & that God will bring all to judgment, should rest satisfied without knowing whether they have the 'Spirit of Christ' or not." According to Mrs. DeRosset the certainty of evangelical claims was contained in the Holy Scriptures, which described "so plainly what it is to be a 'new creature', to be 'born of God,' to pass from 'death unto life,' . . . that any person who reads them at all, may by praying to the Almighty for grace to understand the Word & be able to judge whether they are indeed 'born again'." Catherine DeRosset's religion may have seemed reasonable to her, but it was not the reasonableness of an Enlightenment natural religion. Instead, it was a reasonableness revealed to an individual only by the inner testimony of the Holy Spirit.[44]

The conversions of genteel ladies created a whole new evangelical religious orientation that released tremendous emotional energies into their lives. For some it was as if the white hot coals of the Old Testament prophets had been placed upon their tongues as they spewed forth with apparent effortlessness page after page of pious sentiments in letters to each other. They also composed their own religious poems and copied others from leading Romantic poets. Several of the young women who belonged to the Hillsboro Presbyterian church left a volume of religious poetry written around 1820, much of it original, some transcribed from other authors.

No one can read these poems without appreciating the depth of the religious and emotional transformation that had occurred in young women, such as Eliza G. Hill who reached for the lofty and ephemeral language of poetry to express her new feelings:

> Awhile I strive, awhile I mourn,
>   Mids't thorns & briars here:
> But God vouchsafes with love divine
>   My drooping heart to cheer.
> Though meaner, than the meanest saint,
>   My heavenly Guide I see;
> I hear a voice behind me say,
>   "That Jesus died for me."[45]

Hill's poem revealed a number of important evangelical sentiments and concerns. First, it indicates that evangelical faith above all was Christocentric with an emphasis on the atonement in which "Jesus died for me." The poem also dwelt on the emotional, not the rational, character of faith as "love divine" came "to cheer" a "drooping heart." Finally, it indicated the tension in evangelical attitude toward the world. This was not the benevolent created order of the old Anglicans. It was a world of striving and mourning, not gaiety and disport; full of thorns and briars, not dances and amusements.

Julia A. Miner, a fellow member of Hillsboro Presbyterian penned a filiopietistic poem, "Mother's Prayer," in the same volume. Although it is "heaven" who "bestows" a "large stream of love" on the believing child in the poem, the mother's important role in spiritual matters is elevated to a height that clearly anticipates the dominance of the nineteenth-century religious sphere by women.

> And while Devotion, fear dispels,
> With holy hope assured,
> Some kind commissioned spirit tell,
> "Thy vows of faith are heard!"
> O! rich the meed, that heaven bestows,
> To bless maternal care;
> And large the stream of love that flows
> Called by a Mother's Prayer![46]

Only a quarter of a century had elapsed since the young male students at the University of North Carolina had devoured Thomas Paine's *Age of Reason*. But anyone reading these sentimental poems can see that these young ladies, and others like them, had left the age of the reason for a new age of feeling. Indeed, for young evangelical ladies in North Carolina the connection between religious romanticism and literary romanticism was probably direct. Their evangelical conversions had given rise to a whole new form of self-expression, one with an original language and fresh images to describe a flood of religious passions.

Evangelical ladies empathized with the religious sentiments and feelings contained in the poems of William Cowper and other evangelical poets, and ladies often copied these poems as a way of voicing their religious feelings. It is difficult to comprehend the evangelical ladies' sudden predilection for writing and reading Romantic poetry without postulating that the same conversion process that transformed them into evangelicals also unleashed a surge of emotions that found an appropriate channel in literary Romanticism. Evangelical religion had become a new and powerful emotional vehicle that affected the way genteel ladies spoke and wrote, and also what they read.

Evangelical conversion not only created a new style of oral expression, it also redefined appropriate social activity. Organized female benevolence became a common pastime of evangelical ladies. The work of the Raleigh Female Religious Tract Society was one example of organized Christian benevolence. Similar benevolent organizations existed in nearly every town where there was a group of genteel evangelical ladies.

In Fayetteville, for example, the Female Benevolent Society was almost certainly composed of the same women who made up the Rev. Jesse Turner's church, since they asked him to preach at the annual society meeting. These ladies gathered weekly or biweekly to work on projects to raise money for either a charitable or missionary cause. Since evangelical morality disdained fashionable amusements such as the theater and balls, organized female benevolence provided evangelical ladies with an acceptable replacement for less suitable, traditional pastimes. Benevolent activities offered pious ladies an unobjectionable way to express their feelings and visit friends.

The ladies' revival had changed the religious outlook of a significant number of the women of the upper class. For most genteel husbands, who remained Enlightenment freethinkers, proud men of honor, or an orthodox remnant, their wives' and daughters' religious transformation may have been puzzling, and disconcerting, but the change was irrefutable. The ladies were speaking a new language of piety, interspersed with utterances of praise, and those reverential words seldom heard from Enlightenment thinkers, "Jesus Christ," frequently came to their lips. They were writing religious poems and working diligently in benevolent societies.

These genteel women really must have seemed to be "new creations" to those who had known them before. There was a firmness of conviction, a solidity of belief about these ladies during the early decades of the new century. They had enjoyed "the experience" of conversion, and a mysterious inner testimony left them convinced that they were assured salvation. They were speaking a new language of religious feeling and emotion. Once gentlemen had ridiculed the lowly evangelicals, suddenly they found themselves married to them.

Notes

1. James Jenkins, *Experiences, Labours, and Sufferings of Rev. James Jenkins, of the South Carolina Conference* (n.p.: 1842), 144–45.
2. William M. Wightman, D.D., *Life of William Capers, D.D. One of the Bishops of the Methodist Episcopal Church, South; Including an Autobiography* (Nashville: Southern Methodist Publishing House, 1859), 125, 126, 161–62.
3. Ibid., 128.
4. Donald G. Mathews, *Religion in the Old South* (Chicago: University of Chicago Press, 1977), 42.
5. Journal entry, 26 January 1802, in Francis Asbury, *Francis Asbury in North Carolina: The North Carolina Portions of "The Journal of Francis Asbury,"* (Nashville: Parthenon Press, 1964), 196.
6. Thomas B. Haughton to James Iredell, Jr., 11 February 1807, James Iredell Papers, DUA.
7. B[enjamin] H[olt] Rice to William McPheeters, 28 January 1811, Benjamin H. and John Holt Rice Papers, NCDAH.
8. *Raleigh Register,* 14 February 1811 [21 Feb. 1811?]; Journal entry, 10 February 1811, Asbury, *Asbury in North Carolina,* 252.
9. Willie W. Jones to John Haywood, 7 November 1810, John Haywood Papers, SHC.
10. Thomas B. Haughton to James Iredell, Jr., 11 February 1807, James Iredell Papers, DUA.
11. Ebenezer Pettigrew to James Iredell, Jr., 6 August 1806, Lemmon, *Pettigrew Papers,* 1:393; Diary entry, 3 July [1831], Moses Ashley Curtis Diary, 1830–36, Moses Ashley Curtis Papers, SHC.
12. Mathews, *Religion in the Old South,* 59.
13. Ibid., 84.
14. Thomas B. Haughton to James Iredell, Jr., February 11, 1807, James Iredell Papers, DUA.

15. Mrs. R[osanna] Harrington to Henry Williams Harrington, September 1812, in H. M. Wagstaff, ed., *The Harrington Letters* (Chapel Hill: n.p., 1914), 39–40.
16. J[ohn] Witherspoon to F[rederick] Nash, 20 October 1815, Frederick Nash Papers, NCDAH.
17. Ibid.
18. Nancy F. Cott, *The Bonds of Womanhood: "Woman's Sphere" in New England, 1780–1835* (New Haven: Yale University Press, 1977), 140–41.
19. Ibid.; Maria L. Spear to Catherine Ruffin, 1829, Ruffin-Roulhac-Hamilton Papers, SHC.
20. St. Paul's, Edenton, Vestry Book, vol. 2, 11, microfilm NCDAH; Bernard Overton, "Historical Notices," 1824, Edenton Methodist Church Record Book, NCDAH.
21. Overton, "Historical Notices."
22. John Stanley, *An Introductory Essay, towards the exposure of a Common Lyar, a dastardly self-acknowledged Coward, a low-based Scoundrel, and scandalous Hypocrite: strikingly exemplified in the character and conduct of John Spence West* (Newbern: n.p., 1810), 1, in Francis Lister Hawks Historical Papers, PECA, microfilm at SHC.
23. Ibid; John S. West, *To the Public, Newbern, 30 July 1810* (Newbern: T. Watson, 1810), 1, in Francis Lister Hawks Historical Papers, PECA, microfilm at SHC; John S. West to the Wardens of the Episcopal Church at Edenton (if any) or Josiah Collins, Sr. Esqr., 22 October 1809, Robert Brent Drane Papers, SHC.
24. Stephen M. Chester, rhymes, 1818, quoted in Vass, *History of the Presbyterian Church*, 113.
25. *Wilmington Gazette*, 15 November 1808.
26. Diary entry, 9 July 1798, Catherine Fullerton's diary, DeRosset Family Papers, SHC. This diary can be identified definitely as Catherine Fullerton DeRosset's by a comparison of handwritings with her later letters in the William Lord DeRosset Papers, DUA.
27. Wightman, *Life of William Capers*, 164.
28. Ibid., 165–66.
29. Ibid.
30. Ibid., 126–27; Joseph Travis, *Autobiography of Joseph Travis, A.M.* (Nashville: E. Stevenson & F. A. Owens, Agents, 1855), 101–2.
31. Journal entry, 17 January 1813, Asbury, *Asbury in North Carolina*, 258.
32. Jesse Turner, *Women Ought to Labour in the Church of God; and Men Ought to Help Them; A Sermon Preached for the Benefit of the Female Tract Society, in Fayetteville, on Sabbath, 28th December, 1817* (Fayetteville, N.C.: Duncan Black, 1818); Journal entry, 15 Sep-

tember 1816, Paris J. Tillinghast Journal, part 2, July-October 1816,
Tillinghast Family Papers, DUA.

33. Joseph Gales, "Recollections," 152, Gales Family Papers, NCDAH;
"McPheeters Enters Upon His Duties," in Coon, *North Carolina
Schools and Academies*, 420; J[ohn] Holt Rice to W[illia]m
McPheeters, 17 September 1811, Benjamin H. and John Holt Rice
Papers, NCDAH; B[enjamin] H[olt] Rice to W[illia]m McPheeters,
5 April 1816, Benjamin H. and John Holt Rice Papers, NCDAH.

34. J[ohn] Witherspoon to F[rederick] Nash, 20 October 1815, Frederick
Nash Papers, NCDAH.

35. Session Records, 15 April 1818, and passim, Hillsborough Presbyterian, microfilm at NCDAH.

36. Catherine DeRosset to [her mother], 28 July 1820, William Lord
DeRosset Papers, DUA.

37. Jane Williams to Elizabeth E. Haywood, 4 January 1817, Ernest Haywood Papers, SHC.

38. Catherine DeRosset to [her mother], 28 July 1820, William Lord
DeRosset Papers, DUA.

39. Ann Hill to Catherine DeRosset, 6 August 1817, DeRosset Family
Papers, SHC.

40. Ann A. Turner to [Eliza E Haywood], 23 November 1811, Ernest
Haywood Papers, SHC.

41. Eliza G. Hasell to Miss Elizabeth DeRosset, 11 June 1825, DeRosset
Family Papers, SHC.

42. Ann C. Blount to Polly Ann Rodman, [26 August 1818], in David
Morgan, ed., *John Gray Blount Papers*, vol. 4 (Raleigh: North Caro-
lina Department of Cultural Resources, Division of Archives and
History, 1982), 4:297.

43. Eliza G. Hasell to Mrs. DeRosset, 22 July 1819, DeRosset Family
Papers, SHC.

44. Catherine DeRosset to [her mother], 28 July 1820, William Lord
DeRosset Papers, DUA.

45. Poetry book, ca. 1820, Adelaide Savage Meares Papers, DUA.

46. Ibid.

CHAPTER TWO

Ambivalent Churchmen and Evangelical Churchwomen: The Restoration of the Episcopal Church, 1810–1830

The world in which Episcopal men lived was changing dramatically, and they were uncomfortable with the change. By the first decade of the nineteenth century, market economics, the beckoning frontier, the rise of planter parvenus, democratic politics, and evangelical Christianity had combined to erode much of what remained of the stable, organic, hierarchical world of the colonial era.

The evangelical revival among genteel ladies brought these new, topsy-turvy social arrangements directly into the homes of traditional gentlemen, and it was more than they could stand. With more and more of their female family members embracing evangelicalism, gentlemen across the state could no longer afford to ignore organized Christianity without risking the disruption of domestic harmony. In response, these men, many of them Episcopalians by heritage, revived the Episcopal church as a way of reaffirming the traditional world view, regaining patriarchal control of their families, and maintaining their claim to moral rectitude without having to submit themselves to the strict, evangelical code of behavior.

The return to Episcopal orthodoxy forced men officially to renounce deistical thought, although certain features peculiar to the Episcopal church enabled them to remain privately skeptical toward orthodoxy. Baptized membership in the Episcopal church represented a sort of half-way status that allowed men to govern and to participate in the life of the church without embracing either orthodox theology or the stricter ethics demanded of Episcopal

communicants. Most Episcopal men demonstrated an enduring
ambivalence toward the Episcopal church and refused to become
communicants as they remained wedded to codes of honor and reason. Women made up the overwhelming majority of Episcopal
communicants throughout the antebellum era (see tables 1 and 2).

Table 1
Episcopal Communicants, 1840

	Female	Male	Sex Ratio (F/M)
Calvary Episcopal, Wadesboro	30	8	3.8 : 1
Christ Church Episcopal, Elizabeth City	36	2	18 : 1
St. James's Episcopal, Wilmington	167	40	4.2 : 1
St. Peter's Episcopal, Washington	64	13	5 : 1
Totals	297	63	4.7 : 1

*Statistics compiled from the various local Episcopal church records, on
microfilm at NCDAH.*

Table 2
New Episcopal Communicants
1 January 1840–31 December 1845

	Female	Male	Sex Ratio (F/M)
Christ's Church Episcopal, Newbern	19	10	1.9 : 1
Grace Episcopal, Plymouth	10	3	3.3 : 1
St. James's Episcopal, Wilmington	45	15	3 : 1
St. John's Episcopal, Fayetteville	30	19	1.6 : 1
St. Matthew's, Hillsboro	21	5	4.2 : 1
St. Paul's Episcopal, Edenton	16	7	2.3 : 1
Trinity Episcopal, Scotland Neck	12	1	12 : 1
Totals	153	60	2.6 : 1

*Statistics compiled from the various local Episcopal church records, on
microfilm at NCDAH.*

It was natural that men would revert to the old church as a way of restoring tranquility to their families and lives since that church had once served as such an important instrument and symbol of social order. John S. West had apparently viewed the Episcopal church as the antidote to the disturbing female religious enthusiasm associated with the Methodists as early as 1808.[1] The new effort to revive the Episcopal church succeeded where earlier attempts by West and others failed, however, because it also was able to satisfy female evangelical needs. The new Episcopal church turned out to be as much a part of the ladies' revival as it was a response to it.

The Episcopal laity, therefore, included communicants, adult baptized members, and patrons, or "friends," of the church. It was a theologically diverse group with persons sympathetic to deistic notions, an orthodox remnant, and new evangelicals. The theological variety within the church tended to be linked to gender: Episcopal men were inclined to be either orthodox or deistical; many of the Episcopal ladies came to the church as evangelicals. The difficult task of the church was to contain (and reconcile) the theoretically conflicting religious positions of Episcopal orthodoxy and evangelicalism, while simultaneously working to extirpate deistical belief without alienating the important church patrons who espoused it.

Several distinct blocs made up an Episcopal congregation after 1810: a group of evangelically inclined ladies who formed the overwhelming majority of church communicants; gentlemen related to the ladies who financed the church, but who remained on the periphery of church life as baptized members or even unbaptized friends of the church; a vestry, composed of a mixture of less-committed, baptized men and devoted male communicants, who hired the minister and operated the church; and a minister, the spiritual leader, who must have felt like a chameleon as he tried to please all the disparate parties.

The new Episcopal churches clearly represented a challenge to the church's traditional ecclesiology. In theory, the local Episcopal minister derived his spiritual authority through apostolic succession at the hands of an ordaining bishop. In fact, however, a local Episcopal minister had to satisfy two powerful groups within the congregation if he was to succeed. First, to remain in his office, the Episcopal minister dared not enter into major conflict with the powerful men who sat on the vestry. Second, he had better satisfy the evangelical needs of his female communicants or the ladies would desert the pews and leave the church empty.

During the second decade of the nineteenth century, Episcopalians successfully restored local churches in Wilmington, Edenton, Newbern, and Fayetteville. In these towns, local gentlemen hired Episcopal ministers who were more or less able to meet the difficult demands of a church setting that contained both reactionary males and evangelical females. Soon, Episcopal ministers from these four churches and cooperating laymen spearheaded the creation of the Diocese of North Carolina and called its first bishop, John Stark Ravenscroft.

The male elite of Wilmington was the first group in the state to reestablish a dynamic Episcopal congregation when they called the Rev. Adam Empie in 1811 from his first pastorate in Hempstead, New York, to fill the vacant pulpit at St. James's. Fifty-one local gentlemen subscribed to pay Empie's salary in 1811. Over the next five years an additional sixty-two of the wealthiest and most influential gentlemen in the area contributed money to Empie's support.

The theological views of this group of gentlemen as a whole are suggested by three from their ranks, John De Rosset Toomer, John R. London, and Christopher Dudley, Jr. Toomer financially supported St. James's only nine years after he had espoused his deistical views in his Dialectic Society address. London, who within the last decade had put his bookplate in *Beauties of the Studies of Nature*, a book based on natural religion, did the same. Dudley, wealthy planter, merchant, shipbuilder, and father of a future governor, remained a lifelong deist. None of the three became a communicant.[2]

Fewer than 6 of 123 male financial backers of St. James's became communicants in the church. Episcopal men were not as willing as Episcopal women to take the serious communion vows that indicated their theology was orthodox and their lifestyle pure. Episcopal men probably resisted becoming communicants because they still acted on the basis of older notions of honor and reason that were in conflict with both the theology and the ethics of Episcopal orthodoxy. One Episcopal minister described the baptized Episcopal adult as not "altogether a Christian."[3]

Although Cape Fear gentlemen refused to become communicants of the Episcopal church, a number of them did connect themselves with the church as baptized members. In early 1813 a handful of some of the most prestigious gentlemen in Cape Fear, individuals whose wealth and breeding rivaled anyone in the state, set a pattern that was to be followed in succeeding years by other gentlemen throughout North Carolina as they decided to become baptized members of the Episcopal church. Great planters like Alfred Moore, Jr., Hugh Waddell, John Waddell, Maurice Moore, as well as other men from the ranks of the gentility, were baptized along with their families in February of that year.

It must have been a novel sight as Empie poured water on the kneeling gentlemen, read a prayer, and put the sign of the cross on each of them. One family member was struck by the image of a proud man like Alfred Moore, Jr., assuming such a humble position: "It was very impressive indeed to see a Man as Alfred was on his knees & the minister praying & pouring water on his Head." A few of the local gentlemen even became communicants. The ten male communicants who broke with accepted practice included such distinguished individuals as Col. Joseph Gardner Swift, commander of the United States garrison at Fort Johnston, several miles away in Smithville. Swift, a New Yorker who married into a wealthy and respectable Cape Fear family, admitted that his wife was far more pious than he. Her example may have induced him to connect himself with St. James's in the first place.[4]

As baptized members of the Episcopal church, the gentlemen of Wilmington were eligible to sit on the vestry and rule the local church without having to submit themselves to the stricter code of ethics implied by full, communing membership—they could still enjoy many of their traditional pastimes. According to his mother-in-law, Alfred Moore "has not as you have heard become religious[.] [H]e is the same man he always was, except he has been Christened and does not swear as much, nor will he suffer his Children to take the Lords name in vain if he hears them, or mention it except in saying their prayers, you know in former times there was no such thing as learning a child its prayers could be attempted in the House."[5]

As the description of Alfred Moore indicates, however, orthodoxy did make certain ethical demands that conflicted with at least some former behavior. Perhaps Alfred Moore had not "become religious" in the evangelical sense, but he had altered older behavior, as his intolerance of swearing and his permission of family prayers indicate.

Alfred Moore's actions may be representative of the response made by a small, but influential, number of Cape Fear gentlemen who joined the church as baptized members. Renouncing a few of their most flagrant habits was a minor sacrifice that allowed them, nevertheless, to preserve much of their traditional way of life. Other gentlemen remained unbaptized friends of the church, contributing financially but refusing to join the church. They purchased exemption from all spiritual and ethical responsibilities while other respected and trustworthy Episcopal men controlled their wives' and daughters' church.

The Wilmington gentlemen made a judicious choice when they selected Adam Empie as pastor in 1811: the ladies flocked in to hear the young Episcopal rector. Empie's sermons were full of such evangelical watchwords such as "the misery of man," "justification by faith," "conversion," "the new birth," and "the renewing of the Holy Ghost." According to one devout young Wilmington lady, Empie preached with "peculiar energy," and "with that earnestness of manner . . . which marks the Christian, the zealous Christian." His sermons were not cold and passionless discourses, but warm and emotional appeals that won the hearts of his female listeners. It was absolutely essential that an Episcopal preacher be able to satisfy his lady parishioners if the church was to grow.[6]

One prominent Wilmington layman noted that the preaching of one of Empie's immediate successors in the St. James' pulpit was "calculated to take with the Ladies, (who you . . . know too often rule the roost in church.)" The Wilmington ladies not only flocked to hear Empie, they joined St. James's in record numbers. In a little over two years' time, the number of communicants in the church swelled from 21 to 102. The communing membership was disproportionately female; ninety-two of the most prominent ladies from both the town and outlying plantations belonged to the church. Only ten gentlemen had joined as communing members by 1814.[7]

Empie was a prototype for the new brand of Episcopal ministers in North Carolina who had been influenced by one of the two major theological movements present in the American Episcopal church in the early nineteenth century: Episcopal evangelicalism, or low churchmanship. The low church movement was a part of the broader evangelical movement in nineteenth century America, but was distinguished from the evangelicalism of the Methodists and the Baptists in several important respects. They preached from prepared notes, unlike the Baptists and Methodists. And they tended not to emphasize the terrors of hell and tolerated neither physical excesses nor emotional outbursts during worship. Nevertheless, Episcopal evangelical preachers tried to convert their listeners just as other evangelicals did. As a matter of fact, many Virginia Episcopalians from the old church who heard this new style of Episcopal preaching for the first time called it "Methodist."[8]

To accentuate their special concerns, Episcopal evangelical preachers modified the traditional liturgy of the Episcopal service. They deleted the antecommunion service from the liturgy to allow more time for preaching. They also prayed extemporaneously instead of reading the prescribed collects of the liturgy. In addition, Episcopal evangelicals, including Empie, organized midweek Bible classes beyond the regular Sunday service. The low churchmen controlled the church in a number of other states, including North Carolina's neighbor Virginia. In Virginia during the first decades of the nineteenth century, Bishop Richard Channing Moore and his assistant William Meade provided evangelical leadership to revive a dying Episcopal diocese and to found the low church Virginia Theological Seminary in Alexandria.[9]

Like all evangelicals, low churchmen believed that the experience of conversion endowed the believer with new and holy affections, which enabled the individual to lead a life of personal sanctity. Because low churchmen believed that the preached word, not the eucharist, was the locus of salvation, participation in the eucharist was understood as an outward sign of an inner conversion. Low churchmen did not view communion as a means of grace. Instead, it was a privilege reserved for those already set apart by God. Therefore, low churchmen excluded the unconverted, those who had *not* experienced a spiritual rebirth, from the communion table.[10]

For low churchmen, regeneration was a precondition for confirmation and communion. Confirmation, usually as a young adult, was the true mark of church membership for the Episcopal evangelical. After confirmation it was expected that the believer would lead a qualitatively different style of life following automatically from the inner conversion. The Episcopal evangelical communicant participated in the Lord's Supper with regularity.[11]

It was fortunate that Empie possessed many of the characteristics of a low churchman since, as in the case of his predecessor Solomon Halling, Episcopal activities in the community continued to occur against a background of Methodist success and ongoing appeal to the ladies. When Empie left town for several years to become chaplain at West Point, the Methodists "made some additions to their Society" as a number of the Episcopal ladies deserted St. James's. Even after he returned, several more ladies took flight to the Front Street Methodist church.[12]

One prominent lady, Ann Smith, the wife of Gov. Benjamin Smith, seemed to vacillate between the two denominations. After she had suffered for some time from a severe emotional imbalance, the governor requested that the local Methodist minister, Joseph Travis, pay her a pastoral visit. Travis convinced Mrs. Smith that she was not deranged and "then proceeded to point her desponding and sin-smitten soul to the great atonement made for sinners by the death and resurrection of Christ." A few days later, Mrs. Smith appeared at Joseph Travis's doorstep and announced, "O Sir! you have done me more good than all the doctors put together. You directed me to Jesus. I went to him by faith, and humble confidence, and prayer. He has healed me, soul and body: I feel quite well and happy." Although the Smiths remained grateful friends of the Rev. Travis, they never joined the Methodist church. Mrs. Smith, though now an evangelical, remained at St. James's; her husband, the governor, never became a communicant in any church.[13]

The religious tension in the home of Dr. Armand J. DeRosset, Sr., demonstrates how Methodism disturbed at least one genteel home in Wilmington and suggests why Episcopal men revived the church. Although DeRosset's remarks to his Methodist wife, Catherine, were made six years after Empie's arrival, his response may be representative of the way in which other gentlemen reacted when the Methodists first began to capture their wives' and daughters' loyalties: "I . . . abhor the spirit of proselytism, & hence, while I respect & esteem many of the methodists for their piety & zeal, & regret that those principles are not more common among us [the Episcopalians], I am utterly opposed to, & cannot encourage a social intercourse with, persons who continually endeavor to weaken the attachment of our young people to, & withdraw them from the church."[14]

In Dr. DeRosset's letter, discord between traditional husbands and evangelical wives or daughters was couched in the language of denominational conflict existing between the Episcopal church (which the gentlemen controlled) and the Methodist church (which they did not). But the underlying source of hostility, and, indeed, the most plausible explanation for the gentlemen's effort to revive a virtually extinct Episcopal church in Wilmington, was the evangelical threat to patriarchal control as the Methodists began "to weaken the attachment" within families. The genteel suspicion that the Methodists were loosening family ties was to resurface occasionally long after the restoration of the Episcopal church. In 1831 a young female member of the DeRosset clan wrote to a friend in Pittsboro to find out "if the report is true" that a local Methodist minister "call'd upon children to break through all parental restraints & join the [Methodist] Church."[15]

In Edenton, the Episcopal church was resuscitated, as one local gentlemen candidly admitted, out of fear that the gentry would become Methodist or Baptist. Since the gentlemen, on the whole, did not join the Episcopal church as communing members even after it was revived, obviously they were worried that the ladies would be lost to the evangelicals.

The situation in the home of Dr. James Norcom and his wife, Maria Matilda (Horniblow) Norcom, is illustrative of the confusion caused by the Methodists in genteel homes. When Maria wrote to her husband about the deathbed conversion of a local youth, James replied in an effort "to show the impropriety of our being led away by the prejudices or absurdities of any Sect." Dr. Norcom, a deist, went on to argue that "'tis' not necessary that we should attach ourselves to any society or company of Christians [including the Episcopal church]—To do as we would be done by is our duty to our fellow creatures, & is our truest happiness—To love God & fear him is also necessary, & seems natural to all who are capable of comprehending his character or contemplating his w[o]rks."[16]

According to Norcom, to join a particular church went against the dictates of reason: "We know there are many Christian societies, each thinking itself right. Now reason teaches us that they may all be wrong, but forbids us to believe that they can all be right. The truth is, if there be any essential difference between them, there can be but *one right;* and how extremely improbable is it, among the number which prevail, that I should make choice of the *only true one.*"[17]

Less than ten years later, Norcom was a leading financial supporter of St. Paul's, Edenton. What had made a deist like him change his mind and back the Episcopal church when he had been so resolutely opposed to "attaching himself to any Christian society" only a short time before? Surely the growing fascination of women like his wife with the activities of Edenton Methodists and Baptists must have prompted his new commitment.

The other gentlemen who directed the effort to revive St. Paul's around 1815 included leaders in the town and region. Among them were one future governor and two of the greatest planters in North Carolina. No list of members remains for these first years, but the ladies who dominated the membership only ten years later undoubtedly made up most of the communing membership in the beginning as well. Twenty-seven of the thirty-four communicants of St. Paul's in 1826 were women. John Avery, who had served as headmaster of the Edenton Academy since 1814, doubled as lay reader for St. Paul's before his ordination as a minister in 1816.

More women might have joined Avery's church if his preaching had been more engaging. The former Presbyterian presented his homilies in a dull and measured fashion. One of the St. Paul ladies, Jane M. Roulhac, who could no longer endure the tedium, wrote a scathing letter to Avery informing him of his deficiencies as a preacher. Avery's response was both honest and spirited. He admitted, "I have long been sensible of the serious disadvantages which I labour under from want of an eloquent and captivating address which wins so much upon hearers & often supplies the place of sound sense and scriptural knowledge & even of piety." Avery, however, defended his doctrinal soundness even if he did have a poor delivery: "I did think, notwithstanding these defects [in my preaching style], that my public discourses contained such an exhibition of man's guilt & impotency, of his help through the mercy of God in Christ Jesus, & of his duty as a redeemed creature, that a serious & honest hearer might learn what to believe and practice for his soul's salvation."[18]

The indignant cleric went on to chide his critic and blast certain evangelical preachers:

> If the great end of hearing preaching, were to be affected for the time & to have pleasurable emotions excite[d], then preachers ought to be regarded in the light of play actors & be encouraged or discouraged as they contributed to this end. But surely there is a higher object to be obtained than that of being moved & delighted during the sermon, & that is the reception of Divine truth

to be carried home, thought upon, prayed over, grafted into the heart, & put into immediate practice.[19]

Not stopping here, Avery did everything but call the local Methodists by name—and he did refer to their denomination's founder, John Wesley—when he went on to criticize their "peculiar" doctrine of sensible conversion, "the doctrine that every truly pious person must have a *certain* witness within, of God's pardon, & that every person who does not know certainly this fact is in a state of spiritual death is the doctrine of enthusiasm, unsupported by the word of God, & the general experience of Christians. It is a doctrine that Mr. Westley [*sic*] rejected in his mature years." Unfortunately for Avery, judging from the small size of his congregation, a number of others like Jane Roulhac favored evangelical preaching and the born again experience that he could not provide. If an Episcopal minister was to succeed against Methodist competition, he had to be an inspiring preacher.[20]

In Newbern, around 1817, the Episcopal service resounded once again within the colonial walls of Christ's Church. The Methodists had been active in town for over a decade and the Presbyterians formed a small congregation almost simultaneously with the resumption of Episcopal worship. John S. West and Moses Jarvis were two of the local gentlemen who helped bring the Episcopal church back to life. John Stanley, who had been a political opponent and personal enemy of West less than a decade before, also was in the forefront of the restoration of Christ's Church. According to legend, Stanley's marriage to a Methodist, who was the daughter of a wealthy local planter, resulted in domestic conflict over differences in the couple's religion. The plausibility of the legend is supported by the fact that Stanley—an Episcopalian by heritage—worshipped at the Methodist church before the restoration of Christ's Church, but afterward he switched back, without his wife, to the Episcopal church.

The Newbern gentlemen were generous in their financial support for Christ's Church when they opened their wallets in 1824 and built a commodious new sanctuary. They also continued to display an overriding concern for education, employing the Episcopal minister as schoolmaster in the local academy. The wife of an early Episcopal minister in Newbern worried that, as a result of her husband's all-consuming duties at the academy, the "Preacher will be lost in the Teacher."[21]

There is no reason to doubt that Moses Jarvis and John S. West genuinely celebrated the return of orthodoxy—although it is worth remembering that West had only become a champion of orthodoxy ten years earlier as a response to the Methodist threat. The motives of other Episcopal gentlemen in town, who were not communicants, are less clear. If they were disgusted with their wives' and daughters' evangelicalism, they may have finally reached the same conclusion attributed to West ten years earlier, that "a man has by the law of God such dominion over his wife that she is bound to become a member of any church he prefers," and restored the Episcopal church as a solution. Hiring an Episcopal minister also allowed Episcopal men to make the customary provisions for their children's education. As elsewhere, it was overwhelmingly the women who chose to become communing members. Fifty-three of the sixty-one white communicants at Christ's Church in the late 1820s were female.[22]

The situation confronting traditional gentlemen in a town like Fayetteville, with a well-established, genteel Presbyterian church, was more subtle than in Wilmington or Edenton, where only the Methodists challenged. But the pattern was the same: against a background of female attraction and male resistance to evangelicalism, spiritually less-committed Episcopal men founded a church for more devout women. In Fayetteville the Presbyterian clergyman performed a dual role as community pastor and principal of the local academy. The trustees of the local academy, who represented most of the prominent gentlemen in town (and who were not necessarily church-goers) were interested primarily in a schoolmaster for their children. The ladies wanted a pastor.

Only in 1814 with the arrival of a new Presbyterian minister, the Rev. Jesse H. Turner, did problems with the cooperative venture between the lady evangelicals and the traditional gentlemen begin to surface. Turner was extremely popular with the ladies who made up his church, but his evangelical morality immediately began to rub some gentlemen the wrong way. A few months after the new minister's arrival, William H. Tillinghast, son of a prominent merchant, joked about the absence of dancing balls in Fayetteville: "Our worthy friend Mr. Turner does not approve of such amusements, and we do not desire to offend him, obedient lads to be sure to the will of the parson. [H]owever, I expect the Spirit will move us before long and dancing will revive like methodists, from opposition."[23]

Turner took other action that also portended a clash of values: he placed restrictions on the requirements for baptism. Previous Presbyterian ministers had made allowances in the ceremony of baptism to placate the scruples of certain unnamed, but almost certainly genteel, parents. These ministers had performed baptisms in private homes and even allowed nonmembers to have their children baptized. Jesse Turner, however, decided that baptisms would be performed exclusively in church and only to children of members. Turner made these changes even after the local governing body of the church, the session, advised him that "there would be a propriety in the [minister] pursuing the same line of conduct on this subject, which governed his predecessors."

Turner's innovations in the baptismal requirements probably prevented very few genteel parents from having their children baptized since only one parent needed to be a member in good standing to have a child baptized, and the large number of wives who belonged to the church probably fulfilled the requirements in most cases. But the baptism controversy, like the ban on dancing, indicated a rigor on the part of the evangelical Turner that almost certainly brought him into conflict with proud gentlemen on other occasions.

As a denomination, the Presbyterian church's moral standards for its members may have been no stricter theoretically than those for an Episcopal communicant, but in the Presbyterian church there was no half-way status similar to the one baptized, adult Episcopal members enjoyed. The Presbyterian member, or communicant, (the two were synonymous) attended communion regularly and theoretically observed a strict evangelical standard of behavior. As one student of Presbyterian discipline in the antebellum South demonstrates, Presbyterians, while never completely uniform or consistent, did use their church courts to enforce their moral code. In John Witherspoons's Hillsboro Presbyterian Church, for example, a male member was suspended for owning a billiard table.[24]

With Turner's ethical strictness and his influence over the ladies as a background, a movement arose in 1817 among some of the leading gentlemen in town to establish St. John's Episcopal church in Fayetteville. According to the Rev. Turner, the Episcopal church was to be built "in the ruins of the Presbyterians." Faced with these developments, Turner decided to remain as pastor only after the congregation reiterated its support of him and he "had lately received from the Female part of his beloved flock the strongest expression of their most anxious solicitude for his continuance among them."[25]

The gentlemen of the Episcopal church requested that the Presbyterians relinquish a lot on Green Street because the Episcopalians believed themselves the "rightful proprietors thereof." The Episcopal rationale for attempting to appropriate the Presbyterian property may have resulted from the fact that the Episcopalians had financially supported Turner previously as either school trustees or through direct contributions to the Presbyterian church on behalf of their wives. Eventually, the Presbyterians bargained with the Episcopalians and sold the property to them.

The new Episcopal church in Fayetteville was unique among all Episcopal churches in antebellum North Carolina. It began in 1817 with more male communicants than female: thirteen to twelve. The male majority was all the more remarkable when one recalls that the Presbyterian church had consisted of seventy female and twelve male communicants only three years before. The male-to-female ratio did not persist in the Episcopal church; only nine years later thirty-eight female and fifteen male communicants belonged to the church.

Although the evidence is too slim to uncover the exact reasons that the gentlemen founded St. John's, the situation was remarkably similar, in some respects, to the formation of Episcopal churches in Wilmington and Edenton as a response to the Methodists. It is certain that the Fayetteville ladies were extremely loyal to Turner. It is also clear that he had demonstrated an unwillingness to compromise evangelical principles. Already tired of Turner's repressive moral influence on the community, as suggested by the reaction to the ban on dancing, genteel husbands may have finally perceived him as a rival to their own patriarchal control and started the Episcopal church to get their wives away from him.

The Fayetteville churchmen were fortunate in the choice of their second pastor in 1818; they selected yet another representative of the new breed of young, evangelical, Episcopal ministers, Gregory Bedell. Bedell, who was from New York and a nephew of the noted evangelical Episcopal Bishop of Virginia, Richard Channing Moore, displayed splendid evangelical gifts of his own. The ladies remarked upon his ability to preach without notes and to pray extemporaneously. Despite Bedell's success, the Episcopal gentlemen's commitment to the work of the church remained questionable during these first few years. The young Episcopal minister once threatened to leave unless the vestry compensated him more fairly. Bedell removed to Philadelphia soon after, ostensibly for reasons of health.[26]

Even five years later, in 1822, after the Episcopal church in Fayetteville had grown considerably and hired the Rev. William Hooper, at least one local Episcopal insider felt that the town's gentlemen were still unconcerned about the pastoral ministry and observed that "it is only the Ladies that admire [Hooper] so much as a preacher[.] [T]he Gentlemen are only for the Academy and wish to secure him on that account." Another observer noted that although the Episcopal gentlemen regularly attended divine worship, "it is too true the men are cold enough on the subject of religion— there are but few who think any thing more of it, than as a mere form, which may add something to the order and decency of the community at large." When the Episcopal minister invited the St. John's communicants to come forward to the Lord's Supper, these gentlemen stood like "Stone Idols" and refused to do so.[27]

As unenthusiastic as their religious behavior appeared, however, there was a clear logic to the Episcopal men's actions. They now controlled the vestry and ran their wives' church. They also had acquired a schoolmaster for their children as a part of the bargain. And presumably Episcopal gentlemen in Fayetteville, who were as immovable as rocks when the invitation was made to come to the communion table, moved willingly and freely at local dances: Mr. Turner's puritannical opinions no longer mattered.

As the local Episcopal churches in Wilmington, Fayetteville, Newbern, and Edenton gained stability, their ministers, led by Adam Empie, initiated a successful movement to organize the Diocese of North Carolina in 1817. As necessary as the efforts of these clergymen were in the creation of the diocese, however, they would have failed in their attempt, just as their predecessors under Pettigrew had fallen short in the 1790s, without the support of powerful gentlemen to back the enterprise. As weak as the new diocese was, it accurately reflected the scattered, but growing, gentry support across the state for the new church. Not surprisingly, the gentlemen who ensured the survival of the fledgling diocese were the same group who made possible the restoration of the local churches. Each year saw additions to the roster of Episcopal congregations in North Carolina as churches sprang up in the important towns of eastern North Carolina and a few in western North Carolina as well.[28]

The Episcopal church was assuming its role as the dominant upper-class church in the east, just as the Presbyterian already had in the west. North Carolinians recognized that the Presbyterians and Episcopalians had a higher social standing than the other denominations. One mother, forced to leave the Episcopal church when her husband joined the Baptists, expressed what was undoubtedly a prevailing sentiment concerning the Presbyterian and Episcopal churches: "I am too worldly minded . . . to wish [my daughters] Helen and Fan to be baptists—girls certainly make their way in the world and maintain a place in genteel society better as Presbyterians or Episcopalians than as baptists or methodists."[29]

A Presbyterian minister in Fayetteville who surveyed the prospects of the Episcopal church in the eastern part of the state noted that the denomination did "much good . . . among the rich especially. They draw out their treasure and influence in favour of religion." The Diocese of North Carolina would never be numercially great compared to more popular denominations, but its appeal was significant among North Carolina's elite.[30]

Before the young diocese was able to support a bishop of its own, Bishop Moore of Virginia presided over it. The diocesan hierarchy was completed in 1823 when the Rev. John Stark Ravenscroft came south from Virginia to assume his joint appointment as a pastor of the Episcopal congregation in Raleigh and as the first consecrated Episcopal bishop of North Carolina. Under Ravenscroft's firm and effective leadership, the Diocese of North Carolina began to grow. By the late 1820s the Episcopal church in North Carolina probably contained a thousand baptized and communing members.[31]

Ravenscroft's arrival brought a new theological tradition into the Episcopal Church in North Carolina: high churchmanship. The theological differences between high churchmen and low churchmen were significant enough to spark repeated controversies between the two camps in various sectors of the American Episcopal church. In the Diocese of Maryland high and low church parties were already locked in battle by 1811. A decade later in the Diocese of Pennsylvania, a conflict erupted between the two parties that simmered and spewed intermittently for another twenty years. Indeed, the House of Bishops, the upper house in the bicameral system that governed the Episcopal church at the national level, was largely split into the two contending parties for much of the antebellum period.

Ravenscroft was far from theologically consistent himself and drew from both theological traditions within the American Episcopal church—high church and low church. In particular the Bishop's understanding of the salvation process (soteriology) was a variation of the typical evangelical scheme: he believed that an adult believer must have an experience of rebirth before becoming a full, communing member. He informed Adam Empie that "in general terms, I consider [confirmation] equivalent to a Profession of Religion on Conviction and Experience." He himself had been converted at the age of thirty-eight, and joined the Republican Methodist church in Virginia. Afterward he became an Episcopal minister in Virginia's low church.[32]

Ravenscroft's preaching also reflected his evangelical background. When he preached in Raleigh in 1824 "[h]e was so much affected as to burst into tears & sob bitterly when he alluded to his past life and his merciful deliverance." Here was an Episcopal preacher who knew what it was to be lost and to be saved, and whose preaching breathed all the emotions of his own personal experience.[33]

As a result of his strong evangelical bent, Ravenscroft attracted pious women and rebuked less-committed men. In 1825, for example, Ravenscroft overruled Adam Empie and disallowed William Hill, a member of a powerful Cape Fear family whose other members were patrons of St. James's, from participating in the baptism of his child. Empie took the position that even an irreligious parent could make the baptismal vows in good conscience so long as he saw to it that the child was raised a Christian. But Ravenscroft refused to be a part of the service so long as William Hill was included in it. According to the Bishop, "I have not refused to Baptise the child—on the contrary I offered to do it on the Sponsion of the Mother alone—But knowing the Father to be a professed unbeliever, by the open acknowledgment of his own lips—and having it confirmed by his whole conversation—I refused to be a 'partaker of his Sin'—by admitting him to appear in the Face of the Congregation—as a party to a solemn Sacrament." Ravenscroft went on to inform Empie of his general principle that forbade "known Atheists and Infidels to be received as Sponsors in Baptism—or vicious Livers to the Eucharist."[34]

Ravenscroft would reprimand anyone who, like William Hill, was brave enough openly to question Episcopal orthodoxy. He would stand eye-to-eye with a leading citizen of the state and tell him that he was damned if not a Christian. When Col. William Polk, Revolutionary War hero, president of the State Bank, and father of a future Episcopal bishop, asked Ravenscroft if a man of moral probity and virtuous living would get to heaven by these means alone, the Bishop replied, "No, Sir; he would go straight to hell."[35]

In 1828 the Bishop took the whole diocese to task when he addressed the annual convention on the dangers of "Natural Religion." Ravenscroft warned: "In whatever degree, therefore, we assume the gratuitous reasonings derived from either abstract or natural Religion, as the ground of duty and hope towards God, we depart from the only foundation, and prepare the way for infidelity and indifference to triumph, under the guise of external morality." Ravenscroft's comments were the most vehement declaration of the Episcopal church's official censure of Enlightenment unorthodoxies. When other Episcopal ministers occasionally preached sermons against "socinianism" and "unitarianism," two heresies that deny the divinity of Christ, their exhortations were almost certainly also aimed at those who still held to an Enlightenment heresy. At the same time, however, as long as laymen were quiet about their deviation from orthodoxy, no one—not even Ravenscroft—was likely to probe too deeply; there were too many important Episcopalians who would have failed an inquisition. Only the outspoken, like William Hill, were in danger of personal condemnation.[36]

Ravenscroft also upbraided baptized members—mostly men—who were not as serious about their religion as communicants—mostly women. In 1829 the Bishop reported that the communicants at St. John's, Williamsboro, "are without any known reproach in their walk and conversation in life, regular in their attendance and devout in their deportment." But he "lamented" that the same could not be said for the noncommunicants who neglected the church's "public services" and gave "little countenance . . . to the cause of Religion."[37]

Ravenscroft's premature death in 1830 robbed the diocese of an able leader. Episcopal men, however, may have viewed the Bishop's demise with mixed feelings and silent relief. Ravenscroft's uncompromising spirit and his outspoken demand for moral purity surely made proud and independent-minded Episcopal men uncomfortable. Undoubtedly, Episcopal men were grateful to Ravenscroft for strengthening the church, but it is unlikely that the majority of them missed his commanding presence, his stinging sermons, and his unflinching call to personal holiness.

Many, probably most, of the female communicants of the Episcopal church in North Carolina from 1810 to 1830 were evangelicals whose spiritual counterparts were the other Methodist and Presbyterian ladies who converted to evangelicalism during the ladies' revival. These Episcopal ladies possessed fundamentally different religious outlooks from their husbands. One of them, Margaret Eagles, a Cape Fear lady descended from one of North Carolina's great colonial planter families, underwent the same sort of dramatic conversion that had been changing the religious orientation of genteel women for several decades.

Margaret had felt a "deep concern about her salvation" for more than six months in 1831. As a result of her spiritual crisis, she became ill and was transported up-country to Pittsboro where she was placed under the medical care of Dr. Frederick Hill, one of the few male communicants of St. James's, Wilmington. "Doctor Fred" decided the illness was spiritual not physical and prescribed some religious books for Margaret Eagles to read. While reading a sermon in one of these books, she "felt, first, her burden leave her, & had joy and peace in believing." She was baptized immediately afterwards, and, undoubtedly, was confirmed as soon as the bishop was available.[38]

The old ethic of fashion was a primary obstacle to conversion for Episcopal evangelical women. In the late 1820s, for example, Catherine Ruffin, under the guidance of her Episcopal minister, began to participate in Bible class and was under "serious [religious] impressions." In 1829, however, Catherine moved to "worldly minded Raleigh." One pious female friend worried that there Catherine would become "a lady of fashion" and that "dress, beaux and admiration may fill that heart which used to love Church, Bible Class and S[unday] School."[39]

The worst seemed to come true as Catherine's piety waned in Raleigh. Catherine's devout friend encouraged her to come to the communion table as evidence that she had separated herself from the world of fashion. The friend warned Catherine to beware of "the snare that company is to you. I have no doubt you have had many serious reflections banished by lively companions, & have been led to do & say many things which your conscience condemned." Finally, a year later, Catherine overcame the battle with sin and worldliness and experienced an evangelical conversion.[40]

The new Episcopal religious ethic among genteel women was so appealing that even a few genteel Jewish ladies converted. Ellen Mordecai, member of the prominent family of Jewish educators who operated noted academies around Warrenton, did so. In Wilmington, one of the female members of the Lazarus family, a prominent mercantile family, recorded her feelings and thoughts after deciding to convert in 1835 despite misgivings about her father's reaction.

> I wept & prayed and resolved to take the step [conversion] which I have so long dreaded even to abandonment, of writing to my father, disclosing to him fully my sentiments, & entreating his forgiveness, his indulgence, & his sanction to pursue the course which my feelings & convictions dictate. I felt as if under the influence of the Holy Spirit, I was strengthened, prepared for the effort, & I would not delay to act in obedience to its dictates.[41]

Other Episcopal women across the state left no account of their own conversions, but the entire character of their lives, the way they spoke and wrote, was as unmistakably evangelical as their Methodist and Presbyterian counterparts. Some, overflowing with emotion, turned to poetry to express their feelings. Margaret Cameron, daughter of Rebecca and Duncan, scribbled a "Hymn for an infant's funeral" in 1832:

> Welcome, dear babe, to Jesu's breast—
> For ever there in joy to rest:
> Welcome to Jesu's courts above,
> To sing the great Redeemer's love![42]

Jane B. Norwood, a young woman who belonged to St. Matthew's, Hillsboro, composed a six-stanza poem in 1829 that began:

> To our Redeemer's glorious name
> Awake the sacred song!
> Oh may his love (immortal flame!)
> Tune every heart and tongue.[43]

Episcopal women also supplemented their religious appetites by reading the same works of evangelical authors as their Methodist

71

and Presbyterian sisters. Charlotte Hooper, wife of Wilmington newspaper editor Archibald Maclaine Hooper, enjoyed Henry Martyn's *Memoirs:* "There is no book of the kind I [ever?] read with equal interest. Whenever I have a few minutes to spare I take it up. He possessed more humility and heavenly mindedness than almost any character I ever read of." Martyn's *Memoirs* recounted the life of an Anglican evangelical who left his native England for a career as a missionary in India and Persia.[44]

Mrs. Hooper also admired *The Life of John Urquhart*. Urquhart was a young Presbyterian Scot who decided, after an evangelical conversion while attending the University of St. Andrew's, to become a missionary to China. Urquhart's premature death prevented him from entering the mission field, but his biography and accompanying memoirs became a devotional classic for evangelicals on both sides of the Atlantic.

The women in the Duncan Cameron family also read from evangelical literary giants. Rebecca Cameron (Mrs. Duncan Cameron) recommended that her friend Alice Ruffin (Mrs. Thomas Ruffin) peruse the *Autobiography of John Newton*. Newton was an English ship's captain and former slave trader who fell under the spell of Whitefield's preaching, and eventually became an Anglican evangelical curate. His autobiography, *An Authentic Narrative of Some Remarkable and Interesting Particulars in the Life of. . . . [John Newton]*, detailed the evils of his former life before conversion. The Cameron daughters also read to the family from Hannah More on a typical Sunday afternoon. More's devotional works gained a wider reading audience than any other Anglican evangelical, or any other evangelical for that matter, in both England and America.

Episcopal women were the spiritual lay leaders of the church. The superior piety of the women troubled a few Episcopal men. In 1831 the Committee on the State of the Church asked in its report to the diocesan convention, "how long shall we continue to hear that the male members of our congregations are outstripped in zeal and every holy exertion by those who in order of creation and Providence should look up to them for examples in all that concerns both 'the life that now is, and that which is to come'?"[45]

Most Episcopal men, however, were unwilling to make the changes that would allow them to assume their position as spiritual heads of households. Episcopal husbands and fathers controlled their wives' and daughters' churches without having to become communicants themselves. The men had restored a church that re-affirmed traditional notions of social and domestic order, but older patterns of thought and behavior kept most from embracing the church as wholeheartedly as women.

Notes

1. Stanley, *An Introductory Essay*, 1.
2. John R. London's copy of *Beauties of the Studies of Nature: Selected from the Works of Saint Pierre* (New York: M. L. & W. A. Davis, 1799) is at NCC; *The James Sprunt Historical Monograph No. 6: Diary of a Geological Tour by Dr. Elisha Mitchell in 1827 and 1828 with Introduction and Notes by Dr. Kemp P. Battle, LLD* (Chapel Hill: University of North Carolina, 1905), 9; Powell, *DNCB*, 2:112; St. James Episcopal, Wilmington, Parish Register, Communicants List, 1811–14, microfilm at NCDAH.
3. William Mercer Green to Thomas Ruffin, 11 January 1828, in Hamilton, *Papers of Thomas Ruffin*, quoted in Lawrence Foushee London and Sarah McCulloh Lemmon, eds., *The Episcopal Church in North Carolina, 1701–1959* (Raleigh: Episcopal Diocese of North Carolina, 1987), 137.
4. Jane Williams to Elizabeth Eagles Haywood, 20 February 1813, Ernest Haywood Papers, SHC; Joseph Gardner Swift, "Extracts from the Diary of Joshua [*sic*] G. Swift" in Kemp P. Battle, ed., *James Sprunt Historical Monograph No. 4: Letters and Documents, Relating to the Early History of the Lower Cape Fear* (Chapel Hill: University of North Carolina, 1903), 115.
5. Jane Williams to Eliza E. Haywood, 9 July 1813, Ernest Haywood Papers, SHC.
6. Adam Empie, D.D., *Sermons on Various Subjects, Written and Preached at Different Places and Times During His Public Ministry of Forty–Four Years* (New York: Dana and Company, Publishers, 1856), 41, 184–94, 311–22, 395–407; Diary entry, [December ?] 14, [?], young lady's diary of religious meditations, 1817–20, Moses Ashley Curtis Papers, SHC.
7. W. C. Lord to John S. Ravenscroft, 22 February 1828, John Ravenscroft Papers, PECA, microfilm at NCC; St. James Episcopal,

Wilmington, Parish Register, Communicants List, 1811–1814, microfilm at NCDAH.

8. The information in this paragraph comes from two sources: David L. Holmes, "The Decline and Revival of the Church of Virginia," in *Up From Independence: The Episcopal Church in Virginia* (Orange, Va.: Interdiocesan Bicentennial Committee of the Virginias, 1976), 73–109; and Edward Clowes Chorley, *Men and Movements in the American Episcopal Church* (New York: Charles Scribner's Sons, 1950), 84–105.

9. Chorley, *Men and Movements*, 84–105; Holmes, "Decline and Revival," 73–109; McEachern, *History of St. James Parish*, 54.

10. Holmes, "Decline and Revival," 73–105.

11. Mullin, *Episcopal Vision/American Reality*, 60–66; *NCDJ*, 1829, 16; Jane Williams to Eliza E. Haywood, 9 July 1813, Ernest Haywood Papers, SHC.

12. Thomas Wright to Robert Scott, 8 August 1812 [1816], The Rev. Thomas Wright Papers, LCFHS; Thomas Wright to Robert Scott, 15 February 1819, The Rev. Thomas Wright Papers, LCFHS.

13. Travis, *Autobiography*, 80.

14. A. J. DeRosset to Catherine F. DeRosset, 10 May 1818, DeRosset Family Papers, SHC.

15. Ann Moore to Magdalen DeRosset, 13 September 1831, DeRosset Family Papers, SHC.

16. James Norcom to Maria M. Norcom, 5 September 1812, James Norcom Papers, NCDAH.

17. Ibid.

18. John Avery to Miss Frances M. Roulhac, 13 May 1823, Ruffin-Roulhac-Hamilton Papers, SHC.

19. Ibid.

20. Ibid.

21. Anne Tates Freeman to Joseph H. Saunders, 5 December 1825, William L. Saunders Papers, DUA.

22. Stanley, *An Introductory Essay*, 1; Christ Church, Episcopal, New Bern, Parish Register, [Communicants List], [ca. 1828], microfilm at NCDAH.

23. William H. Tillinghast to Mr. MacLeod, 22 April 1814, Tillinghast Family Papers, DUA.

24. First Presbyterian Church of Fayetteville, Session Records, 23 September 1817, microfilm at NCDAH; William Davidson Blanks, "Ideal and Practice: A Study of the Conception of the Christian Life Prevailing in the Presbyterian Churches of the South during the Nineteenth Century" (Th.D. diss. Union Theological Seminary in Virginia, 1960); Hillsboro Presbyterian, Register and Session Records, 12 May 1819, 19 May 1819, microfilm at NCDAH.

25. First Presbyterian Church of Fayetteville, Session Records, 15 March 1817, microfilm at NCDAH.

26. The Rev. J. C. Huske, "A History of the Parish of St. John's, Fayetteville, N.C." 1879, 3–4, 51–55, in the Benjamin R. Huske Papers, SHC; John Winslow to Duncan Cameron, 16 May 1817, Cameron Family Papers, SHC; First Presbyterian Church of Fayetteville, Session Records, 18 October 1813, microfilm at NCDAH; Stephen H. Tyng, *Memoir of the Rev. Gregory T. Bedell* (Philadelphia: Henry Perkins, 1836), 2, 70–103; Elisa G. Hasell to Mrs. DeRosset, 22 July 1819, DeRosset Family Papers, SHC.

27. MSQ [?] to Mary DeBerniere, 4 July 1822, John DeBerniere Hooper Papers, SHC.

28. A comparison of the lay delegates to the conventions of the Episcopal Diocese of North Carolina during the early years, as recorded in the various diocesan *Journals of the Conventions,* indicates that local Episcopal patrons were also the major diocesan supporters.

29. [Mrs. William Hooper], [undated], John DeBerniere Hooper Papers, SHC.

30. Robert Hall Morrison to James Morrison, 26 May 1823, Morrison Papers, SHC, quoted in London and Lemmon, *The Episcopal Church in North Carolina,* 123–24.

31. This figure is an estimate based on the various lists of members and communicants in local church records and the various diocesan journals. The figure quoted in London and Lemmon, *The Episcopal Church in North Carolina,* is four hundred. This is low and may reflect only the number of communicants. Where no information exists for baptized membership, it seems safe to assume that there were as many baptized members as communicants. Ravenscroft himself maintained that there were more noncommuning Episcopal members than communicants in the diocese.

32. Lawrence L. Brown, "Richard Channing Moore and the Revival of the Southern Church," *HMPEC* 35 (March 1966): 3–64; London and Lemmon, *The Episcopal Church in North Carolina,* 116–21, 130–33; John S. Ravenscroft to Adam Empie, 23 December [18]24, John Stark Ravenscroft Papers, PECA, microfilm at NCC.

33. John H. Bryan to Mary [Bryan], 26 December 1824, John H. Bryan Papers, NCDAH.

34. Adam Empie to John S. Ravenscroft, 4 July 1825, John Stark Ravenscroft Papers, PECA, microfilm at NCC; John S. Ravenscroft to Adam Empie, 11 July 1825, John Stark Ravenscroft Papers, PECA, microfilm at NCC.

35. Quoted in Chorley, *Men and Movements,* 164–65.

36. Ravenscroft, "Address to the Convention," *NCDJ,* 1828, 35; William H. Haywood, Jr., to Duncan Cameron, 10 May 1821, Cam-

eron Family Papers, SHC; Joseph Gales to Rev. Jared Sparks, 4 May 1821, Gales Family Papers, NCDAH.

37. Ravenscroft, "Report on St. John's, Williamsborough" *NCDJ*, 1829, 16.

38. Mrs. Sally DeRosset to Miss E. A. DeRosset, 24 August 1831, DeRosset Family Papers, SHC.

39. Maria L. Spear to Catherine Ruffin, 1829, Ruffin-Roulhac-Hamilton Papers, SHC.

40. Maria L. Spear to Catherine Ruffin, 6 November 1830, Ruffin-Roulhac-Hamilton Papers, SHC; Maria L. Spear to Catherine Ruffin, 1 August 1831, Ruffin-Roulhac-Hamilton Papers, SHC.

41. Ellen Mordecai, "History of a Heart," ca. 1845, Mordecai Family Papers, SHC; R. Lazarus to Mrs. Catherine DeRosset, 1 Aug. 1835, DeRosset Family Papers, SHC.

42. Margaret Cameron, poetry book, 2 January 1832, Cameron Family Papers, SHC.

43. Jane B. Norwood, poetry book, February 1829, Tillinghast Family Papers, DUA.

44. Charlotte Hooper to John DeBerniere Hooper, 7 April 1832, John DeBerniere Hooper Papers, SHC; see Jesse Page, *Henry Martyn His Life and Labours: Cambridge-India-Persia* (London: S. W. Partridge & Co., n.d.)

45. *NCDJ*, 1831, 12.

CHAPTER THREE

The Growth of High Churchmanship and the Decline of Episcopal Evangelicalism, 1820–1860

Although Bishop John S. Ravenscroft exhibited many evangelical characteristics and tendencies, he also brought a new theological tradition into North Carolina's Episcopal church when he arrived in 1823: high churchmanship. Prior to this time, the Episcopal laity included old churchmen and churchwomen who clung to traditional orthodoxy, men who supported the church but remained wedded to more radical Enlightenment thought, and evangelical women who were the spiritual driving force in the church. After Ravenscroft's arrival, however, Episcopal men began publicly to support the high church system because it best suited their social and cultural needs. This support gave the appearance of theological uniformity, although many remained privately ambivalent toward high churchmanship, just as they had orthodoxy.

At the same time, Episcopal evangelical women also gradually expressed more interest in high churchmanship. Initially, Episcopal evangelical women adapted high church sacramentalism to their own peculiar evangelical needs. But after 1830 Episcopal women became more consistently and genuinely high church. The reasons for this change are not altogether clear, but domestic considerations and social anxiety resulting from the mounting sectional crisis and the fear of slave insurrections suggest themselves as possible explanations.

Under the direction of Ravenscroft's successor, Bishop Levi S. Ives, the growth of high churchmanship proceeded unabated from

1830 to 1845 in the Diocese of North Carolina. This was fitting since Ives was the son-in-law of Bishop John Henry Hobart of New York, the founder and leader of the high church party in the American Episcopal church. As a result of the increasingly high church nature of North Carolina Episcopalianism, the rising generation was less and less likely to become evangelicals. Instead, high church religious training at home and at church became the norm. A process of socialization into high church Episcopalianism served as the basis for faith. Episcopal evangelicals became a smaller and smaller minority within the church, although an evangelical remnant survived until the Civil War.

High churchmanship made its appearance on the national scene in the first decade of the new century when Hobart adapted contemporary Anglican thought and American Episcopal tradition to reformulate orthodox claims into a coherent and systematic theology known as Hobartian high churchmanship, or, more simply, high churchmanship. The movement distinguished itself from evangelical Protestant denominations and from Episcopal evangelicalism, or low churchmanship, in a number of important ways: emphasis on the centrality of the sacraments, a rejection of Enlightenment liberalism or rationalism, a rejection of evangelical emotionalism and revivalism, a defense of Episcopal claims to authority based on Apostolic succession, a reluctance to cooperate with other Protestant denominations, and an insistence on obedience to Episcopal traditions and the Book of Common Prayer. High church Episcopalianism constituted a Protestant alternative outside the nation's evangelical mainstream. The high churchmen's stronghold was in New York State, where General Theological Seminary in New York City produced high church ministers, and where the high church press published its literature and its leading denominational newspaper, the *Churchman*.

The differences in the theologies of Episcopal high churchmanship and Episcopal evangelicalism were significant and had important consequences for the North Carolina church. High churchmanship was predicated on a defense of the Episcopal church's exclusive claim as the one and only true church. Hobart and others argued that only the Episcopal church was apostolic among the Protestant denominations and that episcopacy was sanctioned by "Scripture as elucidated and supported by antiquity." High church ecclesiology was vitally important as a means to protect the Episcopal church's claim to distinctiveness in the face of intense competition from other denominations, particularly the Presbyterians.

In many other respects, high churchmanship was simply a rehearsal of the orthodoxy of the old church. In worship high churchmen were traditionalists who strictly observed the liturgy of the Book of Common Prayer, and who eschewed the freer forms of devotion practiced by Episcopal evangelicals. High church worship tended to emphasize the external forms of the church's rites and ceremonies as the vehicles for the inner religious experience.[1]

The high churchmen rejected the evangelical view of salvation and subscribed instead to a soteriology that maintained that conversion was a gradual, lifelong process based largely on intellectual assent to orthodox doctrine, rather than a once-and-for-all, sensible conversion experience. The high churchmen became intellectually persuaded of the truth of God's promises in Christ, and then attempted to live virtuously through a personal exertion of the will in cooperation with divine grace. Grace only assisted an individual's natural virtues and affections; it did not create new, holy affections. Baptism, whether infant or adult, conferred church membership in the high church scheme because the rite was believed to be the beginning of a conversion process that ceased only with death. For the high churchman, conversion was a "humble walk," a slow, incremental, perhaps even meandering, process; for the evangelical, conversion was a new birth, an inner experience that occurred in a moment, in the twinkling of an eye.[2]

High churchmen also had a different view of the sacraments than most evangelicals. While shunning the Roman Catholic notion of transubstantiation, the real presence of the body and blood of Christ in the elements, Hobart regarded communion "as means and pledges of divine favor and grace, necessary to salvation where they may be had." Although during the early years of the Episcopal restoration it was possible for an unconfirmed baptized member to take communion—just as it had been of necessity in the colonial period when there were no American bishops to confirm members—over time, confirmation by the bishop came to be understood as the ceremony that conferred the privilege to participate in the eucharist.[3]

Despite the importance that the high churchmen attached to communion as a means of grace, however, participation in the sacrament was optional. After all, conversion was gradual, and if a high churchman refused to be confirmed or to take communion now, there was always the hope that he (or she) would join the eucharist in the future. In contrast an evangelical was less inclined to skip communion because to do so called into question whether he or she had really been converted.[4]

Ravenscroft was far from theologically consistent and drew from both the high and low church traditions. In terms of his understanding of church government or polity, however, Ravenscroft was as militantly high church as Hobart himself. In 1825, for example, Ravenscroft attacked the North Carolina Bible Society—an interdenominational benevolent organization previously supported by a number of prominent Episcopalians—because it stood outside the auspices of the one true church, the Episcopal church.[5] That same year the bishop chastised Episcopalians whose loyalties were split between the Episcopal church and other more evangelical denominations in his remarks on "occasional conformity" or "the mixed attendance upon the Church and those who dissent from her" in an address to the diocesan convention.[6] Ravenscroft also successfully used his influence in the new diocese to convince wealthy Episcopal men to support the General Theological Seminary in New York.

To a large extent the North Carolina laymen's support for high churchmanship was natural. High churchmanship was an updated version of the old church's orthodoxy and, as such, vastly preferable to evangelicalism. The high church scheme continued to emphasize the role that the religious intellect performed in subduing refractory emotions. As a result, high church worship, like colonial Anglicanism before it, displayed emotional restraint and decorum and avoided the ungentlemanly outpourings of popular evangelical worship. The Episcopal church hierarchy also provided a model for other social arrangements, and, indeed, high churchmanship championed older, more conservative social patterns based on patriarchy.[7]

High churchmanship also refused to condemn traditional genteel diversions, or "worldly amusements," such as dueling, gaming, theatergoing, and public balls. Unlike the evangelicals, the high churchmen maintained that such amusements were insignificant and not sinful. High churchmanship, in general, was much less morally restrictive than Episcopal evangelicalism; it viewed the process of conversion as always incomplete but, it was hoped, also constantly improving. For Episcopal gentlemen still locked into older habits of behavior and belief, high churchmanship allowed them the closest approximation to their traditional lifestyle and outlook.[8]

For all its advantages, however, high churchmanship involved one important departure from Episcopal men's previous religious experience. North Carolina gentlemen, including Episcopalians, were suspicious of anything that threatened their freedom, and they especially despised despotic authority. Gentlemen also retained a strong strain of anticlericalism as a part of their republican heritage.[9] Faced with the threat from evangelical culture, Episcopal men accepted someone with whom their colonial ancestors had never been forced to deal: a bishop. The potential for conflict between proud and independent Episcopal men and a resolute bishop was there from the beginning. Ravenscroft's calls to personal holiness were already creating tension in the 1820s.

Even with the growth of high churchmanship, most Episcopal men followed older patterns of half-hearted allegiance to the church. Many, whose support for various Episcopal projects seemed to earmark them as earnest churchmen, were in reality far from fully committed. George E. Spruill from Warren County, for example, would sit on the executive committee of the Episcopal School for Boys only two years after he expressed great "regard for rational and real religion", but described himself as "no professor" of religion. Likewise, Judge John L. Bailey, a prominent state attorney originally from Elizabeth City, supported Episcopal causes but refused to be baptized.

Although the majority of Episcopal men remained away from the center of church life as noncommuning members, or friends, a small, but influential, number of high churchmen were becoming full participants. Most Episcopal churches could boast at least one or two "Christian gentlemen." Because these men were socially prominent and respected in male circles, they helped to create a new genteel masculine pious ideal that competed with the older masculine ideal of reason and honor. They also lent credibility to the Episcopal church in the face of its overwhelming female character.

Unlike their wives, few of these Episcopal men articulated their religious hopes and struggles, but Thomas Ruffin, a prominent lawyer and future chief justice of the North Carolina Supreme Court, was an exception. In 1828 Ruffin became a communicant of St. Matthew's, Hillsboro, a church he had helped organize four years earlier. Only two years before becoming a communicant, Ruffin had expressed a rather liberal religious attitude in a letter written to persuade his son, who was away at school, not to join the Roman Catholic church. The father's beliefs included elements of Enlightenment universalism and also a traditional emphasis on morality or virtue.

> I do not look upon the differences of Sects among Christians, as of so much consequence in itself: But for that very reason, I have long considered it very proper for each person to attach himself to that persuasion which he can not only call *a* Church of *God,* but also, the Church of his *Fore Fathers.* The Protestant Episcopal Church is that of your family and is in itself, by its formularies, doctrines and practices, excellent, presenting [as] strong restraints to vice and excitements to virtue as any denomination whatever.[10]

Ruffin certainly did not practice what he preached. His own parents had been prosperous Methodists who had sent him to Princeton to be educated. His comments notwithstanding, Ruffin was far less tolerant of certain Christian denominations, even Protestant ones. Earlier that year, he had described an evangelical campmeeting as "noisy turbulent confusion."

When Ruffin decided to be confirmed two years later, his minister, William Mercer Green, was delighted that the Judge would soon be "altogether a Christian."[11] After Ruffin took communion on Easter at St. Paul's, Edenton, where he was visiting, he wrote his wife: "I partook of it, I hope profitably, in charity, faith, patience, and humility. Its strengthening Graces were much multiplied to me by the sincerity & earnestness of my prayers to God for his favor & blessing on Yourself, my dearest Anne, and all our dear children & by the expectation that you were at the same hour engaged in the like duty of obedience to the command of our blessed Redeemer & in commemoration of his passion & rich bounty to the human race."[12]

The importance that Ruffin attached to his family's simultaneous participation in communion takes on a revealing significance when contrasted with former family practice. Daughter Catherine had previously worshipped with other young women at John Witherspoon's Presbyterian church. Despite entreaties from one of Catherine's friends asking her to continue worshipping at the Presbyterian church, Catherine began to attend the Episcopal church with the rest of the family. Thomas Ruffin had reunited his family in a church of his own choosing. The Episcopal church reinforced the domestic control of Ruffin and other Episcopal gentlemen by explicitly supporting patriarchy. Surely Ruffin and other men who became Episcopal communicants found it easier to do so in a church that preached "obedience" not only to the Savior, but also to husbands and fathers.

Judge Ruffin was clearly becoming high church; his faith was not evangelical like his daughters' or his wife's. His reference to communion's "strengthening Graces" reflected a high church sacramental theology. Nearly a quarter of a century later, Ruffin's mature theology would be outlined in a didactic letter to his young granddaughter. According to Ruffin, the duty of a Christian was "to live answerably to the law of God, in obedience thereto and with full faith in His Son Jesus Christ, and to the law of Charity towards your fellow man—always governing your temper and your tongue, and denying selfishness and mortifying all evil affections and striving after a godly life."[13]

Ruffin's "full faith in . . . [God's] Son Jesus Christ" was high church, not evangelical. High church faith emphasized intellectual assent to orthodox Christology; it was a change of mind not heart. The enlightened gentleman who became a Hobartian high churchman avoided a gut-wrenching evangelical rebirth and also was spared obedience to self-denying evangelical morality. High church morality was probably synonymous with honesty and lawfulness, not asceticism. Ruffin himself defied evangelical morality as he continued to own and to race some of the finest thoroughbred horses in the state.

Another high churchman, U.S. Senator Robert Strange, a communicant at St. John's, Fayetteville, explored the subject of genteel masculine piety in his 1839 novel *Eoneguski*, the first novel written by a North Carolina author about a North Carolina subject. Set in the Appalachian mountains, one subplot depicts the new male religious archetype, contrasting the differences of habit and temperament between a group of lawyers and their "pious and benevolent" host, Moses Holland.[14]

Although Holland is not an Episcopalian, the author plainly states that Holland is representative of a group of Christian gentlemen residing throughout the state. Despite the fact that such individuals were clearly a minority, they exerted a powerful influence: "There is in almost every community some individual particularly distinguished for his piety and benevolence—like Abram, in Canaan, or Lot, in Sodom. . . . In the presence of such men the most hardened profligacy is awed into respectful silence, and he who laughs at the terrors of the Almighty in theory, finds his spirit rebuked and subdued by even so inconsiderable a reflection of his moral perfections."[15]

The novel provides background for its comparison of the traditional genteel male ethic and the new pious ideal with a frank discussion of the character of North Carolina lawyers. According to Strange, North Carolina lawyers were impeccably honest and chivalrous, but "thoughts of futurity are not allowed to disturb their quiet, and as the only security against convenient intrusions, they generally become free-thinkers. Intolerant of the slightest breach of the code of honor or honesty, that portion of the moral law which is not found written in either of these codes, is overlooked as immaterial." In many ways, Strange's description of the lawyers epitomized the ethics of traditionalist gentlemen still wedded to more radical Enlightenment thought and the southern code of honor, but not to Christianity.[16]

The interaction in the story between the pious host and the worldly lawyers demonstrates several important characteristics of the new ethic of masculine genteel piety. Holland's piety was not humorless evangelicalism. "[He] was not one of those who imagined religion to consist in a vinegar countenance or starched formality of manner." Instead, he enjoyed the lawyers' banter and tales. Holland, nevertheless, demonstrated far greater moral forbearance than his guests. He did not drink or swear; the lawyers did so freely. He also forbade "by the most positive prohibition, the desecration of his mansion by card playing." At the end of the evening, the intoxicated lawyers retired. Before going to bed, "Mr. Holland and his household surrounded their family altar, and offered the Almighty their evening sacrifice."[17]

By 1840, then, a small minority of high churchmen like Thomas Ruffin and Robert Strange were embracing the new ideal of genteel masculine piety. These individuals regularly sat on local church vestries and represented their local parishes at annual diocesan conventions. High churchmanship provided these Episcopal men with an acceptable Protestant Christian alternative to the more prevalent code of honor and, also, to evangelicalism. The majority of Episcopal men, however, never could bring themselves to become full, communing members of the Episcopal church. They remained not "altogether . . . Christian."

The triumph of high churchmanship in North Carolina was assured when Episcopal women began to embrace it and to abandon evangelicalism. By 1830 the process was clearly under way, but Episcopal women's confusion concerning communion shows that the process had begun much earlier. At first, Episcopal women adapted orthodox sacramentalism to meet their own evangelical needs. In 1815 Rebeccah Moore, wife of Alfred Moore, Jr., experienced the same sense of doubt about the state of her soul as other evangelical women; the orthodox attitude of trusting in the promises of the Old Church was gone. She wanted the same inner assurance as other evangelicals, but she became convinced that the sacrament of communion might be an effective vehicle for such an experience. Rebeccah had never taken communion before, but she was considering it "as a means of Grace." Rebeccah Moore was contemplating using orthodox means to accomplish evangelical ends: she had adopted a traditional sacramental view of communion as an instrument to bring about an inner religious rebirth.[18]

In 1820 another Episcopal lady was concerned enough to write Bishop Ravenscroft asking for an explanation of the relationship between the sacraments and spiritual rebirth. Eleven years later, Anne Cameron, wife of Paul Cameron of Fairntosh Plantation, struggled with similar issues. She confessed "I have often thought on the subject [of confirmation] and believe it a means of grace." After a "serious talk" with her Episcopal minister, Anne decided to be confirmed. She had embraced the high church view of the sacraments as a means of grace, but did so in order to assuage evangelical doubts.[19]

The increasing importance of sacramentalism for these Episcopal ladies indicates that slowly but surely they were evolving into committed Episcopalians who valued the distinctive features of their denomination. It was a first step in the "humble walk" of high churchmanship. In 1828 one female member of the distinguished DeRosset family joked that her Methodist friends suspected that she was a "bigotted Episcopalian." Behind her humor was a historical reality as Episcopal women grew to prize the Episcopal way above all other denominational approaches.

Without any genteel church to attend prior to 1831, the young ladies of Pittsboro, who dominated the genteel religious scene there as they did elsewhere, enjoyed hearing "very good" Methodist preaching. In 1831, however, a group of ladies in town decided to establish an Episcopal church despite having too few males interested in the project even to form a vestry. The successful establishment of St. Bartholomew's was even more remarkable considering the simultaneous occurrence of a large Methodist camp revival outside Pittsboro which threatened to leave the Episcopalians without "a single person in the whole county to proselyte."[20]

The lure of Methodism, so powerful at an earlier time, was no longer strong enough to deter the Episcopal ladies of Pittsboro. At least one among them, in what seems to have been an emerging attitude among Episcopal ladies, openly criticized the Methodists for the harm that they had done in trying to convert one of her male relatives: "I never saw before how wrong it is, to urge persons to go to greater lengths in religion than their own hearts dictate—for that reason I will ever be opposed to alter business [altar call]—for I am persuaded it is productive of much injury." These Episcopal ladies may have reached the conclusion that it was better to join the Episcopal church, where there was some hope of influencing their men to seek religion, than to align themselves with a denomination that completely alienated their men from Christianity.[21]

There is also evidence that the initial fascination with evangelical worship began to subside and even to offend Episcopal women's refined sensibilities. In 1829 Anne B. Pettigrew praised the Methodists as "pioneers in religion," and noted that the Pettigrew plantation "should live without the Gospel sound were it not for the Methodists." But Mrs. Pettigrew went on to declare, "I should dislike to belong to the sect such scrutinizing into the feelings & moralities & forms must be disagreeable." In the restored Episcopal church, particularly as it became more high church, it was possible to be pious without being forced to go beyond the bounds of propriety.[22]

Other factors may also account for Episcopal women's acceptance of high churchmanship. The decade of the 1830s was a time of growing conservatism throughout the South. The growth of aggressive abolitionism and the fear of servile insurrection caused southerners to become increasingly defensive. Nat Turner's insurrection in southside Virginia spawned widespread rumors of slave uprisings in eastern North Carolina. At a time when both external and internal forces seemed to be threatening southern society, high churchmanship defended hierarchy, patriarchy, and slavery. In contrast, though it was a far cry from the reformist temper of the North, Episcopal evangelicalism posed a challenge to traditional masculine culture based on honor. As Episcopal ladies fretted over slave revolts and abolitionist tirades, the orderliness and security of the high church system may have been more and more appealing.

Whatever the reasons, Episcopal ladies drifted away from evangelicalism in the years after 1835. Church remained important to them, but increasingly they discussed participation in worship and church activities, not their subjective religious feelings. For most, evangelical language began to disappear from their religious conversations. Rare was the correspondence that breathed the original intensity of the early Episcopal evangelicals. The impact of the ladies' revival in the Episcopal church was diminishing; high churchmanship was in the ascendancy.

Since high churchmen understood religious life as a "humble walk" that began temporally with baptism and ended only at the grave, serious North Carolina Episcopalians placed great emphasis on providing their children with proper religious training. Throughout its history, the Anglican church has used catechetical instruction as a way of indoctrinating young churchpeople. In the third decade of the nineteenth century, Episcopalians supplemented traditional catechetical instruction with their own high church version of the new evangelical plan in religious education: Sunday schools. The effect of the entire spectrum of Episcopal religious education in North Carolina during the era was to shift the nature of Episcopal piety from an experienced faith to a learned one: increasingly, Episcopal piety became a matter of socialization into high church practices and beliefs.[23]

Devout parents encouraged their children's spiritual growth and development in ways that included family devotions and studying the catechism. Through such daily rituals children were taught the rudiments of adoration, confession, thanksgiving, and petition. Paul C. Cameron and Anne (Ruffin) Cameron's small children said their prayers every morning and night. One young Episcopal adolescent away at school intimated the prayer habits in his own family when he promised his father that he would "never forget to say my prayers." William Anderson, a layman from St. John's, Fayetteville,

Table 3
Episcopal Sunday School Scholars and Teachers, 1833

	Female Scholars	Male Scholars	Female Teachers	Male Teachers
Christ's Church, Newbern	105	48	20	7
St. John's, Fayetteville	50	70	8	8
St. Peter's, Washington	36	31	7	8
Christ's Church, Raleigh	34	16	8	4
Calvary, Wadesboro	28	20	4	2
St. Bartholomew's, Pittsboro	13	10	4	1
St. Matthew's, Hillsboro	unknown	unknown	6	2
Totals	266	195	57	32

Statistics from NCDJ, *1833.*

quizzed his children at home on questions from the catechism. Dr. James Norcom, vestryman at St. Paul's, Edenton, suggested his own family's Sunday routine when he advised his absent son to be sure to "read your catechism and the psalms for the day" and also to pray before bedtime. When another young Episcopalian away from home recited his catechism to his guardian every Sunday, the boy was undoubtedly repeating a family practice.[24]

The development of the Episcopal Sunday school movement complemented domestic efforts at religious education. In 1827 Episcopalians at the national level formed the General Protestant Episcopal Sunday School Union to give the church a counterpart to the interdenominational and evangelical American Sunday School Union. The Episcopal Union offered local Sunday schools a complete program, curriculum, and supporting materials. By 1830 every congregation in the Diocese of North Carolina had organized a Sunday school. Although only a few have left local records that confirm their connection with the Union, almost certainly all the Episcopal Sunday schools in the diocese were auxiliaries. In 1833 six local churches sent the diocese detailed reports, which offer a statistical view of Sunday school participation (see table 3). Most of the Sunday school teachers in the diocese were women. Several years earlier, some local churches complained about "want of suitable teachers, especially *male* teachers."

Although the Union produced a score of publications, the core of its curriculum was four Protestant Episcopal Sunday School books and three catechisms. The four books emphasized biblical precepts and history. The first catechism contained Scriptural passages and was intended as an introduction to the second, which was the traditional Church catechism. The third catechism was Bishop Hobart's *Explanation and Enlargement of the Church Catechism.* The high church leader also compiled *An Office of Devotion, or Liturgy, for the use of Sunday Schools* for the Union.

The Union plan separated boys and girls and placed them by age in seven grades. Sunday school met for two hours before the worship service, and then reconvened for another two-hour session after lunch. The emphasis was on memorization and recitation of hymns, psalms, collects, prayers, and Scripture selections.

The socialization of piety created a new generation of high church Episcopalians who swelled church ranks. In 1840 there were over twelve hundred communicants in the church and probably another two thousand baptized children and adult members. For all its success, however, religious education was achieved at the expense of the original spiritual intensity of the ladies' revival. For the rest of the antebellum era, Episcopal communicants were generally regular participants in organized religious life. They may even have been well informed in doctrine, but they lacked the religious enthusiasm and evangelical conviction that their mothers and grandmothers had so abundantly manifested.

When Bishop Ives took office in 1832, he envisioned the establishment of Episcopal schools that would promote high church doctrines and train future ministers. In the early 1830s North Carolina Episcopalians embarked on an ambitious program to establish a denominational preparatory school for boys. When, after an auspicious debut, this failed, Episcopalians successfully established a denominational preparatory school for girls. Without the active financial support and interest of leading laymen, Ives's plans for high church education never would have been realized.

The Episcopal School for Boys opened its doors in June 1834, on the outskirts of Raleigh. Bishop Ives and the Rev. George W. Freeman, minister at Christ's Church, Raleigh, together prepared a prospectus that advertised the school's experiment in denominational education. Although non-Episcopal students were welcomed, the school was "avowedly Episcopalian," as its name implied. Each student was given a copy of the Holy Scriptures and the Book of Common Prayer. The school adopted a classical curriculum with additional emphasis on Christian education. The latter included "regular and systematic instruction . . . in the HOLY SCRIPTURES; in natural Theology, Moral Philosophy, the evidences of revealed Religion, the History of the Church, the Doctrines, Discipline, and Worship of the Protestant Episcopal Church." Students also worshipped regularly at nearby Christ's Church.

The initial success of the Episcopal School was flattering; a number of the most prominent Episcopalians in the state enrolled their sons. Genteel fathers had always placed a premium on their sons' education, even before the restoration of the Episcopal church. The Episcopal School provided all the advantages of secular academies plus an emphasis on the type of religious education that fostered moral development without tending to religious enthusiasm. Enrollment soared to ninety-nine students during the school's second year, prompting additional construction of buildings. Over 80 percent of the student body was resident to North Carolina, and almost all of those lived in the eastern half of the state.

Unfortunately, discipline problems plagued the Episcopal School from the outset and contributed to its eventual closing. In 1836 school trustees published an address to parents in an attempt to curb student misconduct. According to the document, some parents expected the school to "tame the *unmanageable* and reform the *vicious*." The trustees exhorted parents to instill "*strict* discipline" and "to resort to punishment" at home in an effort to stop such behavior. The discipline problems at the Episcopal school were not uncommon in Southern male academies. Southern schoolboys commonly defied school authorities. Indeed, many Southern parents condoned such behavior because it was an important part of the socialization process in which young gentlemen learned how to command social inferiors, in this case their hapless teacher.

The difficulties at the Episcopal School do reveal, however, a contradiction inherent in traditional genteel masculine ethics: the tension between being moral and being manly. The young men who misbehaved were displaying the sort of behavior that masculine culture reinforced. Episcopal fathers sincerely admired morality and propriety, but many also encouraged their sons to be domineering and courageous. The conduct of the unruly boys at the Episcopal School reflected the environment in which they were raised. The Episcopal trustees admitted as much when they noted that similar northern schools escaped such difficulties because of "peculiarities of habit and situation." Presumably, northern school boys were more thoroughgoing evangelicals who obeyed the inner voice of conscience, not the disruptive rules of southern honor. At the Episcopal School two gentlemanly ideals collided, and the forces of manly chaos overwhelmed moral order.

The Panic of 1837 rocked North Carolina's economy and added deep financial troubles to the Episcopal School's other problems. The school closed in December 1838, and the buildings stood idle until the prominent and wealthy layman, Duncan Cameron, purchased the property in 1841 for a sum exactly equal to the school's debts. Soon afterward, Cameron and Bishop Ives contacted the Rev. Albert Smedes, a New York Episcopal minister, about the prospects of renting the facility and opening an Episcopal girls' school. When Smedes accepted, one of the most successful attempts at denominational female education in the antebellum South began: St. Mary's School. A private enterprise, the school also received valuable assistance from Bishop Ives and the diocese.

Albert Smedes, a gentleman who combined deep piety with "polite urbanity," supplied the able leadership so essential to the school's prosperity. The educational atmosphere at St. Mary's reflected Smede's personality, simultaneously pious and refined. An eager pool of Episcopal parents and daughters willingly responded to this type of religious environment. Many of these families were the same ones who had previously supported the Episcopal School. The social distinction of the young Episcopal women who attended St. Mary's indicated the school's upper-class character.

Life at St. Mary's offered female education, the acquisition of genteel manners, and serious religious instruction. One example of the desire to promote "the cultivation of social refinements" was school-sponsored "musical soirees" which became major events on the Raleigh social calendar. Smedes was sensitive enough to evangelical scruples not to allow dancing at the soirees. Instead, he provided musical accompaniment as the young women promenaded around the room. The ability to balance social and spiritual graces was a hallmark of emerging Victorian values, and St. Mary's excelled at satisfying both.

The daily religious routine at St. Mary's began with a morning service in the campus's new chapel. The school closed each night with an assembly for prayer. In between, a portion of every day was set aside for the rote memorization and recital of Scriptural passages. Smedes himself "explained and illustrated" these passages with the grand design of imparting "a systematic view of all the great doctrines of the Gospel as held by the Church, with their practical results and bearings."[25]

Many young women at St. Mary's also participated in the most signal religious event of their lives when Bishop Ives confirmed them in the college chapel. Over the years Smedes developed a remarkable ability to convince students to take this important step. During the 1840s and for the remainder of the antebellum era, fifteen to twenty young ladies were confirmed each year at St. Mary's. Every year the school produced another class of female communicants for the Episcopal church in North Carolina. The religious life at St. Mary's became so well-developed and habitual that Smedes in 1857 published two pamphlets, *Manual of St. Mary's School, Raleigh, N.C.* and *Hints on the Rite of Confirmation*. Those who internalized these high church values were in a unique position to shape the civilization of the state as they married a rising generation of state leaders and gave birth to the next.

Maintaining the delicate balance between faith and fashion was difficult for the young women at St. Mary's. Some devout Episcopalians worried that their daughters were being confirmed in order to conform to accepted social practice and not because of serious religious impression. The rite of confirmation was itself becoming a fashionable ceremony for adolescents. In the Wilmington family of Dr. Armand J. DeRosset, Jr., the problem involved daughter Kate, a St. Mary's student who informed her parents in 1844 that she had decided, with the encouragement of headmaster Smedes, to be confirmed. Her parents received Kate's news with grave concern. They maintained that under the right circumstances nothing "would give us more heartfelt pleasure than to see our first born take upon herself her baptismal vows, and renounce the devil and all his works." But they feared that their daughter was simply trying to "gratify" Smedes without "thinking sufficiently upon the subject." They added that "we have seen so many girls go up with no serious impressions [who] returned to the world with a renewed zeal for all its pleasures."[26]

Similarly, Dr. James Norcom expressed the same reservations in advising his granddaughter about confirmation in 1848. Dr. Norcom encouraged her to look forward to confirmation, but he cautioned, "I admonish you not to be led by fashion in this matter, nor contagious excitement, but by a devout & reflecting & holy spirit!" Norcom's comments were extraordinary testimony to the changing significance of confirmation. Episcopal confirmation had once meant that young women embraced an evangelical cultural ethos that was in conflict with the older genteel female ethic of fashion. James Norcom's warning indicates that by the 1840s confirmation had become fashionable. The ethics of fashion and piety were being conjoined in the rite of confirmation.[27]

After 1840 Episcopal evangelicalism in the North Carolina church survived only as a minority faith among the laity; it was kept alive in several ways. Episcopal evangelical mothers were able, in some instances, to pass their faith to sons and daughters despite the overwhelmingly high church character of the institutional church. These sons were the first Episcopal evangelical males in North Carolina. Sometimes, as in the case of the Hooper family from Wilmington, siblings included both evangelicals and high churchmen. Charlotte Hooper, an Episcopal evangelical, raised two such sons. One, John DeBerniere Hooper, who was involved in an evangelical revival at the University of North Carolina in 1831, displayed a religious character of a decidely evangelical cast. Another, George Hooper, was a high churchman suspicious of revivals.

The case of John H. Tillinghast, a Fayetteville Episcopalian, indicates that the life of a young Episcopal evangelical in a high church diocese was full of spiritual conflict. Tillinghast was the son of an older mother whose evangelical faith had been formed years before in the ladies' revival. Four years before the Civil War, John decided to enter the ministry, but his dual theological heritage, high church and evangelical, made the decision agonizingly difficult.

Tillinghast's problem involved choosing whether to become a Presbyterian or an Episcopal clergyman. The problem with the Episcopal church was that John "*utterly repudiated*" high churchmanship "either in doctrine or practice." His decision concerning the ministry hinged on whether he "could consistently enter the ministry with a foregone determination of nonconformity to much which is regarded by the *larger portion* of the *ch[urch]* as *essentially* belonging to it as a *separate* communion."[28]

When it came time to choose a college, the young Episcopalian selected Hampden-Sydney, a Presbyterian college in southside Virginia, because he was leaning toward Presbyterianism. But the ultimate decision remained in doubt for more than two years. "I am," he admitted, "constantly oscillating between the two." According to him, the Presbyterian church agreed "more nearly with my notions of consistent orthodoxy both as to form & doctrine," while his "early associations" and "warmest sympathies" were with the Episcopal church.[29]

Tillinghast's determination to go to Hampden-Sydney did influence his final choice but, surprisingly, in favor of the Episcopal ministry. While there he gained firsthand exposure to Virginia's low church, or Episcopal evangelical, tradition. He also read that diocese's evangelical periodical, the *Protestant Churchman,* which he described as a "comfort" and "a resource." His Episcopal evangelical mother rejoiced when she heard the news that her son would remain in the church. She may never have considered that her son's difficulty in choosing a denomination was a result of the mixed theological training he had received growing up with an evangelical mother in a high church diocese.

In addition to evangelical mothers, occasional revivals in various locales also created some new Episcopal evangelicals. In 1842 a revival in Warrenton "in all the churches" brought "upwards of a hundred" new members into the Episcopal church.[30] In 1857–58, similar outbreaks of the Spirit occurred among Episcopalians at St. James's, Wilmington, St. John's, Fayetteville, and among Episcopal students at the University of North Carolina. One young member of the Badger family, who was converted at the university exclaimed:

> Thank God! I daily increase in knowledge of what is right, and in power to resist evil—The worship of my God, is no longer an irksome task never performed, but I delight more and more, every day, in throwing myself at the feet of my Saviour, and in asking his promised aid and comfort, which I feel are so necessary to my prosperity as a christian.[31]

This sort of language became rarer and rarer among Episcopalians during the last two decades of the antebellum era.

A final and more marginal evangelical presence within the Episcopal church was the slaves. Undoubtedly many, if not most, slaves who belonged to the Episcopal church were evangelicals, although they probably were forced to express their exuberant and life-affirming evangelicalism outside organized Episcopal worship in the secret confines of their "invisible church." Episcopal slave owners occasionally discussed their slaves' religious life on the plantations, but this discussion never became personal, and there is no evidence indicating that slave evangelicalism influenced masters and mistresses away from high churchmanship.[32]

The triumph of Hobartian high churchmanship in the Diocese of North Carolina could even be seen in church architecture. During the twenty years after Ives was consecrated bishop in 1832, there was a boom in church building as forty new Episcopal churches were constructed. These churches were ambitious undertakings by North Carolina standards. The dominant architectural style was Gothic revival, which came to be identified with high churchmanship throughout the national Episcopal church in the decades of the 1840s and 1850s.

Although the Episcopal churches in Hillsboro (1815) and Halifax (1830) had incorporated Gothic motifs at an earlier date, the construction of St. James's, Wilmington, in 1837 signaled a new construction phase of highly architectonic Gothic Episcopal churches. Designed by nationally renowned architect Thomas U. Walter, St. James's exhibited a level of quality and style previously unattained. Chapel of the Cross, Chapel Hill (1842–46), also designed by Walter, and Christ's Church, Raleigh (1848), designed by Richard Upjohn, were two other exceptionally distinguished and architecturally coherent structures made out of brick and cut stone, respectively. Even the frame sanctuaries in Williamston, Plymouth, Morganton, and elsewhere demonstrated an architectural distinctiveness and sophistication, as well as a quality of construction, that set them apart from other churches and public buildings in the state.

The high church theological justification for these fine churches was that they created a solemn and mysterious ambience that enhanced the worship experience. Undoubtedly this was the effect as Episcopalians entered the interior of one of these sanctuaries. The exteriors of the new Gothic churches, however, communicated a different message to a wider public. The quality of the materials used in the churches and the skill of the architectural treatment bespoke the status of an Episcopal gentry that could afford to hire professional architects and raise fine buildings. The distinctiveness and richness of the architectural style and material construction reinforced other aspects of genteel culture that separated it from lower-class elements. The Gothic Episcopal churches were intended to glorify God, but they also served as monuments to the wealth, sophistication, and cultural distinctiveness of an important segment of North Carolina's ruling class.

Notes

1. The information in this and the two preceding paragraphs comes from two primary sources: Chorley, *Men and Movements*, 159–81; and Mullin, *Episcopal Vision/American Reality*, 9–66.
2. Chorley, *Men and Movements*, 175–81.
3. Ibid., 260–63.
4. Ibid., 264–68.
5. London and Lemmon, *The Episcopal Church in North Carolina*, 116–21.
6. *NCDJ*, 1825, 25.
7. Mullin, *Episcopal Vision/American Reality*, 75–76.
8. Ibid., 78–80.
9. Wyatt-Brown, *Southern Honor*, 99, 101–2, 147, 248, 341, 410.
10. Thomas Ruffin to William K. Ruffin, 31 December 1826, in J. G. de Roulhac Hamilton, *The Papers of Thomas Ruffin*, 4 vols. (Raleigh: North Carolina Historical Commission, 1918), 1:369, quoted in London and Lemmon, *The Episcopal Church in North Carolina*, 138.
11. William Mercer Green to Thomas Ruffin, 11 January 1828, in Hamilton, *Papers of Thomas Ruffin*, quoted in London and Lemmon, *The Episcopal Church in North Carolina*, 137.
12. Thomas Ruffin to Anne M. Ruffin, 9 April 1828, Thomas Ruffin Papers, SHC, quoted in London and Lemmon, *The Episcopal Church in North Carolina*, 137.
13. Thomas Ruffin to Frances Gray Roulhac, 22 April 1850, in Hamilton, *The Papers of Thomas Ruffin*, 2:293.
14. [Robert Strange], *Eoneguski, or The Cherokee Chief: A Tale of Past Wars By an American* (Washington: Franck Taylor, 1839), 210–18; Richard Walser, "Senator Strange's Indian Novel," *NCHR* 26 (January 1949): 1–2.
15. Strange, *Eoneguski*, 191.

16. Ibid., 201–2.
17. Ibid., 211–18.
18. A. C. Moore to E. E. Haywood, 21 September 1815, Ernest Haywood Papers, SHC.
19. Anne Cameron to Paul Cameron, 1 April 1833, Cameron Family Papers, SHC.
20. Ann Moore to Miss Magdalen DeRosset, 13 September 1831, DeRosset Family Papers, SHC.
21. Ibid.
22. Ann B. Pettigrew to Mary W. Bryan, 20 October 1828, John H. Bryan Papers, NCDAH.
23. Clifton Hartwell Brewer, *A History of Religious Education in the Episcopal Church to 1835* (New York: Arno Press & the New York Times, 1969), 38–39, 186–222, 328; Anne M. Boylan, *Sunday School: The Formation of an American Institution, 1790–1880* (New Haven: Yale University Press, 1988), 77.
24. Anne [(Ruffin) Cameron] to Paul C. Cameron, [26 December 1845 ?], Cameron Family Papers, SHC; Thomas B. Bailey to John L. Bailey, 28 February 1836, John L. Bailey Papers, SHC; Mary M. Anderson to Margaret B. Cameron, 8 January 1844, Cameron Family Papers, SHC; James Norcom to [his son], 25 March 1845, James Norcom Papers, NCDAH; William H. Haywood, Jr., to Duncan Cameron, 10 May 1821, Cameron Family Papers, SHC.
25. *NCDJ*, 1844, 25.
26. Mrs. A. J. DeRosset, Jr., to Miss Catherine D. DeRosset, 5 September 1844, DeRosset Family Papers, SHC.
27. James Norcom to Emily M. Norcom, 29 March 1848, James Norcom Papers, NCDAH.
28. John H. Tillinghast to [Jane (Norwood) Tillinghast], 11 August 1856, Tillinghast Family Papers, DUA.
29. Ibid.
30. [Mary H. Walker] to Mrs. Susan P. Cabanne, 16 February 1842, Battle Family Papers, SHC.
31. Dick Badger to [his sister], 15 [?] September 1858, Polk-Badger-McGehee Papers, microfilm at SHC.
32. Steven Stowe argues similarly that Southern planters seldom discussed slave life. *Intimacy and Power in the Old South: Ritual in the Lives of the Planters* (Baltimore: Johns Hopkins University Press, 1987), xvi–xvii.

CHAPTER FOUR

Encouraging the Spirit of Christian Submission: Religious Discussion and Domestic Relations within Episcopal Families, 1815–1860

The two decades after the creation of the Diocese of North Carolina in 1817 were ones in which Episcopal families engaged in a lively domestic dialogue on the subject of religion. This discussion was so inextricably bound to the fundamental transformation of marital relations in nineteenth-century America that it is impossible to separate the two. Throughout the nation a new companionate style of marriage was replacing the older patriarchal one, and the two styles were dramatically different. Emotional restraint and unquestioning deference to husbands were characteristics of patriarchal marriage. In contrast, romance, emotional openness, and mutual support were qualities of companionate marriage. In Episcopal homes, religious discussion not only dealt with spiritual matters, it also involved domestic politics as couples sought to work out their differences in a time of shifting values.

Traditional men of honor and reason held fast to the older patriarchal norm, a code of conduct that allowed considerable freedom to act in ways that pious wives found objectionable. Episcopal evangelical women, like other evangelicals, longed for the intimacy and support of companionate marriage and they encouraged their husbands to accept the Christian values that would lead to such marriages. As a result, Episcopal evangelicalism became a challenge to traditional patriarchy and the most important instrument in the

100

struggle to civilize male honor and to create gentler and more intimate conjugal relations. In a sense, every time a worldly husband interacted with a pious wife, an older way of living that had flourished in an age of reason and honor confronted a new style that was the product of an evangelical awakening.

Episcopal gentlemen were extremely reluctant to forsake their traditional way of life for several reasons. First, in order to become pious, gentlemen had to give up what they enjoyed doing—indeed to surrender enjoyment itself. For most men, prayer simply was not as interesting as dancing, playing cards, and theatergoing; it was not as exciting as dueling or revelry, or at least being part of an ethos that defined gentlemen. Men who did practice Christian morality also suffered ridicule from their peers. To convert to Christianity meant to renounce the masculine code of honor for feminine Christianity.

Evangelicalism created another fundamental problem for men because it demanded that its adherents surrender themselves to an emotional religious experience. Traditional gentlemen accustomed to displays of physical courage and reluctant to show emotions except in ways prescribed by the code of honor were bound to have trouble with a religion that required they be submissive and meek. For traditional, upper-class men to profess evangelical religion was to demonstrate a weakness of will, the antithesis of the firmness and self-command exhibited by a man of honor.

One young Pittsboro gentleman's reaction to feminine pressure to convert him illustrates the problem. According to a sister, her brother had developed an aversion to evangelicalism on account "of his having been urged to humble himself as a mourner when in fact he never felt any contrition for sin." The brother now appeared "ashamed & seems anxious to show that he has over come the weakness." The sister worried that her brother would "ever after be affraid [sic] to yield to the least emotion of tenderness, & harden his heart & stiffen his neck" against evangelical religion.[1]

Ironically, although traditional men restored the Episcopal church as a conservative response to the evangelical awakening, in so doing, they legitimated their wives' Christian values. One Episcopal evangelical clergyman underscored the role that women could play in their spouses' conversions. The Rev. William Hooper of St. John's, Fayetteville, believed that God had placed women in the ideal situation "not only [to] have greater facilities for working out your own salvation, but have an important influence on the salvation of your male relations!" According to Hooper, "Many a thoughtless man has been brought to reflection, many a wicked man reclaimed, by the charm of religion exhibited in the conduct of a wife." When wives converted "thoughtless" and "wicked" husbands, they theoretically endowed them with a set of ethics that was in conflict with older habits and activities. Wives and mothers could use piety to tame the most refractory and unregulated gentleman of honor.[2]

The rise of high churchmanship presented a Christian alternative to both patriarchal and companionate marriage ideals. Unlike the rest of evangelical America, high churchmanship asserted that husbands and fathers were patriarchs in all spheres of life, including church and home. At least in theory, there was no separate sphere of religious and domestic life dominated by women. High church husbands, however, also demonstrated a care and concern for their spouses that resembled the companionship of evangelical marriages. High churchmanship provided a middle way between patriarchal and companionate marriage ideals.

Despite variations in the individual personalities of Episcopal spouses, the interplay of male honor/patriarchy and female evangelicalism typically created predictable patterns of domestic tension. The marriage of Catherine (Fullerton) and Armand J. DeRosset is a clear example of the way in which female evangelicalism challenged traditional patriarchy. Only two years before leaving Charleston to marry Armand in Wilmington, Catherine criticized some of her insubordinate female friends who "thought the Wife shou'd command & the Husband obey." As Catherine noted, "in that case there can be no happiness if the Man shou'd happen to have a little Spirit." Once in Wilmington, Catherine became more self-assertive in religious matters when she got a "little Spirit" of her own at the Methodist meeting.[3]

Catherine's example influenced Armand to become more religious himself: "I indeed shudder my wife, at the picture [you] have held up to my view—to think of the life we might have led, but for your example of forbearance, which you had too often occasion to exercise—an example which I hope has not been altogether lost upon me—Let us give thanks to God, for this among the multiplied instances of his goodness & mercy to us, so unmerited." Despite Catherine's religious influence over her husband, however, he became an Episcopal communicant, not a Methodist. Mrs. DeRosset and at least one other daughter defied patriarchal convention and remained in the Methodist church, separate from the rest of the family.[4]

Marital discord in the home of Jane B. (Norwood) and Samuel W. Tillinghast involved the conflicting values of a husband of honor and an evangelical wife. Jane, a Hillsboro Presbyterian-turned-Episcopalian, married Samuel, whose family included charter members of St. John's, Fayetteville. Tension surfaced even before their marriage in 1830 as Samuel wondered if one of Jane's female companions would approve of a marriage to a man "whom she suspects has no fixed religious principles." Tillinghast implored his future wife to "tell her I am not what I once was. That my views on that subject [religion] have materially changed. That I hope [through] the constance and example of a pious companion I may become pious myself. That I have ceased to cavil. That my affection for you is so mingled with respect for your understanding, that your influence over my changing will enable you to remove any doubts which may trouble my mind." Promises! Promises! Despite his protestations, Samuel remained unchurched throughout the marriage.[5]

In 1844 one prominent Fayetteville churchman took the opportunity in a note of condolence upon the occasion of the death of Samuel and Jane's infant son to urge the father to make an "open *profession*" of religion. The nature of the argument indicates how closely Episcopalians linked motives to convert with domestic considerations. According to the Episcopal churchman, Samuel ought to convert on account of his duty to his children and "to a Wife, who is all any Man could wish—& whose bosom you would carry the purest joy—who is entitled at your hands to a conclusion on this momentous subject—who, if she should be taken away from You & Your children, ought to have from You a guarantee that these children would have the example of a godly life in the [?] of their surviving parent."[6]

Despite peer pressure, Samuel Tillinghast remained resolutely unchurched. Even in 1850, after a long and devoted marriage, there was evidence that Samuel's conversion still had not occurred. Jane was still imploring, but also remaining deferential as the apologetic note at the end of a letter to Samuel indicates: "My Dearest we have been blest above all others; but have we made a meet return for all the mercies of our God—he has long been speaking to us in prosperity, listen to his voice, lest he be forced to speak to us in adversity. [H]ow could you bear the loss of all that makes life dear—excuse my writing thus, but my heart is full." Samuel, however, operated on an entirely different set of values with "honour, fame, wealth" and "power" as its basis. In an 1852 letter to his son, he declared, "Human life is a great battle for superiority and supremacy. [E]ach individual is antagonistic to his fellow." There is no evidence that the religious differences within the Tillinghast home were ever resolved.[7]

Often, the focus of religious and domestic tensions for traditional husbands and pious wives was the service of communion. Bishop Ravenscroft's declaration in 1825 that he would allow no "vicious Livers to the Eucharist" indicates that participation in communion acted as a sort of litmus test for personal piety in the Episcopal church. Since most wives celebrated the sacrament and most husbands did not, it was predictable that disagreements would arise over this issue.[8]

Depending on whether they were evangelical or high church, pious Episcopalians viewed the sacrament of communion in one of two ways. Evangelicals understood communion as a celebration for those who had experienced salvation. High churchmen believed that the eucharist was a means of grace to support Christian pilgrims. Either way, becoming a communicant was serious and implied a new level of commitment to the church and a concomitant change in the customs of daily life. Even though high churchmanship permitted Episcopal gentlemen a good deal of moral leeway, Episcopal gentlemen of honor apparently took communion seriously, and refused to celebrate the sacrament until they were willing to mend their ways. The "fashionable" excuse for these "worldly" Episcopalians was that they were "not good enough to join the communion." This excuse enabled uncommitted Episcopalians to refuse communion on theologically defensible grounds since the Episcopal communion service warned the spiritually unprepared to stay away. The excuse also served as a pretext for unreformed living.[9]

John H. Bryan, one of the preeminent lawyers of antebellum North Carolina, and his wife, Mary W. (Shepard) Bryan, offer an example of religious discussion involving the husband's refusal to take communion. John was from a distinguished Newbern family and connected himself to the powerful Shepard and Pettigrew families through his marriage to Mary. From the beginning, murmurs were heard over the religious differences between the traditional groom and pious bride. One of Mary's friends commented on John shortly before the marriage in 1821, "Your *hearts chosen* unites all that is estimable & excellent, *one thing* only [is] wanting to render him all I could desire for you, and I trust ere long, with the man of talents & worth will be added the Christian."[10]

Bryan's faith may have seemed suspect to pious females, but he was hardly irreligious. Even as a college student he had talked about piety with his uncle, John S. West, if only in passing. Throughout the decade after his marriage, he attended Episcopal services on his legal itinerary, and his support for that body identifies him as a loyal backer of the church. In 1829 he once even uttered the words "our Saviour" in a letter to his wife, which indicated at least a partial acceptance of orthodox Christology.

Whatever Bryan's beliefs may have been, however, his wife's pleas demonstrate that he was resisting the church's claims in at least one important respect. In 1834 Mary became deeply troubled over the prospects of her own death and the possibility that she and John would be eternally separated because he was not saved: "And my dearest husband if we should not meet again in this world, I trust we shall both arrive at that place of everlasting rest & peace prepared for those who love & fear God—I am striving my dear husband to get to Heaven, but if I were there & could know that you would never meet me, it would be a great alloy to my happiness if not entirely destructive to it." Mary Bryan believed that John's life was without reproach except for his persistence "in not obeying the command of our Saviour at his last supper—but I hope it will not be long before you partake of this Holy Sacrament." Mary emphasized the urgency of John's compliance with her request because "we know not the day nor the hour when we shall be summoned to appear before the Almighty Judge of the quick & dead to give an account of all our earthly actions." No evidence survives to indicate whether Mary succeeded in bringing John to the communion table.[11]

Similarly, Anne (Ruffin) Cameron urged her husband, Paul C. Cameron, to become a communicant. Once again, religious tension between the couple appeared during the engagement. After a revival in Hillsboro, Paul penned an extremely forthright letter to his soon-to-be mate in which stated his "caveat" concerning the emotional brand of religion. Cameron assured Anne that "I am [neither] an infidel, a Turk, [nor] a contemer: no far be it from me, to say aught against any thing, that tends in any degree, to advance the *genuine* spirit of 'Christianity'. For I love, honour, and *revere* this holy institution of the 'Deity'." But Cameron went on to declare his intolerance for unrestrained evangelicalism:

> The past experience of all ages, from the days of "Peter the Hermit" down to this hour; has taught us that blind fanaticism, is too-often the forerunner, either of [spiritual?] neglect, if not the more odious state of bare-faced and shameless infidelity. Religion is a matter of reason, and gratitude, and not of excited fears and passions; and such is our nature that we must be drawn into its "path" more by mild persuasive language of promised rewards, than by wild and threatening fulminations from the pulpit.

Cameron added with hesitancy, "I trust 'Anna' *you* will find nothing objectionable in this expression of my mind upon the subject of Religion, but on the other hand, I trust that *our* sentiments are in union."[12]

Paul Cameron probably sensed an inchoate evangelicalism in his future bride. Only two years after their wedding, Anne decided to be confirmed since, as noted earlier, she felt "it to be a means of grace." She also wanted a spiritual companion and entreated husband Paul, "If I make up my mind to be confirmed will you not think about it and be confirmed with me? It would be much more pleasant to me to be confirmed *with you* than by myself." Anne Cameron's request did not necessarily mean that her husband must become an evangelical. After all, some high churchmen were communicants. But at the very least, Anne was asking her husband to take a step that he had previously avoided and that implied a deeper religious commitment.[13]

Another Episcopal domestic discussion that also centered around a husband's refusal to take communion occurred between Catherine (Ruffin) Roulhac and her husband Joseph B. G. Roulhac. Catherine, who had gone through a tortuous conversion herself, strenuously endeavored to bring her husband into the fold as well. In 1841 Catherine used the occasion of an older male relative's conversion to plead with her husband to do likewise:

> [I]s it not strange that instead of wishing to devote our best and longest days to our Maker we are satisfied if the few of our last

years are spent in his service, it is the height of ingratitude! [A]nd it is [a] worthless sort of love and "yet our kind Father" will accept it, if it is sincere, Be persuaded my dear husband not to put off the day of repentance too long but give the rest of your days to your God, who gave his life for your salvation, let us both feel and act "As for me and my house we will serve the Lord" so that we can by example as well as precept teach our children to love & fear the Lord, but you can not take any step in a religious life because forsooth you are not *good* enough—or in your own words you are not prepared, My dear husband do not the *sick* use the means to be cured, and is not our souls sick unto death—Yes! death eternal if we do not apply to the Physician of souls to heal our sickness, He has performed his part in showing us the way to be saved and it is ours to use the means of grace that he has appointed—[14]

Catherine's frank letter ended on a deferential note, "But I did not mean to write you a sermon . . . but it is a subject we can not be too familiar with—"

Over the next five years Catherine Roulhac worked incessantly to convert her husband. Particularly grieving to her was Joseph's unwillingness to participate in communion:

Oh! when shall my beloved husband bow with me round the altar and unite in partaking of the broken body and precious blood of our crucified Redeemer. We hope to be meet partakers of his kingdom in Heaven but how can we unless we use the means He has appointed to fit us for that kingdom, the affectionate and dying command of our Saviour was to "Do this in remembrance of me" and it seems because it is so simple and so easy, we are more reluctant to obey, think of these things my dear husband put them not off to a more convenient season, you may depend there will never be a time more suitable and we have no lease for our lives as the late warnings we have all had so plainly show, don't be deceived by that device of Satan "to wait until you are better prepared."[15]

In 1843 Catherine brought to Joseph's attention the conversion of one of his male friends and queried, "Why will you not follow the example of so many of your friends my dear husband? I am sure your soul is as precious as theirs and you feel the importance of the means of grace as much as any body." The next year she encouraged Joseph to come forward to the communion table with the assurance that he was indeed "prepared," even though he might not be "a perfect christian."[16]

On the surface, Catherine's motives were the same as Mary Bryan; she feared that death would forever separate her from a damned husband. Her concern, and the concern of other Episcopal ladies for their husbands' eternal salvation, was obviously sincere, but there were temporal issues at stake here as well. Once when Catherine discussed her failure to bring her husband "to Christ," she confided her hope that she and Joseph might soon "go hand in hand strengthening each other and training our children for an everlasting inheritance at Gods right hand."[17]

This was not a vision of life beyond the grave, but of ideal family life. Many Episcopal men were men of honor who engaged in a lifestyle that exhibited a tendency toward recklessness, excess, and marital infidelity. When Episcopal women like Catherine Ruffin tried to convert their husbands, they may simultaneously have been trying to reform male conduct. In Catherine Ruffin's vision, the couple's clasped hands symbolized her converted husband's faithfulness, closeness, and affection. No records survive to tell whether Catherine's efforts finally convinced Joseph to renounce the older ethic and give his heart unreservedly to God—or to her.

Sometimes the posthumous memory of a pious wife exerted a greater influence over traditional husbands than did the living example. Thomas F. Davis of Wilmington was a lawyer descended from one of Cape Fear's most distinguished planter families. Davis's wife, Elizabeth, was a communicant in St. James's, but he was not. In 1830 she died, at the age of thirty. As a result, Davis not only decided to become an Episcopal communicant, he also decided to enter the Episcopal ministry. His long clerical career culminated with his appointment as Bishop of South Carolina in 1848.

Ebenezer Pettigrew, son of Bishop-elect Charles Pettigrew, was another individual whose pious wife's death triggered a conversion. As a young man, Ebenezer Pettigrew demonstrated a strong, almost bitter, opposition to evangelicals. Pettigrew's religious predilections did not keep him from marrying the pious Anne Blount Shepard, or Nancy as she was known to him, daughter of the powerful William Shepard of Newbern. Anne was an Episcopal evangelical who in 1823 wondered whether a prominent gentlemen had felt "the forgiving and attoning [*sic*] Redeemer's love. [W]hat a hope & consolation for dying sinners as we all are by nature." Her concern for the spiritually lost may have included husband Ebenezer whose later actions demonstrated a refusal to embrace an emotional religion.[18]

Only seven years later, in 1830, Anne herself would need that same "hope & consolation" offered to all sinners as she lay dying. Her death sent Ebenezer careening into a despair from which he issued this lament: "I grieve for the suffering of one of the best of women. O my Nancy, my dearest wife! I grieve that she was taken in the prime of life from her dear family. I grieve for myself because I have lost that which the whole world could not replace." Out of Ebenezer's profound lost, however, came a discovery which he himself admitted was due to his wife's death: an emotional religious conversion. "I grieve that I did not know the author of my blessing. I grieve that my dear Nancy did not live to see that change in my heart towards the great author of all good. I grieve because I required such a heart rending affliction to bring me to a knowledge of my own weakness and dependence on him. I hope & pray God that this curse of sorrow, which is now overflowing may be lessened."[19]

Ebenezer's grief was a natural response to his loved one's death, but at least part of his remorse resulted from his realization that something had been lacking in an otherwise happy marriage. He regretted that Anne could not see that he had become as religious as she had been; perhaps he also felt guilty because his former irreligiousness had made their marriage less than ideal, less than the sort of marriage that Anne had wanted and deserved. Anne Pettigrew had led her husband to Christ from the other side of the grave, but, in this world at least, it was too late for Ebenezer's conversion to change the quality of their marriage.

Although other high church marital relationships may suggest the way in which high churchmanship mediated the tensions between traditional husbands and evangelical wives, the marriage of Mary (Polk) and George E. Badger presents unusually clear testimony to this phenomenon. Badger, future Secretary of Navy in the Tyler administration, married Mary B. Polk, daughter of Colonel William Polk and Sarah (Hawkins) Polk, in 1826; it was widower George's second marriage at the age of thirty-one. Mary's mother had attended the Rev. William McPheeters's Presbyterian Church in Raleigh. William Polk, a proud man of honor who was a friend of the Episcopal church, personally disliked McPheeters enough to refuse to let him perform the ceremony at George and Mary's wedding. Since all North Carolina's Episcopal ministers were away in general convention at the time, the ceremony was performed by a justice of the peace.

George Badger's remarks to his fiancee concerning the absence of an Episcopal minister at their upcoming marriage suggested a certain lack of respect for Episcopal orthodoxy: "Now to staunch church-people like you and me is it not a little provoking that the ring that symbol of purity and perpetuity of affection, should be in danger of wanting the presence of an episcopal *magician* to give the mystick words of incantation their appropriate charm." Although Badger claimed to be a "staunch" Episcopalian, his comparison of the Episcopal minister to a "magician" implied a religious rationalism that tended to dismiss Episcopal rites and ceremonies as superstitions.[20]

George Badger's attitude toward the Episcopal church changed significantly over the course of the next two years. By 1828 George was confident enough in spiritual matters to counsel Mary who was in the midst of a spiritual depression:

> Perservere in your efforts & I feel the fullest confidence you will succeed—To feel that you are totally helpless in yourself to rely on the merits of your Saviour & to realize that God for his sake is really & truly willing to receive & pardon you is the best preparation you can have . . . and therefore either carelessness or depression—the former suits not the condition of a sinner seeking salvation—the latter belongs not to one who believes the generous declarations of the Gospel.[21]

Mary was also demonstrating an increasing interest in Christianity. By 1830 she was displaying the tell-tale signs of evangelicalism as she warned her brother, "It is certain that we must all die and appear at the judgment seat of Christ—and O my beloved Brother may I meet you there as one of the redeemed spirits whom Christ came to save—Will you think of this great scheme of salvation before it be to [sic] late."[22]

The Badger's religious lives were inseparably connected to the other emotional dimensions of their marriage. George himself discussed the relationship between their marriage and spiritual progress:

> How blest then am I, my dear Mary, in you—whose amiable temper has now added to it that serious earnestness after religious attain-

ment which seconds & even prompts all my own desires—which cheers and aids me on the search after virtue & piety—happiness & Heaven. United thus in our efforts—mutually supporting and assisting each other and constantly realizing our dependence on that Spirit "which worketh in us both to will & to do" may we not hope, my dear, that our pursuit shall be successful—[23]

George and Mary's increasing religiousness allowed the couple to be "mutually supporting" in matters of faith. In the Badger household, the caring high church husband eventually persuaded his more evangelical wife. In 1834 just before her premature death, Mary reported to her husband how glad she was that Bishop Ives was instructing the students at the University of North Carolina against the dangers of revivalism. George echoed his wife's high church aversion to revivals. His tenderness and sensitivity to his wife, his concern for her spiritual welfare minimized their religious differences and even appear to have weaned her away from a more evangelical faith. In the process, Badger asserted his role as Christian patriarch in his high church household.

Domestic religious differences usually began with traditional husbands and pious wives, but invariably moved beyond spouses to affect larger family systems. In the Charlotte (DeBerniere) and Archibald MacLaine Hooper family of Wilmington, a pattern of protracted and intergenerational religious and domestic tension existed. Archibald MacLaine ("A. M.") Hooper was descended from an illustrious Cape Fear family that included one signer of the Declaration. A. M., who was editor of the town newspaper, however, had fallen on financial hard times. He and one of his sons, George, continued to resist Episcopal orthodoxy, while wife Charlotte, her daughter, and one son, John DeBerniere, were Episcopal evangelicals. Charlotte Hooper was confident that God would bring her husband "out of his [financial] difficulties," and she tried "to inspire him with trust in God." She also worried because Archibald and George were not "professors of religion." For Charlotte Hooper, all life's troubles were interpreted through the eyes of evangelical faith.[24]

Charlotte revealed her evangelical sensibilities in an 1831 letter to her son John DeBerniere, or DB:

My dear DB do write unreservedly to me—How much I wish it were possible for you to visit me for it is impossible to say all we

111

wish in letters, but I do not repine I have so much cause for thankfulness, that I must bear the privations patiently, & yet it appears to me you might be the instrument of good to your family if it were possible for you to be with us—We are so cold & dull & indifferent that we require an intercourse with those whose hearts are full of the love of god to rouse us—[25]

Charlotte's relationship with her evangelical son, DB, was unusually close. Her language indicates that she was more and more dependent on him for emotional support. She could share herself with a son whose "heart" like hers was "full of the love of god" in a way that she could not relate to her reserved husband. In a very real sense, DB became his mother's closest companion.

Charlotte's other son, George, also became a source of joy when he joined the church two years later. Sister Louisa, however, was not entirely convinced that George had made "that *total surrender of heart*" necessary for a true conversion. Her reservations about George's salvation were not based on anything concrete; nevertheless, something made her doubt that his conversion was entirely genuine. Since George's faith was high church, and not as evangelical as Louisa or DB, his sister probably recognized the absence in him of the emotional affect that accompanied an evangelical conversion experience.[26]

While his family, one-by-one, became communicants in the church, A. M. Hooper, an impecunious patriarch, became more bitterly disposed toward the Episcopal church in Wilmington. In 1835 he described the town as a community which "though presenting the externals of religion and the decencies of life, is growing every day more lax in principle and more corrupt in practice."[27] When Charlotte left town a year later for a visit, Archibald stopped going to church entirely. Charlotte, who was upset by Archibald's spiritual plight, continued to speak to him on matters of faith. The family moved to Chapel Hill in the late 1830s, and Archibald aided in the organization of the Chapel of the Cross, Episcopal, in May 1842. But he was still not a communing member. Finally, a year later, as he approached the age of seventy, Archibald MacLaine Hooper made his peace and joined the Episcopal church as a communicant.

The relationship between Dr. James Norcom and his sons, Dr. Benjamin Rush Norcom and Dr. John Norcom, was another variation on the more typical pattern of religious disagreement: adult

112

children assumed the roles usually performed by an evangelical wife. James Norcom's religious pilgrimage also provides one of the richest accounts of the conversion of a deist. In 1810, after a sensational divorce from his first wife, James Norcom, at the age of thirty-two, married the sixteen-year-old Maria Horniblow. Evidence suggests that the pious Maria became interested in evangelicalism shortly after her marriage, but by the 1820s, Norcom and his family were in the Episcopal church. Maria was a communicant; James was not, although he was a vestryman.

If the spouses were concerned about their religious differences, no record of discussion survives to document it. There is evidence, however, that the Norcom's marriage was disturbed in the late 1820s when James began to make sexual advances to an attractive, light-skinned, slave girl, Harriet Jacobs, who was a domestic servant in his home. Although Jacobs spurned Norcom's attempts to make her his mistress, Maria became extremely jealous of James's affection for Harriet.

Against a background of domestic unrest, Dr. Norcom's adult children assumed the role usually played by an evangelical wife and tried to convert their father. Perhaps the age difference between Maria and James Norcom prevented her from relating to him on anything like an equal basis and thus kept her subservient. In any case, the Norcom children, including the eldest, John, who was a product of the first marriage, were far more pious than their father. John Norcom was converted in 1833 as a result of a life-threatening illness that, according to him, was "of immense value to the interest of my soul." During his brush with death John "realized the entire necessity of absolute dependence upon the mercy of God and upon the merits of his beloved son Jesus Christ."[28]

Only a month after his own conversion, John became worried about his father James's spiritual condition and wrote to him about the need for conversion:

> You certainly are a very favoured man. In addition you have all the comforts & enjoyments,—yea! luxuries of life in abundance: you have a family of fine, promising, prosperous children. You ought to be a happy man: you ought to be a contented man. But are you? If not, why are you not? Search the scriptures, and faithfully & honestly examine your heart by them: humbly beseeching the favour and help of your Lord and Redeemer in behalf of your attempt, and you will be abundantly rewarded in the result. . . .

May God continue to favour you with his blessings, and enable
you to see & know yourself truly and correctly![29]

James Norcom was not convinced, at least immediately, by his
son's warning. A year later, James outlined his own natural theology when he advised another son, Wistar, "that your mind may be
too much occupied by religious studies and discussions." According
to the father, an individual became acquainted with the "Deity" by
contemplating the created order that revealed to the human mind
"a lively sense of the goodness & wisdom of that great & benevolent Being who is the author & giver of . . . all!" James Norcom,
perennial vestrymen and friend of St. Paul's, Edenton, had not yet
surrendered his older religious notions and lifestyle to embrace
Episcopal high churchmanship.[30]

Norcom finally became a communicant in 1839, at the age of
sixty-three. According to Harriet Jacobs, Norcom continued sexu-
ally to harass her. When she reminded him that he was now a communicant, and, therefore, should refrain from such lascivious
behavior, Norcom responded, "It was proper for me to [be confirmed.] I am getting [on] in years, and my position in society re-
quires it, and it puts and [*sic*] end to all the damned slang."[31]

If Jacob's testimony was the only evidence of Norcom's motives
for becoming a communicant, then it would appear that he was a
religious hypocrite. Norcom's situation, however, is rendered much
more ambiguous by other important circumstances. The trium-
phant death of another devout evangelical son, Benjamin Rush,
which occurred shortly before Norcom's decision to be confirmed,
deeply impressed the father and probably caused him to think
about his own mortality and salvation. James commented on Benjamin's last moments: "Having lived in the faith & fear of God, it
was to be expected that in the great trial he has undergone, he
would be blest with the manifestations of his Creator's goodness &
supported by His Spirit. It was strikingly so: He . . . expressed to the
last a perfect confidence that he was about to enter into that Eternal Joy, which God has promised to all who love & fear Him!"[32]

It is quite likely that Benjamin's death affected his father in much
the same way that the deaths of pious wives influenced their unconverted husbands: it caused him to consider the state of his own
soul. Before Benjamin's death James had never uttered the word
"Saviour" in any of his lengthy discussions of religion or morality,
but a change was imminent. Norcom was confirmed soon after and

judging from his written utterances his conversion was genuine. Three years later as he meditated on the inevitability of his own death "when I shall be summoned to appear before the Judge of Quick & dead, to render my account," Norcom admitted that "in reflecting on the manner in which the greatest part of my life has been, my soul is filled with the most awful apprehensions." James Norcom was trusting in "the gracious promises contained in the gospel of an Immaculate Saviour"; it had taken him nearly a lifetime to do so. During the remaining eleven years of his life, James Norcom evinced an unmistakable concern that his family and friends obtain the same assurance of salvation that he had obtained as a communicant within the Episcopal church. If his conversion was insincere, he was a gifted actor.[33]

Another variation on the usual pattern of religious differences occurred when a son frustrated the wishes of a traditional father by becoming pious. It bears repeating that to do so was to reject the traditional male code of ethics and become like a woman. When Thomas F. Davis chose to give up his successful law practice and enter the Episcopal ministry, his father was vehemently opposed to the decision.

Col. William Polk, a friend and patron of the Episcopal church in the state, reacted in a similar fashion when son Leonidas made the same determination. Polk's wife Sarah (Hawkins) Polk attended the Presbyterian church. Son Leonidas was aware of the spread of evangelical religion in Raleigh, but he had manifested no great interest in it. In his own words, he had "repeatedly put off the further consideration of [the Christian Religion] . . . to what *I conceived* a more favorable opportunity; designing at a future day, when less engaged with worldly affairs, to examine fairly into their truths."[34]

For Leonidas "a more favourable opportunity" arose when he entered the United States Military Academy at West Point in 1826 at the age of eighteen. Once there, Leonidas began reading two volumes of published letters by Olaithus Gregory of the Royal Military Academy at Woolwich, England on "the evidences of Christianity" and "its Doctrines & Duties." Cadet Polk found the argument intellectually compelling, and after seeking the counsel of a local minister he decided "to renounce all my former habits & associations, to step forth singly from among the whole Corps acknowledging my convictions of the truth of that Holy religion which I had before derided, and was now anxious to embrace."[35] Leonidas's conversion differed from most evangelical conversions in that his decision depended so heavily on intellectual consideration of the arguments in Gregory's book. Other details, however, suggest that Polk's conversion was indeed evangelical, demonstrating an "ardour of feelings" characteristic of one who had just undergone an emotional conversion.

The news of Leonidas's conversion was "the cause of uneasiness to the family" in Raleigh. Father William shot back an anxious letter to Leonidas which arrived less than three weeks after the ink had dried on Leonidas's own letter informing the family of his conversion. Leonidas's brother followed less than a month later with another letter trying to convince him to renounce his new beliefs. In the face of his family's assault, Leonidas was unwavering and self-assured. He "was aware of what are the opinions of men of the world, generally as to [Christianity], and [those] who are its followers." But he was more firmly convinced of "the truth of Revelation" than of any fact in the world. When Leonidas replied to his brother, he ended on the offensive by begging him "to examine for yourself" the truth of Christianity.[36]

Colonel Polk was not yet through trying to dissuade his strong-willed son. A year later, in the spring of 1827, William advised his son not to take any steps under the influence of religious fervor that would be "to the detriment of the health either of [your] mind or body." Apparently the father believed that evangelical conversion was a form of emotional instability. William also warned Leonidas that his "ardour of feelings" threatened to undermine the prospect of "an honourable, dignified, & useful" career.[37]

The Colonel's worries about his son's new-found evangelical faith may have been even greater than the prospects that his son had wrecked his chances for worldly success. The father's dismay may have reflected a deeper fear that his son's evangelical piety, the faith of the ladies, suggested effeminacy. Leonidas's later military career left little doubt about his personal bravery or manly virtues, but that may not have been clear to his father at the time. William Polk, after all, was a Revolutionary war hero and a proud man of honor, and the family's reputation was at stake. It is not difficult to imagine William's reaction—he already was worried about the possibility of Leonidas impairing his mental faculties—when his son informed him shortly after that he had decided to go into the

Episcopal ministry. Leonidas attended the low church Virginia Theological Seminary in Alexandria, not the high church General Theological Seminary in New York.

The religious differences between Episcopal family members could be reconciled, but only through conversion, and only with difficulty. Some wives succeeded in convincing their husbands to become Episcopal communicants; others did not. The experience for the male could be wrenching when it involved a more evangelical (emotional) conversion instead of a high church (rational) one. And no wonder: reluctant gentlemen long-accustomed to shielding their "passions" from public view now had to expose emotions. One prominent Raleigh churchman "was almost convulsed by the effort to restrain his feelings" at his confirmation in 1840. Upper-class men often resisted conversion until late in life, as in the cases of James Norcom and A. M. Hooper.[38]

Other gentlemen postponed conversion until death was staring them in the face. Gov. Benjamin Smith never joined St. James's, Wilmington, even after his wife's dramatic conversion and recovery. Smith, who had participated in several duels and had gambled his immense fortune away, died impenitent according to one female friend. But his last will and testament told a different story. In it he openly repented and acknowledged Christ as Savior. Another former governor, John Owen, was actually on his deathbed when he summoned Episcopal minister William M. Green to his Pittsboro home in 1841. Owen had been a conspicuous friend of religion while he served as vice-president of the North Carolina Tract Society in 1828, but apparently he had never joined the Episcopal church as a communicant. According to Green, the former governor's long-delayed conversion appeared efficacious as his last days were ones "of deep humiliation for the past, of patient endurance of God, with unfeigned hope of the blessedness beyond the grave."[39]

The actions of Episcopal men suggest that they postponed becoming Episcopal communicants for one of two reasons: either they held to Enlightenment beliefs that made it difficult for them to accept orthodoxy, or they were proud men of honor whose lifestyles conflicted with the moral standards expected of a communicant. Judge William Norwood, for example, was a founder, vestryman, and baptized member of St. Matthew's in Hillsboro, but not a communicant. The Norwood family's reaction to their

117

taciturn father's unrepentant death in 1842 must have been typical of the experience of many other Episcopal families. During the last year of his life Judge William's health declined rapidly. His wife, Robina, and daughter Helen (Norwood) Mickle hoped that "Pa" had grabbed "hold on the hope set before him in the Gospel." But they were unsure.[40]

The judge had spent a great deal of time alone in his sick chamber, perhaps in religious reflection, and had also read some religious literature. He refused to discuss religion, however, saying he had "thought much on the subject while he had possession of his mental faculties," but that he was too sick and confused to do so during his last days. At one point near the end he even expressed a desire to join the church, "but with his characteristic procrastination said he was not ready *then*." As the judge lay dying, his family hoped that somehow in private their father had "sought the salvation" which he had refused to receive publicly.[41]

The Norwood family's doubts concerning William Norwood's salvation outweighed its hopes. The adult daughters worried that there was something presumptuous and disrespectful about assessing their father's spiritual condition, but their deep concern about what they considered ultimate matters made it necessary to do so. According to one of them, "no degree of moral worth" even for one with a character "so excellent" as their father's could substitute for salvation by grace.[42]

Dr. George Moore, respected physician in Chapel Hill and a founder, but not a communicant, of the Chapel of the Cross, also wrestled on his deathbed with his lack of orthodox faith. According to an early twentieth-century Chapel Hill historian, Moore "had great respect for religion, often attended church, but did not become a member." On his deathbed, Moore called his nurse, Miss Sally Williams, an Episcopal communicant, and "a simple-minded, devout Christian," to his side. Moore queried, "Miss Sally, do you think a man will go to hell for not believing all that is in the Bible?" She hesitantly replied, "I suppose I must." Moore responded, "I don't, I can't. I have never to my knowledge lied or cheated. I have been charitable to the extent of my means. I never was a coward. I have paid my debts as far as I possibly could. Now if they send me to hell, I will go grumbling."[43]

It is impossible to tell to what extent Moore and Williams's close professional relationship was also personal, but in his last moments the bachelor doctor turned to his unmarried nurse for comfort as a dying man might turn to his spouse. She, however, could offer him no religious solace. Moore, whose faith reflected the liberal religious assumptions of a bygone era, died bravely, but in doubt.

Other Episcopal men who delayed becoming communicants may have done so not because of intellectual reservations, but because they wished to remain unrestrained men of honor. If not the outright imputation of effeminacy, Episcopalianism called, at the very least, for a lifestyle that shunned many of the activities that defined a man of honor. As a result, male peers often ridiculed Episcopal men who were sincerely pious. When Edward J. Mallett complied with his Episcopal evangelical mother's wishes and quit gambling, his companions immediately derided his reformed behavior and asked mockingly if he had become "pious."[44]

One of the reasons that prominent state judge John L. Bailey, who had displayed a keen interest in evangelical religion even in his twenties, delayed baptism in the Episcopal church until his fortieth year was his fear that it would damage his professional reputation among his fellow lawyers. John R. London, a lay delegate from Wilmington to the first Episcopal convention, which organized the Diocese of North Carolina, would not become a communicant for more than forty years. Only five years after London helped reorganize North Carolina's Episcopal church, he was a second in a Wilmington duel that also involved another Episcopalian, Edward B. Dudley, future governor. A number of other prominent Episcopal laymen were also involved in duels. It appears that as these Episcopal men grew older, the code of honor exerted less influence over their lives, enabling some of them finally to become Episcopal communicants late in life. According to Bertram Wyatt-Brown, a related process absolved older gentlemen from participating in duels because it was considered inappropriate for them to display youthful passions.[45]

With the growth of high churchmanship in the Diocese of North Carolina, religious discussion within Episcopal families subsided. After 1840, and for the remainder of the antebellum era, Episcopal women's outspoken efforts to convert their husbands faded away. The tranquility in Episcopal homes almost certainly was related to the women's growing appreciation for Hobartian high churchmanship. When both husbands and wives genuinely subscribed to high churchmanship, the result was Episcopal marriages that appear to have been a satisfying synthesis of companionate and traditional styles of marriage.

Many Episcopal men, however, remained gentlemen of honor who persisted in older attitudes toward their wives. Surely, domestic tension remained in these Episcopal households. If so, Episcopal women kept their silence, tolerated existing conditions, and supported patriarchy. Why? Once again, in the absence of absolutely clear and persuasive evidence, contemporary social fears offer the most convincing explanation. As sectional strife and internal social tensions increased, perhaps Episcopal women became less critical of their husbands' religious shortcomings and more appreciative of the role that Episcopal gentlemen played as agents of social order and control.[46]

Notes

1. Anne Moore [Davis] to Magdalen DeRosset, 13 September 1831, DeRosset Family Papers, SHC.
2. Rev. William Hooper, *The Happy Choice: A Sermon Occasioned by the Death of Mrs. Mallett, Wife of Peter Mallett, Esq. of Fayetteville, N.C.; Who Died, March 1st, 1824* (Philadelphia: W. W. Woodward, 1824), 4–5.
3. [Catherine Fullerton] Diary, 22 June 1798, DeRosset Family Papers, SHC. This unsigned diary can be identified as Catherine Fullerton's by a comparison of the handwritings in later Catherine (Fullerton) DeRosset letters in the William Lord DeRosset Papers, DUA.
4. A[rmand] J. DeRosset to Catherine F. DeRosset, 10 May 1818, DeRosset Family Papers, SHC.
5. Samuel W. Tillinghast to Jane Norwood, 20 December 1829, Tillinghast Family Papers, DUA.
6. Edw[ar]d Lee Winslow to S. W. Tillinghast, 1 October [18]44, Tillinghast Family Papers, DUA.
7. Jane [Tillinghast] to Samuel W. Tillinghast, 10 June 1850, Tillinghast Family Papers, DUA; Samuel W. Tillinghast to John H. Tillinghast, 11 April 1852, Tillinghast Family Papers, DUA; Samuel W. Tillinghast to John H. Tillinghast, 11 April 1852, Tillinghast Family Papers, DUA.
8. John S. Ravenscroft to Adam Empie, 11 July 1825, John Stark Ravenscroft PECA, microfilm at NCC.
9. Maria L. Spear to Catherine Ruffin, 6 November 1830, Ruffin-Roulhac-Hamilton Papers, SHC.
10. Julia P. Miner to Mary W. Shepard, 1 November 1821, John H. Bryan Papers, NCDAH.
11. Mary W. Bryan to John H. Bryan, 1 April 1834, John H. Bryan Papers, NCDAH.

12. All quotations in this paragraph are from Paul C. Cameron to Anna Ruffin, 8 July 1831, Cameron Family Papers, SHC.
13. Anna Cameron to Paul Cameron, 1 April 1833, Cameron Family Papers, SHC.
14. Catherine Roulhac to Joseph B. Roulhac, 26 July 1841, Ruffin-Roulhac-Hamilton Papers, SHC.
15. Catherine Roulhac to Jos. B. G. Roulhac, 9 April 1843, Ruffin-Roulhac-Hamilton Papers, SHC.
16. Catherine Roulhac to Joseph B. G. Roulhac, 21 September 1843, Ruffin-Roulhac-Hamilton Papers, SHC; Catherine Roulhac to Jos. B. Roulhac, 5 April 1844, Ruffin-Roulhac-Hamilton Papers, SHC.
17. Catherine Roulhac to Joseph B. G. Roulhac, 8 October 1842, Ruffin-Roulhac-Hamilton Papers, SHC.
18. Anne Blount Pettigrew to Mary W. Bryan, 7 October 1823, John H. Bryan Papers, NCDAH.
19. Ebenezer Pettigrew to Mary Shepard, 19 November 1830, and [fragment] 6 December 1830, Pettigrew Family Papers, SHC; Ebenezer Pettigrew to John H. Bryan, 26 October 1847, John H. Bryan Papers, NCDAH.
20. George E. Badger to Mary B. Polk, 21 October 1826, Polk-Badger-McGehee Papers, microfilm at SHC.
21. George E. Badger to Mary [B. Badger], 13 April 1828, Polk-Badger-McGehee Papers, microfilm at SHC.
22. George E. Badger to Mary B. Badger, 21 April 1828, Polk-Badger-McGehee Papers; Mary B. Badger to Alexander Hamilton Polk, 5 February 1830, Polk-Badger-McGehee Papers, both on microfilm at SHC.
23. George E. Badger to Mary B. Badger, 19 April 1828, Polk-Badger-McGehee Papers, microfilm at SHC.
24. Charlotte Hooper to John DeBerniere Hooper, 19 November 1828, John DeBerniere Hooper Papers, SHC; Charlotte Hooper to John DeBerniere Hooper, 22 August [ca. 1830?], John DeBerniere Hooper Papers, SHC.
25. Charlotte Hooper to John DeBerniere Hooper, 5 June 1831, John DeBerniere Hooper Papers, SHC.
26. Louisa Hooper to John DeBerniere Hooper, 22 June 1835, John DeBerniere Hooper Papers, SHC.
27. Archibald MacLaine Hooper to John DeBerniere Hooper, 11 July 1835, John DeBerniere Hooper Papers, SHC.
28. John Norcom to Benj. R. Norcom, 20 November 1833, James Norcom Papers, NCDAH.
29. John Norcom to James [Norcom], 30 December 1833, James Norcom Papers, NCDAH.

30. James Norcom to [Caspar] Wistar [Norcom], 25 September 1834, James Norcom Papers, NCDAH.
31. Harriet A. Jacobs, *Incidents in the Life of a Slave Girl,* Jean Fagan Yellin, ed. (Cambridge: Harvard University Press, 1987) 74.
32. James Norcom to Caspar W. Norcom, 13 December 1838, James Norcom Papers, NCDAH.
33. James Norcom to John Norcom, 29 December 1842, James Norcom Papers, NCDAH.
34. Leonidas Polk to [his father], 11 May 1826, Leonidas Polk Papers, SHC.
35. Ibid.
36. Leonidas Polk to [his father], 5 June 1826, Leonidas Polk Papers, USoA, microfilm at SHC; Leonidas Polk to [his brother], 25 August 1826, Leonidas Polk Papers, USoA, microfilm at SHC.
37. Leonidas Polk to [his father], 9 May 1827, Leonidas Polk Papers, USoA, microfilm at SHC.
38. George W. Freeman to Duncan Cameron, 17 February 1840, Cameron Family Papers, SHC.
39. W[illiam] M[ercer] Green to Duncan Cameron, 13 October 1841, Cameron Family Papers, SHC.
40. Eliza Bingham to Jane Tillinghast, 19 January 1842, Tillinghast Family Papers, DUA.
41. Ibid.
42. Ibid.
43. Kemp P. Battle, *History of the University of North Carolina,* 2 vols. (Raleigh: for the Author by Edwards & Broughton Printing Company, 1907) 1:479, 609.
44. Mallett, *Memoirs,* 45.
45. Wyatt-Brown, *Southern Honor,* 354.
46. The defense of patriarchy remained a prominent feature of Episcopal social thought in North Carolina well into the twentieth century. Interestingly, the percentage of Episcopal women who supported antisuffrage was even higher than Episcopal men. Although Episcopalians constituted only 3 percent of North Carolina's churchgoing population in 1920, Episcopalians accounted for 60 and 30 percent of the antisuffrage and suffrage women, respectively, and 42 and 27 percent of the antisuffrage and suffrage men, respectively. These figures are found in Elna C. Green, "Those Opposed: The Antisuffragists in North Carolina, 1900–1920," *NCHR* 67 (July 1990):315–330.

CHAPTER FIVE

"Mild and Indulgent Doctrines of Religion": The Triumph of Hobartian High Church Ethics, 1800–1860

The restoration of the Episcopal Church in North Carolina caused ethical confusion within church and family for nearly a quarter of a century. The clash of traditional and evangelical culture affected both Episcopal personal morality and social ethics. Episcopal evangelicals advocated a personal moral code that condemned many habitual pursuits that the gentry had long enjoyed. Episcopal traditionalists, who opposed evangelical morality, endorsed Hobartian high church morality because it condoned much that was customary to genteel behavior. When traditional activities such as dueling and swearing violated high church morals, however, traditional Episcopalians were torn between conflicting ethical systems: Hobartian high churchmanship and southern honor.

The growth of high churchmanship throughout the 1830s assured the triumph of high church morality over its evangelical counterpart. An 1840 controversy at Christ's Church, Raleigh, on the subject of dancing confirmed the high church position. High church morality, however, struggled with mixed success against southern honor. Throughout the antebellum era, proud Episcopal men defied the church by dueling among themselves and philandering with female slaves. And they did so without any specific censure from the church and without any significant loss of standing within the community.

Hobartian high church social ethics created a different set of problems for Episcopalians, particularly reform-minded men. Dur-

124

ing the years immediately before and after the restoration of the diocese, Episcopal men and women cooperated with evangelical Protestants in a number of benevolent reform activities. Episcopal men, who were not evangelical, apparently supported benevolent reform as the part of a broader program of moral, social, cultural, and economic reform. Benevolent reform was one facet of their larger vision of progress.

High church clergymen, however, demanded that Episcopalians sever all ties to other denominations and quit ecumenical reform. Episcopal clergymen promoted only Episcopal reform. The growth of northern antislavery sentiment, which was linked to national reform, eventually persuaded the Episcopal laity to accept the clergy's more narrow approach to social reform. Simultaneously, the Episcopal church in North Carolina became a vocal supporter of the institution of slavery.

The moral differences between Episcopal evangelicals and traditionalists was particularly evident as it related to the temperance issue and to a diverse group of personal activities, known collectively as worldly amusements. Drinking alcohol was a prominent feature of masculine culture in antebellum North Carolina. According to Bertram Wyatt-Brown, "drinking was a function of masculinity, and upper-class women who partook of anything stronger than a sweet wine risked loss of respectability. Consumption of hard liquor signified virility."[1]

Unfortunately, the cult of male drinking exacted a high social cost in the form of alcoholism. The upper classes in North Carolina may have been quietly troubled about excessive drinking well before evangelicals began the temperance crusade in the early nineteenth century, but it was probably no coincidence that members of the elite began to condemn drunkenness at the same time. One Episcopalian by heritage delineated the dangers of drunkenness in an 1815 Dialectic Society speech. This should not, however, be construed as a call for abstinence. Moderate drinking continued to be entirely acceptable to most churchpeople.

As the temperance movement, which was linked to the broader program of evangelical reform, began to promote abstinence, however, North Carolina Episcopalians were faced with a difficult choice. Some Episcopal gentlemen renounced the masculine habit and wholeheartedly joined the movement. In Hillsboro in 1841, a representative from a Baltimore temperance society succeeded in establishing an auxiliary society that included a number of prominent local Episcopalians; John Mickle, and Walter and Joseph Norwood from St. Matthew's (the latter a vestryman) all joined "the *tee total* cause." Robert Strange spoke favorably of temperance societies in his novel *Eoneguski.* Judge William H. Battle, a communicant in the Chapel of the Cross, Chapel Hill, abstained from drinking alcohol.

Other Episcopal laymen were less enthusiastic about what they considered fanaticism. George Badger, the redoutable high churchman, was a firm believer in the virtues of moderate drinking; he thought the teetotalers absurd. When a local temperance man came into Badger's Raleigh law office and cited the opinions of eminent physicians that abstinence was salubrious, Badger exploded:

> Those celebrated physicians are nothing in the world but miserable popularity seekers—They never dreamed a drink injurious until they found the whole earth turned topsy turvy with Father Mathews [*sic,* Mathew]—such a wonderful discovery of the dreadful evils of stimulating liquors were never originated by a consultation of any medical faculty—but it remained for these miserable tee totallers to denounce suddenly and without much forethought—a practice which has been in existence from time immemorial—which can only be deleterious when carried to excess.[2]

Badger's counsel was moderation. According to him, the temperance reformers' mistake was in going from one extreme to the other. In their attempt at "avoiding sottishness," they had wandered "into downright prejudice & narrow mindedness."[3]

Although a number of individual members supported the temperance cause, the Episcopal church reflected the attitudes of the majority of its laity and was one of the only denominations in the state that did not support the temperance movement. In 1851 the Rev. Jarvis Buxton of Asheville even publicly criticized a noted temperance lecturer. Episcopal views concerning drinking were more tolerant than any other denomination in the state, with the possible exception of the Kehukee Baptists. In 1859 Albert Smedes, Episcopal minister in Raleigh, invited another Episcopal cleric to his home where "a box of claret" was waiting for the guest to drink.[4] As in so many other cases, high church morality on drinking appears to have provided a moderate way between evangelical abstinence and traditional excess. By 1840 North Carolina Episcopalians generally rejected temperance, allowed moderate alcohol consumption, and condemned overindulgence.

In addition to the temperance issue, Episcopalians debated other pastimes known collectively as "worldly or fashionable amusements." These included card playing, novel reading, horse racing, theatergoing, and, most importantly, dancing. Episcopal evangelicals apparently opposed some of these activities for the same reasons outlined by a literate North Carolina Methodist. Such pleasurable pursuits "polluted and corroded the soul" and distracted the believer from seeking "the comforts and pleasures of the New Birth." Evangelicals feared that worldly amusements were so entertaining that the sinner never would become concerned enough with his or her lost state to seek salvation. The extent of the public discussion among Episcopalians on the worldly amusements varied widely depending on the activity in question.[5]

For a pursuit like horse racing, which evangelicals attacked, no record survives to indicate that any ethical debate arose within Episcopal circles. Horse racing was the leading sport among eastern North Carolinians and particularly among the elite, who relished fine horse flesh. Willie Jones of Halifax, a notorious deist, reputedly installed the first bay window in the state so that he could watch his horses practice on the track in his backyard. The horses from Northampton County, among them the legendary Sir Archie, were so fleet that Virginians outlawed them from participating in races across the line in the Old Dominion.

Hillsboro, Halifax, Pittsboro, Warrenton, and Newbern, all held fall and spring races. By the late antebellum period, the annual races in Warren County had grown popular enough to attract spectators from Richmond, Charleston, and Columbia. Thomas Ruffin, prominent high church communicant, apparently felt no uneasiness at horse racing, for he continued to own and race some of the finest thoroughbreds in the state. The pedigree of one of Ruffin's finest horses, Cherokee, survives in the family papers.

Unlike horse racing, card playing, novel reading, and theatergoing generated mild controversy within the genteel class. Robert Strange condemned card playing in his novel *Eoneguski*. Edward Jones Mallett's conflict with his pious mother over card playing was a typical clash between evangelical and traditional morality.

Shortly after graduating from college in 1820, Mallett joined a club in Fayetteville and developed an appetite for cards. His Episcopal evangelical mother heard of her son's habit and called him into her bedroom for a session of kneeling prayer. After she finished praying, the widow Mallett remarked, "I have been made very unhappy to hear that you frequent the gambling table. For my sake now, and for your own, here and hereafter, I desire you . . . to give me your [solemn oath forswearing the practice.]" Mallett complied with his mother's wishes, and the results illustrated the dilemma of gentlemen caught between evangelical females (his mother) and traditional males (his fellow club members). Mallett's peers, deriding his reformed behavior, asked if he had become "pious."[6]

Young Episcopalians discussed the morality of novel reading and theatergoing in the debating societies at the University of North Carolina. In 1828 Philip W. Alston, a young Episcopalian related to the powerful Johnston family of Edenton and a future Episcopal minister, defended the practice of novel reading in an address to the Dialectic Society. In an obvious jab at the evangelicals, Alston denounced "religious fanatics," who were "disgraceful to human nature, much less to the mild & indulgent doctrines of religion, whose cause they pretend to support" by opposing the reading of novels. According to one Methodist evangelical, however, "novels" and "romances" spoil "the taste, distemper the mind, and unfit it for the reception of wholesome and nourishing [spiritual] food."[7]

Two years later, in 1830, the Dialectic Society debated whether theatrical exhibitions were moral. According to those who opposed it, theaters "abound in all the evils that can waste prosperity—corrupt our morals—blast our reputation—impair our health—embitter our lives, destroy our souls." Among the society members opposed to the theater was John DeBerniere Hooper, a young Episcopal evangelical and future Episcopal minister.[8]

Other Episcopalians across the state, however, attended the theater either without or in spite of qualms of conscience. In the first decades of the nineteenth century, local gentry formed amateur theatrical societies in Wilmington, Fayetteville, Raleigh, Newbern, Salisbury, and Warrenton. Episcopalians were in the forefront of producing and attending local drama productions. Thomas P. Irving, the Episcopal schoolmaster and occasional minister, directed theatrical efforts in Newbern before the Episcopal restoration. In Wilmington local Episcopalians were prominent in the productions of the theatrical society, the Thalian Association. Since the Thalian Association's actors were all male, members performed female roles as well. William Mercer Green, a Wilmington layman who would later become bishop of Mississippi, was noted for his excellent portrayal of heroines. Frances Iredell (Mrs. James Iredell, Jr.) presumably saw nothing wrong with the theatre in 1829; she allowed her children to attend with a family friend in Raleigh. Apparently, the vast majority of the Episcopal laity never developed a strong opposition to attending the theater.

No issue of personal morality engendered greater controversy among Episcopalians than the subject of dancing. The problem with forbidding dancing was that the diversion was so inextricably connected with older notions of gentility and sociability. Before the restoration of the Episcopal church, the ability to dance was a prerequisite to entering polite society, and dancing was central to most genteel celebrations. In Edenton the Iredell girls were "mortified" when they learned that there would be no dancing at a local Edenton wedding because the family happened to be Baptist.

Dancing was a hallmark of gentility. As a boy, Edward Jones Mallett attended a dance school in Fayetteville where he learned not only terpsichore, but also polite manners such as "how to enter a room, how to introduce a gentleman to a lady, how to walk arm in arm with a lady, how to drink a toast." Dancing was also critical because, like the theater, it involved the ladies who by and large avoided all the other male amusements. If dueling was the ultimate badge distinguishing the gentleman of honor, dancing was one of the supreme accomplishments identifying a lady of fashion.[9]

The evangelical awakening, however, brought into existence a moral code that outlawed dancing. Methodists and Baptists expelled members of their churches for the practice. According to one prominent young Episcopal woman, a Methodist preacher in Williamston repeatedly upbraided his young nephew who enjoyed dancing. The Methodist uncle "never fails to lecture him after one of his transgressions, and to represent to him the dreadful consequences." Even Presbyterians, who approached the Episcopalians in terms of social standing, took a much harder line on dancing. Belle Norwood, a Presbyterian, wrote to her Episcopal cousin, William N. Tillinghast, that she had "attended a dance" but "was too good a Presbyterian to dance as you might know, but enjoyed myself very much as a spectator."[10]

Whether Episcopalians ought to dance had become a lively question by the late 1830s. According to a female member of the Burgwyn family in 1839, the propriety of dancing was a frequent and hotly debated topic among the gentry. The Episcopal church issued its definitive answer to the dancing question after a controversy at Christ's Church, Raleigh, in 1840. Because the argument took place in the see of the diocese, and because the disputants published documents for the whole state to read describing their respective theological positions, the outcome had broad implications for the rest of the church regarding the subject of amusements.

The Christ's Church controversy was a striking confrontation between an Episcopal evangelical minister and his high church laity over the nature of Episcopal morality. The popular minister of some twelve years, George W. Freeman, took the evangelical position that a communicant should not dance. Nearly all the communicants in the church were female, and, according to Freeman, all had refused to participate in any balls during the first five years of his ministry. This certainly must have had a depressive effect on dances—all the really high-class women were cut off from "spirited youth."

In the late 1830s, however, communicants began to attend dancing parties. In response, Freeman decided to take a hard ethical stance on the issue of amusements and included attendance at the theatre and the circus, along with dancing, as activities unbecoming the life-style of a communicant. When his congregation failed to mend their ways, Freeman tendered his resignation because of the irreconcilable differences that had developed between shepherd and flock. Faced with a choice between evangelical morality and traditional sociability, the vestry made the only decision possible under the circumstances: it received its pastor's resignation with regret.

Freeman's decision to resign sparked a larger church debate on the morality of amusements. Bishop Ives defended Freeman, which was surprising since Ives was a high churchman, and high churchmen were generally tolerant of worldly amusements. The vestry as a whole stood firm, however, (which was revealing of the true locus of power within the Episcopal church) stating that dancing fell into that class of "objects indifferent in themselves, involving mere questions of expediency, in regard to which it is an error 'to attempt to fix a definite limit of universal obligation.' " The vestry therefore declared that dancing provided "no just ground of interruption to full, affectionate, mutual, christian intercourse and communion."[11]

Vestryman George Badger, apparently piqued at Freeman's evangelical distinction between the duties of communicants and baptized members with regard to amusements, printed his own separate theological treatise asserting that the moral responsibility was the same for both types of membership. He then went on to deny that either was obligated to forgo dancing.

The Christ's Church vestry had clearly advertised that they would not renounce their long-enjoyed entertainment. The vestry's actions signified the victory of the conventional-turned-high-church ethics of gentlemen and ladies over evangelical attitudes toward amusements. William Hooper Haigh, a young Raleigh high churchman, represented the same position when he declared the folly of expecting Episcopalians "to renounce all the pleasures of the world, as soon as they enter the church[.] To be serious and monkish—perfect Anchorites as respects worldly affairs, and confining their thought totally to the gloom & melancholy of the grave." Haigh's remarks revealed the disdain that worldly men felt as they considered the self-denying lifestyle of an evangelical communicant. The solution was high churchmanship, which allowed its communicants to continue to enjoy many older habits.[12]

Haigh's comments also are an important indication of the way in which high churchmen viewed evangelicals. He believed that the evangelicals' insistence on withdrawing from all harmless recreations was reminiscent of the asceticism of some early Christians and of monks. The evangelicals' own experience of their faith may have been joyful, but to high churchmen it appeared doleful. While evangelicals associated their religious experience with a spiritual new birth, Haigh conjoined evangelical faith with death, or the grave.

The triumph of high church morality allowed Episcopalians to work out a spiritual compromise and to reclaim the world of fashion. Even during the height of evangelical influence during the 1810s and 1820s, Episcopal ladies renounced the code of fashion only with difficulty. For the remainder of the era, fashion and piety were reconciled. In 1843 Wilmington Episcopal ladies prepared a benefit dinner to raise money for Chapel of the Cross, which was under construction in Chapel Hill. After the meal, the young Episcopalians immediately started a dance in the presence of their elders; no one so much as raised an eyebrow.

In the face of the high church position, even the Episcopal evangelical minority reshaped their position on amusements. They no longer entertained the idea of renouncing dancing. They did, however, continue to recognize that there was a tension between worldly amusements and Christian living that called for vigilance and restraint. The Episcopal evangelical Jane (Norwood) Tillinghast sent her children to dance school, but she also rejoiced that son William, who frequented local cotillions, "has discovered that the exciting amusements do not promote our true happiness."[13]

The striking alteration in the moral sensibilities of Episcopal ladies is revealed in the comments of Mary B. Pettigrew, Ebenezer's second wife, whom he married after the death of Ann. According to Mary, in an 1855 letter advising her younger sister on religious matters, "Love [God] above all things. He does not forbid us reasonable enjoyments in the world. With our natures he knows we need innocent recreations." Mary Pettigrew had moved beyond the original high church argument that amusements were "indifferent things" to argue that they actually were beneficial. Her high church piety not only permitted many traditional genteel diversions, it affirmed them.[14]

Episcopal men had no difficulty conforming to high church standards of conduct with respect to worldly amusements; high church morality, after all, upheld traditional behavior. High church morality was much harder to obey, however, in those instances where it forbade practices that the ethic of honor elevated, such as dueling and swearing. In addition, southern men of honor also tolerated certain types of behavior, objectionable in the eyes of the church, like adultery and miscegenation, so long as a man of honor acted discreetly. As a result, Episcopal men were often caught in a moral dilemma that forced them to violate either the code of honor or high church morals.

The tension between high church morality and the code of honor was evident in the gentlemanly habit of swearing. Swearing was habitually associated with manliness and was particularly common among young men. For adolescent males, swearing was a form of aggressive behavior, along with fighting, drinking, wenching, gambling, and horse racing, that helped establish the reputation of a young man of honor among his contemporaries. Swearing had been common practice in certain genteel spheres. In the late 1790s, the members of the Dialectic Society of the University of North Carolina passed an amendment abolishing "the law prohibiting swearing." Maurice Moore, from a Wilmington family long-associated with old St. James's, introduced the amendment to permit swearing in the society's meetings.

The restoration of the church persuaded certain Episcopal men to quit cursing. After Maurice Moore's brother, Alfred, was baptized in 1813, he stopped swearing as much as he had previously. Four years later, another young gentleman from a prominent Cape Fear Episcopal family would deliver an address in the Dialectic Society that condemned swearing as an "impious and foolish habit." In 1844 Dr. Richard Mason, pastor of Christ's Church, Raleigh, preached a sermon that described swearing as "a low, vulgar & unchristian practice . . . one which forms itself into a *habit*, & endangered the eternal welfare of all who indulged in it." William Hooper Haigh, a young high churchman originally from Fayetteville, praised Mason's sermon and added that no man "of refined taste and Christian feeling can take pleasure" in cursing. But even Haigh recognized that it was by no means an easy habit to break: "[I] looked upon my having overcome the habit, as the greatest triumph of my life."[15]

Episcopal high churchmen who were also men of honor could check the impulse to swear only with great difficulty. Dr. James Norcom in a moment of detachment and cool deliberation advised his son, "Do not contract a habit of saying bad words or using profane language: it is not only sinful, but unmannerly in the highest degree."[16] But some years earlier when a female slave publicly accused Norcom of fathering her child, Norcom cursed her. Swearing clearly fell outside acceptable practice for a high churchman in theory. But Norcom's actions suggest that Episcopal men—and not just young ones—often cut loose with invectives, especially in public situations where a man's reputation was called into question and tempers boiled. In these moments, indignant and passionate men of honor forgot high church morality.

A more serious example of Episcopal men's defiance of high church morality in order to conform to the code of honor was their frequent involvement in duels. Dueling was almost exclusively a genteel activity; the lower classes used their fists. Almost always the circumstances leading to the duel resulted from one gentleman questioning the manliness, integrity, or reputation of another. The offended party was compelled to challenge the antagonist in order to protect his honor in the eyes of the community.

Dueling developed an elaborate ritual with a well-defined etiquette that cloaked savagery under a mantle of civility. The aggrieved gentleman, or principal, sent a note carried by a friend, or second, to explain the nature of the perceived insult to the offending party. The offender replied to the note with an explanation sent through his own second. If the offender's response did not mollify the aggrieved gentleman, then another note was sent challenging the offender to a duel. The seconds worked out the details for the time and location of the actual confrontation. The duel was usually carried out in relative privacy with only seconds and a few other spectators present, but the conclusion was a matter of public knowledge since this was the only way to retrieve lost honor.

Before the restoration of the Episcopal church in 1817, many Episcopalians condoned dueling, although it is hard to explain how the Old Church rationalized loss of life with the sixth commandment. Nevertheless, the Rev. Thomas P. Irving of Christ's Church, Newbern, made no criticism of the duelist, Gov. Richard Dobbs Spaight, or of his killer, John Stanley, in the former's funeral sermon in 1803. In fact, Irving extolled Spaight as one "Jealous of his own reputation" who was motivated by "the principles of honor."[17]

John A. Cameron, son of a Virginia Episcopal minister, expressed a prevailing opinion of dueling in an 1804 essay written at the University of North Carolina less than a year after his brother Duncan was involved in a duel. Young Cameron queried, "Had you rather your relative was alive and live detested, or die gloriously in the defence of a Character which was dearer to him than life [?]" Although Cameron admitted that "to the weak mind duelling may present a terrible aspect," he asserted that gentlemen of honor "would without hesitation declare that they would choose [such a relative] to die." Before the Episcopal restoration, many gentlemen and the Episcopal clergy saw no great tension between dueling and virtuous living. Indeed, virtue, character, and code duello seemed interlocked.[18]

The Episcopal church eventually condemned dueling. In late 1831 the Rev. Philip Wiley of Christ's Church, Elizabeth City, had a friend placed under temporary arrest to prevent him from participating in a duel. In 1844 one Episcopal layman in Raleigh noted that the clergy "denounce [dueling] because they believe it unwarranted by Christian duty—contrary to humanity—and totally defective in producing any result truly beneficial."[19]

The Episcopal clergy's admonition had some effect, but the code of honor was too deeply embedded in genteel culture to disappear easily or swiftly. In 1840 a high church vestryman at Christ's Church, Raleigh, declared that dueling was "in itself, and in every degree, inconsistent with a Christian's duty, and, by consequence, with a Christian's vows." For an Episcopalian like Dr. James Norcom, who had converted to high church orthodoxy, dueling was a vice that threatened the eternal welfare of the participants. When a prominent North Carolina physician was killed on the first shot in an 1846 duel, Norcom deplored that the sudden death "left him no time for repentance or reparation!"[20]

One opponent of dueling from the Tillinghast family was representative of a rising generation of Episcopal males raised by evangelical mothers. These men rejected dueling not only in theory but also in practice. According to him, "In the catalogue of crimes" dueling "occupys a conspicuous place." Young Tillinghast linked dueling to other traditional vices. Dueling was, he said, "the result of the card table and the drinking saloon. In a word, it is confined [?] to those who fear the scoffing, more than they regard the prompting of their consciences, or to those who 'fear not God, neither regard man.' " For young Episcopal evangelical men, a sense of guilt arising from an evangelical conscience that abhorred dueling was much stronger than any sense of public shame that might motivate them to issue a challenge.[21]

Despite all the clergy's efforts, and individual examples of lay compliance, however, some Episcopal men continued to struggle with conflicting allegiances. In 1844 William Hooper Haigh, a high churchman, realized that dueling was "an evil, a palpable, ruinous, barbarous evil, which strikes at the fountain of morals & law." But Haigh also claimed that dueling had certain beneficial effects as "it checks impudence, teaches men their relative duties to each other as *honourable* beings, and induces persons to be Courteous & Civil—when if there was nothing to restrain them, no fear of consequences to deter them, they might be perfect pests in society."[22]

The circumstances surrounding an 1832 fight between Josiah Collins III and Charles Kinney suggest the contending forces that Episcopal men of honor experienced as they tried to live with two ethical systems. Both men had strong ties to the Episcopal church.

Collins, a young man of twenty-three, was from a loyal Episcopal family of enormous wealth. Kinney's connection with Christ's Church, Elizabeth City, although less clear, was implied by his friendship with the minister Philip Wiley and his subsequent church membership.

In October 1831, according to an eye witness, Collins walked into Hoskin's Tavern while Kinney gazed at him from a chair near the entrance. Collins interpreted Kinney's look as insulting and demanded that Kinney "should not stare him in the face." When Kinney refused, Collins took his horsewhip and began to beat his adversary. Kinney retaliated with his fists before the two combatants were separated. Kinney challenged Collins to a duel immediately afterwards. Another prominent Episcopalian, William B. Shepard, was also involved in the affair as a "second."[23]

After Kinney's temper had subsided, he regretted his part in the whole affair, which never actually resulted in a duel. According to him, "When I view myself as a man responsible to my family, and as a being [account]able to God, I can but acknowledge, that [I stand?] condemned. Had I but the courage eno[ugh] to disregard 'the scoffs & sneers of *fools and cowards,*' I should never have consented to run the risk of leaving my wife a widow and my child fatherless; nor offered up at the shrine of ignoble ambition, the greatest and best gift of God to man."[24]

Several years later Kinney would become one of the few male communicants in Christ's Church, Elizabeth City. His contrition after his fight and near-duel with Collins suggests that Episcopal orthodoxy had already begun to exert an influence over his actions prior to his decision to join the church. Whether Josiah Collins had similar pangs of conscience is unknown.

Despite the church's exhortations, proud Episcopal men would not stop dueling. One member of Wilmington's high society observed after a local duel in 1831 that "most [of the public] shuddered at the event. But they have no way of discouraging such things by a decided expression of disapprobation. These men are still treated with the same respect as before by the most disapproving." In 1842 Edward Stanley, who taught a boy's Sunday school class at Christ's Church, Newbern, in the late 1820s, challenged a fellow congressman to a duel. Another Episcopal layman in 1844 described the continuing prevalence of dueling among the elite: "An institution of this kind is absolutely & indispensably requisite, so long as present notions of honor & etiquette are retained . . . for he is branded as a coward who has the moral firmness to resist a challenge—and as a mercenary, & cringing puppy who screens himself behind the shelter afforded by the law."[25]

Although dueling was becoming rare by the Civil War, sporadic duels occurred in the South as late as the 1880s. Episcopal evangelicals who listened to stirrings of conscience had renounced the practice earlier. Serious high churchmen had already abandoned the deadly ritual as well.

Miscegenation by Episcopal men was another indication of high churchmen's ability to flaunt Episcopal morality when it interfered with habitual behavior sanctioned by the code of honor. Southern genteel society was extremely tolerant of male adultery and even less disapproving of miscegenation. Gentlemen did, however, attempt to carry out these affairs with a certain amount of discretion. Dr. James Norcom, for example, suggested to his slave Harriet Jacobs that he wished to build her a small house outside Edenton where they could carry out an affair in privacy.

Actually, southern gentlemen deceived almost no one, including their wives. Maria Norcom, according to Jacobs, was well aware of her husband's intentions toward the female slave. Mary Boykin Chesnut in her famous diary explained that southern ladies consciously ignored their husbands' infidelity in order to maintain a facade of propriety. The ladies really had no recourse but pretense, since their husbands' behavior did not affect their standing in the church or the community. Norcom certainly managed to preserve his reputation as a respected physician in the community and a vestryman at St. Paul's, rising to the position of senior warden in 1838. When Jacobs continued to spurn his offer to become his concubine, Norcom shipped her off to manual labor on one of his outlying plantations as punishment.

U.S. Congressman Kenneth Rayner, who worshiped at and contributed financially to Christ's Church, Raleigh, openly acknowledged his mulatto son, John B. Rayner, born to a slave mother in 1850. The boy was raised with extraordinary attention and advantage in the Raleigh home of Rayner, his wife, and their legitimate children. Kenneth Rayner's adultery and the resulting offspring did nothing to lessen his standing as a leader of the Whig party in North Carolina. He also remained active in Episcopal affairs and received no public censure from the church. Indeed, Rayner's willingness to include his mulatto son so visibly in his own household indicates how tolerant southern society was of such extramarital alliances.

In 1854 James W. Bryan described widespread infidelity with slave mistresses among Episcopal men in Newbern:

> Our society is in a deplorable condition & I think in a few more years the negroes will take and rule the place. The displays made by them here on Sunday is perfectly [ill?]—they *dress Elegantly* & have taken the Episcopal Church—our Pastor had a tremendous Sunday School of the Negro Elite—they have flocked in in short. There are a large number of our young men & several of our Merchants who have negro wives or "misses" & keep them openly, laying up families of Mullatoes!—The depravity of the place is becoming [?] shocking & our preacher may preach forever & they will produce no change.[26]

Although extreme caution must be used in making conclusions based on an isolated statement such as Bryan's, his description bears remarkable resemblance to upper-class male sexual practice in other port cities like Charleston and New Orleans. Gentlemen there often maintained a respectable white family while simultaneously protecting and supporting a black mistress and mulatto children. The white community tolerated this system so long as gentlemen were quiet and discreet.

In the cases of James Norcom, Kenneth Rayner, and the Newbern Episcopal men, and probably in many other cases as well, power and sexuality undermined high church morality. Power legitimized drives and urges that were a stronger determinant of masculine behavior than the high church ethos.

Episcopalians not only debated personal moral issues during the years after the Episcopal restoration, they also had to decide what their social duties were. The ladies' revival offered the elite a new program of evangelical social reform that differed from any conceptions formerly held. Social ethics within the Old Church had emphasized personal charity as the churchman's main social responsibility, while the local parish provided welfare, relief, and other social services as a part of local government. The Revolution altered the old social order, but even in the republican period charity was a quality that the community still highly valued.

The evangelical awakening created an entirely new social vision as evangelicals sought to reform society in their image. Evangelicals substituted organized benevolence for personal charity as their primary instrument for effecting social change, and they began forming benevolent societies in the early years of the nineteenth century. The North Carolina elite, at first among the women, and then the men, began to support and join benevolent societies during this time. In Raleigh, Hillsboro, Fayetteville and Newbern, prominent ladies started some of the first local benevolent societies in the state.

In 1815 leading men from across the state imitated the ladies as they formed the North Carolina Bible Society. Some of the leading Episcopal men (using that term in its most general sense to include friends and baptized members) like Duncan Cameron, Josiah Collins, Jr., and James Iredell, Jr., who were clearly not evangelicals, became members alongside other upper-crust Presbyterians, Methodists, and Baptists in the newly formed enterprise. In Wilmington local Episcopal men cooperated with the Methodists to start the Wilmington Bible Society in 1817.

Episcopal men were also especially prominent in the colonization cause. In Fayetteville in 1820 the Episcopal minister, Gregory Bedell, served as corresponding secretary of the Fayetteville Colonization Society. In Raleigh in 1822 friends of the church like Archibald Henderson and William Polk served as officers of the colonization society. The Edenton Colonization Society was formed in 1825 with a number of officers and managers who were also vestrymen in St. Paul's, Episcopal: Josiah Collins, Jr., president; James Iredell, Jr., vice-president; Dr. James Norcom and Charles E. Johnson, managers. All these laymen were large slave owners who could endorse colonization and even gradual emancipation in theory. This does not mean, however, that they had any sympathy whatsoever for the immediate abolition of slavery.

The reason for Episcopal gentlemen's participation in benevolent reform is far less clear-cut than for evangelicals, but it seems to be linked to a comprehensive view that included moral, educational, and economic reforms. These men not only were members of benevolent societies but also sat on the boards of agricultural societies, banks, and the University of North Carolina. For them benevolent reform seems to have been not so much an expression of faith or a social event as a means of implementing the moral

139

component in a broader vision of social and economic progress associated with the growth of commercial capitalism within the state.

This comprehensive vision of progress would transform North Carolina's older society composed of illiterate, superstitious, self-sufficient farmers. The religion promoted by these upper-class male benevolent reformers would replace the superstitious religion of the backwoods farmer with one that was orderly, rational, and modern—a faith that was compatible with the new economy and society envisioned by the reformers. By the 1840s, this vision of reform would be associated with the political ideology and social theory of the Whig party. By then, however, most gentlemen in the Episcopal church had already separated themselves from evangelical reform, first out of loyalty to their church, and then over the issue of slavery.

In North Carolina the Episcopal clergy were the first to shun evangelical reform; a portion of the laity followed. The first bishop, John S. Ravenscroft, initiated the Episcopal separation from interdenominational benevolence in North Carolina. When asked to address the North Carolina Bible Society in 1825, Ravenscroft used the opportunity to fire his opening volley in an assault on interdenominational Bible societies. Behind Ravenscroft's assault on evangelical reform was the urgent need to protect the distinctiveness of the Episcopal church in order for it to compete with evangelical denominations. Ravenscroft faced the same difficulties as every Episcopal bishop: how to prevent church members from being absorbed by the larger evangelical denominations, particularly the Presbyterians.

Bishop Ives completed the separation of Episcopal reform from interdenominational reform begun under Ravenscroft. High church Episcopal clergymen developed the position that reform was appropriate only so long as it was directed by the Episcopal church: ecumenical cooperation with evangelical denominations was forbidden. The practical ramifications of the high church position on reform were important. About 1829 the North Carolina Episcopal Missionary Society, which had been founded in 1817, was expanded into the North Carolina Missionary, Bible, Common Prayer Book and Tract Society in a clear attempt to assume the role formerly supplied by various interdenominational societies like the North Carolina Bible Society and the North Carolina Tract Society. At the local church level, there was also the acceleration of a trend among the ladies to form Episcopal benevolent societies instead of joining the older interdenominational societies. Between 1822 and 1829 Episcopal societies were formed in Wilmington, Newbern, Fayetteville, Edenton, and Washington.

The record is silent on whether the church's stance on benevolent reform enraged Episcopal evangelicals whose social vision did not differ significantly from other evangelical Protestants intent on converting and reforming the nation. Just as interesting, perhaps, is the response of men like Duncan Cameron who, although not evangelical, nevertheless, supported the whole spectrum of economic, educational, agricultural, and benevolent reforms. Cameron ignored the bishops and continued to serve as an officer in the North Carolina Bible Society and as president of the newly organized North Carolina Tract Society in 1828. A few other prominent Episcopal men also continued to participate in interdenominational, evangelical reform in what appears to be subtle evidence of a rift developing between a few high churchmen and their clergy. These Episcopal laymen whose social vision involved the economic, social, and cultural transformation of their state were not content to limit moral reform to the narrow Episcopal field recommended by the clergy.

The potential for serious conflict between Episcopal clergymen and laymen over reform never materialized because the growth of antislavery protest had the effect of reconciling the two groups. Episcopal lay attitudes toward colonization began to shift as early as 1826 in North Carolina. In that year, Duncan Cameron withdrew his subscription to a Philadelphia Episcopal journal "in consequence of an article on the subject of slavery." Two years later the operations of the Hillsboro Colonization Society were claimed to have caused local slaves to "become unruly and immanageable when they became acquainted with [its] operations." In 1829 Gov. James Iredell, Jr., refused to endorse the organization of a local colonization society for fear of negative political repercussions.[27]

Interest in the colonization and gradual emancipation as a way of eliminating the Free Negro population, who were thought to be the agitators behind slave insurrections, revived after Nat Turner's Rebellion and the threat of a slave uprising on Lower Cape Fear in 1831. The next year John Haywood Parker, a future Episcopal minister, gave a valedictory speech at the University of North Carolina that argued in favor of the gradual abolition of slavery in the state. In 1834 Duncan Cameron, powerful Episcopal layman and one of the largest slave owners in the state, was elected president of the reorganized North Carolina Colonization Society.

The growth of antislavery reform in the north in the early 1830s, however, doomed the prospects that North Carolina's upper class would back either the colonization cause or organized benevolence in general. Henceforth, all ecumenical reform became associated with abolitionism, and all denominations, including the Episcopalians, rejected it. In March 1837 the vestry of St. Paul's, Edenton, unanimously asked their minister, the Rev. William D. Cairnes, to resign, partly because of his continued support for the colonization cause. The death of a local Episcopal female brought to light that Cairnes had encouraged her to bequeath her slaves to the American Colonization Society and to provide funds for their transportation to Africa.

Radical northern reform convinced Episcopal men of the merits of the high church clergy's condemnation of interdenominational evangelical reform, and they quit participating in interdenominational benevolence. Only the safe and tame North Carolina Missionary, Bible, Common Prayer Book, and Tract Society was acceptable. Episcopal men with a vision of progress for the state were forced to abandon moral reform while they continued to promote economic and educational advancement through the Whig party's programs.

In 1836 the Episcopal church in North Carolina further cemented the relationship between the church and Episcopal slave owners when it made an open apology for slavery. On November 27, 1836, the Rev. George W. Freeman preached two discourses on "The Rights and Duties of Slaveholders." Four North Carolina senators heard Freeman's sermons and encouraged him to publish them. Bishop Ives was equally pleased and encouraged Freeman to comply with the senators' request to print the sermons. When the two discourses were published soon after, they included two letters of endorsement, one from the Senate Chamber signed by the four senators, and one from the Bishop. The church and four representatives of the state had put their official imprimatur on Freeman's defense of slavery. The publication was the Diocese of North Carolina's most important statement regarding the social ethics of slavery during the antebellum era.

Freeman's defense was only one of a number of proslavery statements that came from Southern pulpits at this time as a response to the abolitionist campaign to use the mail system to flood the South with antislavery propaganda. Freeman's apology included a scriptural defense of the peculiar institution and an injunction to slave owners concerning their duties. The latter was subdivided into obligations relating to the slaves' "temporal conditions" and to "their future and everlasting state."[28]

As concerned temporal affairs, Freeman advised masters not to overwork their servants and to "exercise patience and forbearance towards their faults." He also recommended that owners treat slaves with "kindness and consideration" and refrain from excessive punishment. Freeman brought his sermon to a close with a discussion of a master's accountability for the religious welfare of his or her bondsmen. In spiritual matters masters had the responsibility of bringing slaves "into the Christian covenant by Baptism," and then nurturing them in the faith through instruction "in the doctrines, principles and duties of Religion."[29]

Freeman's apology recommended a course of action toward blacks that the Episcopal church had already begun to pursue in a limited fashion. In the years immediately following Nat Turner's rebellion, many Episcopal churches began to incorporate larger numbers of slaves into the life of the church, particularly in urban settings. Often this involved creating a separate service for black Episcopalians. In St. Paul's, Edenton, the Rev. John Avery began to hold a separate service for the slaves who belonged to the members of his church. Avery conducted the service in the house of a free man of color who was already a regular member of St. Paul's. The text at the first service, according to Harriet Jacobs, was "Servants, be obedient to them that are your masters according to the flesh, with fear and trembling, in singleness of your heart, as unto Christ." Since many of the slave insurrections were thought to have been led by black evangelicals, white Episcopalians seem to have viewed the move as a healthy means of social control.[30]

The church also encouraged Episcopal planters to instruct their slaves. In 1841 Bishop Ives compiled a catechism for plantation slave children. No copy of the catechism survives, but Ives's comments upon the nature of the Episcopal slave mission suggest that the catechism resembled others compiled for slaves by the southern churches. Ives assured the diocesan convention that "every thing [in the Episcopal mission to the slaves] is conducted with a strict regard to the legal enactments on the subject, and under theconstant supervision, in each case, of the *planter himself*. In reference also to our exertions hitherto, so far as we can discern it, we feel warranted in offering it to be decidedly favorable to due *subordination*."[31]

The overall success of the Episcopal mission to the slaves is difficult to gauge. The statistics are not impressive. At most, six Episcopal planters established plantation chapels for their slaves. In 1858 almost half of the 342 Negro communicants in the diocese were slaves on Josiah Collins III's plantation. To suggest just how small the number of Episcopal slave communicants was relative to the total number of slaves owned by Episcopal masters, the forty-two largest Episcopal slave owners in North Carolina alone owned some three thousand slaves in 1830. In 1861 only thirty-three of the sixty-two Episcopal churches in North Carolina had any Negro communicants. In the towns of Wilmington, Newbern, Fayetteville, and Edenton, however, local Episcopal churches included substantial numbers of African-Americans. Stiles Bailey Lines estimates that the Episcopal church in North Carolina was reaching as many as fifteen hundred Negro communicants and catechumens on the eve of the Civil War.

For sincere high churchmen the Episcopal church's pronouncements on slavery were both a comfort and a challenge. The church defended the peculiar institution against outside attacks and proclaimed that planter patriarchy was divinely ordained. At the same time, however, the church exhorted Episcopal slave owners to take responsibility for their slaves' physical, emotional, and spiritual welfare. The church called Episcopal masters to ameliorate the harshest and most brutal features of slavery, but it defended the institution itself.

The triumph of Hobartian high church personal morality and social ethics appeared complete in the Diocese of North Carolina by 1840. Episcopal gentlemen and ladies had rejected Episcopal evangelicalism and preserved much of their traditional culture. Worldly amusements and fashionable entertainment were not detrimental to piety. The world of high church Episcopalians was basically a good place, and amusements were either a morally neutral or a beneficial part of the created order. Only a few Episcopal evan-

144

gelicals, a shrinking minority, held fast to the austere morality of the first lady converts.

Southern honor and fashion competed fairly successfully with high church morals. Despite the church's urgings, some Episcopal men swore, dueled, and philandered. Many Episcopal men were powerful enough to violate high church morals without fear of church discipline when the code of honor or their own desires prompted them to do so. Likewise, Episcopal ladies struggled to keep the demands of fashion from overwhelming high church piety. At its best, high church morality served as a force of moderation against traditional excess. At its worst, it offered a mask of respectability to recalcitrant high churchmen whose power allowed them to indulge traditional vice with impunity.

The Episcopal church was far and away the most lenient denomination in the state concerning personal morality. All the evangelical churches, and even the evangelical Episcopal church in Virginia, ocasionally tried individual members for ethical violations and enforced their decisions with suspensions or excommunications. The Episcopal church in North Carolina relied entirely on moral persuasion to foster right living.

North Carolina Episcopalians developed a social ethic that was distinctively southern and high church. The efforts of high church clergy and the growth of antiabolitionist sentiment killed Episcopal participation in organized interdenominational benevolence. Hereafter, the spiritual realm was separated from the social and political spheres for Episcopalians, except as it affected the institution of slavery. On the issue of slavery, the church forcefully addressed contemporary social and political events. Episcopal masters applauded the Episcopal church's use of Holy Scriptures to defend the institution of slavery. The church also advised masters to care for their slaves' spiritual and physical well-being, but the evidence suggests that the slave owners' response to this admonition was partial and incomplete. When the Episcopal mission was carried to the slaves, the church clearly intended to promote obedience and subordination, as well as piety.

Notes

1. Wyatt-Brown, *Southern Honor*, 278–79.
2. William Hooper Haigh Diary, 27 July 1844, SHC.
3. Ibid.
4. Albert Smedes to J. L. Wheat, 7 June 1859, Wheat-Shober Papers, SHC.
5. William T. Bain, *Letters and Meditations on Religious and Other Subjects* (Raleigh: Office of the Raleigh Register, 1839), 6.
6. Mallett, *Memoirs*, 45.
7. Philip W. Alston, "Novelwriting," 1828, Dialectic Society Papers, Addresses and Debates, UNCA; Bain, *Letters and Meditations*, 74.
8. Thomas R. Owen, 23 June 1830, Dialectic Society Papers, Addresses, and Debates, UNCA; T. J. Pitchford, June 1830, Dialectic Society Papers, Addresses, and Debates, UNCA.
9. Mallett, *Memoirs*, 42.
10. A[nne] I[sabella] Iredell to James Iredell [Jr.], 30 June 1804, Charles E. Johnson Papers, NCDAH; Belle [Norwood] to William N. Tillinghast, [1850s], Tillinghast Family Papers, DUA.
11. *At a special meeting of the Vestry of Christ's Church held on the 18th day of June, 1840* (n.p., n.d.), 6.
12. William Hooper Haigh Diary, "Conversations 2nd," 8 July 1843, SHC.
13. Jane [B. Tillinghast] to John [Tillinghast], 12 February 1850, Tillinghast Family Papers, DUA.
14. Mary B. Pettigrew to Isabel [Bryan ?], 5 April 1855, John H. Bryan Papers, NCDAH.
15. Thomas J. Davis, 1815, Dialectic Society Papers, Addresses, and Debates, UNCA; William Hooper Haigh Diary, 18 September 1844, SHC.
16. James Norcom to [his son], 25 March 1845, James Norcom Papers, NCDAH.

17. Thomas P. Irving, "Funeral Discourse for Richard Dobbs Spaight," in *Controversy between Gen. Richard D. Spaight and John Stanley, esq.*

18. John A. Cameron, "Is Duelling Justifiable?" 1 June 1804, Cameron Family Papers, SHC.

19. William Hooper Haigh Diary, 20 [July 1844], SHC.

20. [George E. Badger], *Notes Upon Dr. Freeman's Appendix to the Documents Connected with His Resignation as Rector of Christ's Church, Raleigh, By One of the Vestry* (n.p.: n.d.), 13; James Norcom to Liz [?], 8 February 1846, James Norcom Papers, NCDAH.

21. J[ohn] H. Tillinghast, "Duelling," 25 April 1852, Tillinghast Family Papers, DUA.

22. William Hooper Haigh Diary, 20 [July 1844], SHC; see also Haigh Diary, 17 May [1844], SHC.

23. Charles R. Kinney, *To the Public* (Elizabeth City, N.C.: n.p., 1832), Edmund Ruffin Beckwith Papers, SHC, 1–2.

24. Kinney, *To the Public*, 4.

25. Moses Ashley Curtis Diary, 14 July [1831], Moses Ashley Curtis Papers, SHC; William Hooper Haigh Diary, 17 May [1844], SHC.

26. James W. Bryan to John H. Bryan, 7 June 1854, John H. Bryan Papers, NCDAH.

27. G[regory] T. Bedell to D. Cameron, 9 November 1826, Cameron Family Papers, SHC; Thomas Hunt to R. R. Gurley, 3 September 1829, Letters of the American Colonization Society, in Minnie Spencer Grant, "The American Coloniation Society in North Carolina" (Master's thesis, Duke University, 1930), 21, 25, 37–38.

28. George W. Freeman, *The Rights and Duties of Slaveholders: Two Discourses Delivered on Sunday, November 27, 1836, in Christ Church, Raleigh, North Carolina* (Raleigh: J. Gales & Son, 1836), 25.

29. Ibid., 26–28, 32–35.

30. Jacobs, *Slave Girl*, 68–69.

31. *NCDJ*, 1839, 13; *NCDJ*, 1841, 19; *NCDJ*, 1843, 13, 25.

CHAPTER SIX

The Episcopal Tractarian Controversy and Its Aftermath: Exposing High Church Contradictions and Tensions, 1840–1860

In 1840 the Episcopal church in North Carolina appeared to be more unified and peaceful than at any time previously in its history. Episcopalians had made a number of important changes that alleviated the original conflict between evangelicals and traditionalists. Some Episcopal men had become "Christian gentlemen" whose high churchmanship provided a sincere alternative to evangelicalism. Episcopal ladies, whose evangelicalism had originally stood in contrast to traditional culture, gradually accepted a faith that attempted to balance an aristocratic lifestyle and an affective piety. The Diocese of North Carolina defended slavery, patriarchy, and a high church ethical system that was far more tolerant of the code of honor than was evangelicalism. As a result of these adjustments, a superficial observer might have concluded that the church had never experienced greater harmony.

Beneath the surface, however, serious tensions and contradictions were growing within high church orthodoxy. For some, in a rising generation of churchpeople, the rationalism and formalism of Hobartian high churchmanship failed to satisfy emotional needs in an age of passion. For others from an older generation, Hobartian high churchmanship only partially resolved and, indeed, may have hindered, the successful resolution of marital conflict accompanying the transition from patriarchal to companionate marriage.

For a portion of the clergy, Hobartian high churchmanship was a disturbing failure because it lacked sufficient strength to change traditional behavior and to create genuine Christian character.

Controversy gripped the Diocese of North Carolina from 1848 to 1851 as Bishop Levi Ives initiated a high church reform movement, tractarianism, that exposed old tensions in Hobartian high churchmanship and created new ones. Ives started the reform movement as a response to what he perceived to be the low level of piety among the Episcopal laity and clergy. Before the tractarian controversy, Ives was popular. He and Hobartian high churchmanship had served as powerful forces of cultural conservatism. The tractarian controversy was protracted because it split the laity nearly evenly between those who viewed Ives as a source of confusion and those who revered him as an agent of order.

Ives's reforms were controversial for several reasons. Because tractarianism resembled Roman Catholic practices, Ives's actions revived older prejudices against Catholic corruption shared by many Protestant Episcopalians, as well as evangelicals from other denominations. In a time of intense second-party-system competition, these anti-Catholic prejudices actually became a political issue that hurt several Episcopalians running for state office in North Carolina. Tractarianism also created anxieties for Episcopal husbands and fathers who feared that lascivious Episcopal tractarian priests would abuse the intimacy of one of their innovative reforms, the confessional booth, in order to seduce innocent females. Finally, Ives's tractarianism awakened Episcopal men's dormant anticlericalism by challenging their authority and, they believed, their freedom.

By the 1840s Hobartian high churchmanship was becoming badly out of rhythm with the passionate nature and needs of the age. The emphasis on ardent feeling, not cold mental calculation, was becoming pervasive and was part of a broad cultural shift. Evangelical Christianity, with its demand for the born again experience, was the dominant form of religious expression in North Carolina and throughout the region. Intense feeling also was infusing the code of honor with a passionate spirit that previously had been absent. Steven M. Stowe argues that the expression of feelings rather than the earlier concern for the maintenance of self-control was becoming the animating principle of the code of honor by 1850[1].

In contrast Hobartian high churchmanship seemed to be a relic from the past. Early in the century Hobart and others had drawn on the rationalism and formalism of colonial Anglicanism as an antidote to the emotionalism and enthusiasm of the evangelical revival. But with each passing decade, the coldness and lifeless formality of Hobartian high churchmanship became increasingly unsatisfying to laypeople who craved passion and emotion.

One young high churchman's personal religious struggles during the early 1840s indicated the growing tension. William Hooper Haigh attended St. John's, Fayetteville, graduated from the University of North Carolina, and began to study law in George Badger's Raleigh law office. Haigh's faith was so deeply moving and troubling that at times he resorted to poetry as an adequate means of self-expression, as in the following poem, entitled "Faith."

> Star of my Hopes—that shines bright—
> In the lone chambers of the Christian's heart
> That bids his terrors flee—makes darkness light—
> And cheers him mid the solitude of night—
> Oh! wherefore from me wilt thou depart?[2]

As evident in the last line of the poem, Haigh experienced religious doubt, just as evangelicals so often did before conversion. For an earlier generation of Hobartian high churchmen, faith was a matter of trust and intellectual assent to a corpus of correct doctrines, but Haigh's faith was one that could depart from him amid his doubts. As a high churchman, evangelicalism was not an option for him. Where could he turn to find a faith full of feeling and assurance?

In 1844 Haigh commented upon the inadequacies of Hobartian high churchmanship for the young men in his hometown of Fayetteville. According to him, Fayetteville contained "a class of moral & upright young men" who belonged principally to the Episcopal church. These young men appeared to be "evidencing a serious & religious spirit & intense thoughts—high hopes & pure thoughts." But Haigh, who was an intimate associate of these young men, knew their faith was superficial "and has sadly too little to do with the heart." The situation in Fayetteville was only one example of a more general religious trend among the elite: "In fact such is modern religion—form from beginning to end—The enlightened & educated portion—horror struck & confounded with the canting tumultuous assemblies of camp meetings and quarterly preaching—verge to another extreme—and in their eagerness to give reason her full sway—they neglect feeling, & the heart is often unaffected, when the Judgement feigns itself thoroughly satisfied."[3]

Four months later, Haigh expressed the same misgivings about current preaching after hearing an exceptionally good sermon which was full of both feeling and reason: "The great fault of sermonising at the present day is a want of this combination. The discourse is either a *ranting*, harum scarum, 'ironside Baptist' sermon—or it is a cold, passionless, *argumentative* affair, which puts most hearers asleep, and keeps others on the constant look out at their *time* pieces."[4] Obviously, other Episcopalians besides Haigh were falling asleep in the pews and reaching in their vests for watches during dull sermons. If high churchmanship was going to satisfy these Episcopalians hungry for emotion in religion, it had to find a meaningful way to incorporate feeling and passion into religious life.

Tractarianism was a broad national and international Episcopal reform movement that spread to the American Episcopal church from the Church of England. In 1836 a small group of Anglican theologians centered around Oxford University began issuing a series of publications, the *Tracts for the Times*. These tracts provided the Oxford churchmen with a name for themselves, tractarians, and for their movement, tractarianism. The movement was also known by two other names synonymous with tractarianism: the Oxford Movement, after its place of origin; and Puseyism, after one of its leading English exponents, Dr. Edward B. Pusey.

Tractarian reform grew out of the high church tradition, but with new emphases. Tractarian reformers sought to recapture the spirit of medieval Christianity by introducing new rituals, doctrines, and devotional and liturgical practices into the Episcopal church. They placed great stress on the need for personal holiness, which verged on a celebration of monastic asceticism. Tractarians, like evangelicals, maintained the primacy of religious feelings: it was a religion of heart over head. Historian T. J. Jackson Lears contends that Catholic ritualism during these years appealed to the erotic. In any case, the strong accent on evocation of feelings such as mystery and awe, and the revival of medieval forms and rituals, indicated tractarianism's connection to the larger Romantic movement.[5]

Tractarian piety differed from both Hobartian high church and evangelical piety in fundamental ways. Tractarians insisted that salvation resulted from a gradual process of sanctification—just as other high church theologians had always maintained—and not from a sudden, evangelical conversion. Where the tractarians differed with other high churchmen, however, was in their insistence on the absolute necessity of personal holiness. Bishop Ives and his colleagues had begun to doubt the ability of Hobartian high churchmanship to reshape the human will, particularly the wills of stubborn men of honor: tractarian reform was the solution.

Tractarian reforms were extremely controversial because they were so similar to Roman Catholic practices. Some of the reforms most offensive to more Protestant Episcopalians, and to evangelicals from other denominations, were auricular confession (oral confession to a priest), priestly absolution (forgiveness of sins by a priest), prayers to the Holy Mother, and more ornate priestly vestments: all characteristic of Roman Catholic worship.

Tractarianism touched off a storm of controversy in the American Episcopal church. Both Episcopal evangelicals and more conservative Hobartian high churchmen opposed the innovations. In 1840 in a celebrated case, a young graduate of the General Theological Seminary, Arthur Carey, had difficulty obtaining ordination in the Diocese of New York because, in the minds of some Episcopal presbyters, his tractarian beliefs were inconsistent with "the doctrines and discipline" of the church.

Although Carey was eventually ordained, more controversy followed. In 1843 at the behest of Episcopal evangelicals, the House of Bishops, the upper house in the bicameral government of the General Convention, investigated the General Theological Seminary to determine if it was infected with tractarianism. The bishops found no such evidence, but rumors persisted. Tractarianism was hotly debated at the next General Convention, and Episcopal evangelicals proposed a series of resolutions condemning the movement; they were not adopted. For the next ten years the theological crisis continued to agitate the entire national church.

North Carolinians were especially sensitive to tractarian reforms because anti-Catholic sentiment was so prevalent. As recently as

1835 the debates at the North Carolina Constitutional Convention revealed deep popular distrust of Roman Catholics. None of the constitutional amendments considered was more controversial than the attempt to remove the clause from the state constitution which barred all non-Protestants from public office. Several delegates expressed unreserved contempt for Catholics during debate. Others, who personally favored a more liberal amendment, were afraid to contradict the will of their more bigoted constituents. This side of the debate at the Constitutional Convention is evidence of a popular anti-Catholicism that existed in North Carolina throughout the antebellum era. Since there were only 800 Catholics among a total state population of 750,000, Protestants were reacting to fears with small basis in reality.

Nevertheless, Catholics were the target of a number of other Protestant assaults during the 1840s. These attacks ranged from several anti-Catholic polemics in state newspapers to the disruption of a midnight mass in Newbern by a band of drunken Protestant sailors. One newspaper article, in particular, anticipated a central fear of Episcopal men during the tractarian controversy. The author, a Presbyterian minister, argued that Catholic confessional practices promoted female sexual lapses. Despite the demographic insignificance, the Catholic threat was real in the Protestant imagination.

Although the Episcopal laity only occasionally discussed Roman Catholicism before the tractarian controversy, they appeared decidedly ambivalent toward Catholics. Publicly, most Episcopalians endorsed religious tolerance. At the North Carolina Constitutional Convention of 1835, at least five delegates, all Episcopal laymen, spoke or voted in favor of religious tolerance toward Catholics. One of the five, Kenneth Rayner, from an eastern county, gave an especially eloquent and moving speech advocating an end to all legal distinctions based on religion. Only one Episcopal delegate dissented from his fellow churchmen and voted against extending Catholics the right to hold public office. The position of Episcopal delegates suggests the attitudes of other laymen toward Catholicism. Delegates who supported religious tolerance also demonstrated a certain political courage in the face of popular opposition to the constitutional amendment.

Privately, however, Episcopal churchmen regarded Roman Catholicism far more critically. At least two prominent high church laymen voiced their dislike for Roman Catholicism because it was "superstitious" and "corrupt." In 1826 Thomas Ruffin wrote his daughter after curiosity prompted him to attend a Catholic mass. According to him, the Catholic service was "absurd unintelligible *jargon & mummery.*" Judge William Norwood believed that the Episcopal church was simply the Roman Catholic church "purified" of those "superstitious rites, that idle parade, that ostentatious form of pomp, those absurd doctrines, in a word without those abominable and detestable corruptions which are a disgrace to any religion, and imputation upon the character of civilized men." Although far less strident, at least publicly, than evangelicals, most Episcopalians found Roman Catholicism very disturbing.[6]

Bishop Ives's tractarian reforms not only provoked anti-Catholicism, they also may have reinforced older prejudices against the Episcopal church. These prejudices were born out of contempt for the colonial Anglican establishment, but there is some evidence that they never completely disappeared during the antebellum era. Well before the tractarian dispute, popular suspicions of Episcopalianism surfaced in a United States Congressional election. In 1810 some eastern North Carolina voters worried that a prominent Episcopalian running for Congress intended to reestablish a state church.

On at least two other occasions, evangelical political candidates appealed to voters' religious loyalties when running against Episcopalians. After losing an 1810 election, one Newbern Episcopalian accused his opponent, formerly an Episcopalian, of attending a local Methodist church in order to curry votes among the more populous denomination. In 1843 Godwin C. Moore, moderator of the Chowan Association (Baptist) in eastern North Carolina, tried to use his "immense Baptist connection" to unseat the Episcopal incumbent, Congressman Kenneth Rayner. Despite Moore's tactics, Rayner prevailed. Afterward, Rayner described his opponent's electioneering: "He is one of your psalm-singing pharisees, a member of the Baptist church, who went whining through the district begging his brethren to vote for him on consideration of church membership." These political incidents suggest that tractarianism may have tapped an older, subterranean vein of popular fear and resentment of Episcopalianism.[7]

From 1840 to 1844 Ives's emerging tractarianism was so mild that it drew little, if any, criticism. In the early summer of 1840 Ives addressed the students at the General Theological Seminary in New York, and urged them to cultivate a humble piety reminiscent of the

Middle Ages as a way of overcoming contemporary worldliness. Ives's restrained support for the Rev. George W. Freeman in the Christ's Church amusements controversy several months later was also extremely significant because it was the first time he acted in the diocese as a result of his budding tractarian views. Since Ives previously was a staunch Hobartian high churchman (indeed, the son-in-law of Hobart) who tolerated worldly amusements, his support for Freeman only makes sense in light of his earlier pronouncements at the seminary. Ives succinctly expressed his sentiments on lay piety within the diocese to Freeman's successor, Richard Sharpe Mason: "It is true men are too much given to pleasure everywhere, but I do not think Ch[rist] Ch[urc]h Raleigh more disposed this way, than churches generally. . . . Where a people are much given to pleasure, the case is to be viewed rather as a *symptom* than as an *instrument* of their low piety."[8]

Less than a year later, in November 1841, Ives also was forced to depose the Episcopal rector in Warrenton for adultery with a woman of bad reputation. As the bishop surveyed the diocese, he saw true piety sadly wanting in both the laity and the clergy, and he was determined to employ tractarian reforms to correct the situation. In his 1841 report to the diocesan convention, Ives had congratulated the Rev. Henry H. Prout, the tractarian rector of St. Matthew's, Hillsboro, for "zealous efforts . . . to establish a daily morning and evening service: and to restore to his congregation something of the primitive spirit and practice."[9] The development of tractarianism under Ives created a second high church party in North Carolina intent on reforming the older Hobartian high churchmen.

Lay discussion of the tracts was growing, but opinion tended to be favorable. At the diocesan convention of 1843, the Rev. Moses Ashley Curtis preached a sermon on sacerdotal absolution that showed the unmistakable influence of the tractarians. Those attending the convention, including all the lay delegates, were pleased enough with the sermon to ask for its publication. At the General Convention of the Episcopal church in 1844, the Rev. Richard S. Mason led a North Carolina delegation that defended the tracts against growing opposition. In July 1843, William Hooper Haigh described the tractarians as "a set of great & good men, activated by the purest motives—the most devotional feelings, and the strongest desire to promote the interests of Christendom."[10] Even an

Episcopal evangelical female remained neutral on the tracts as she prepared to read them in October 1844. Other high churchmen, who chafed under the constraints of a faith increasingly anachronistic in a new age of feeling, may have responded to Ives's first gestures toward tractarianism with similar approval.

Even as early as 1844, however, some minds were associating Bishop Ives's reforms with Roman Catholicism. William Hooper Haigh recounted that a Raleigh woman of "vulgar mind," presumably a lower-class evangelical, had seen the bishop cross himself before entering the sanctuary and had commented on the similarity to the Roman Catholic gesture. Another observer later would describe individuals who believed Ives was taking orders directly from the Pope as "ignorant and prejudiced." These references are important because they hint at the way in which tractarianism aggravated class tension that already existed between Episcopal aristocrats and the evangelical masses. The growing public perception that Episcopalianism was associated with Roman Catholicism was significant both within and outside the Episcopal church.

The controversy surrounding tractarianism began to grow in 1848 as the reforms became linked directly to state politics in at least two elections. The first was the gubernatorial race between Whig Charles Manly and Democrat David S. Reid, a contest that proved to be one of the closest in the antebellum era. The main campaign issue was a Democratic proposal to remove the fifty-acre voting qualification requirement in state senatorial elections, a constitutional amendment that Whigs opposed. In such a tight race, any meaningful issue that distinguished the candidates was important. Manly, a Raleigh Episcopalian, was at a particular disadvantage with voters because of his connection with Ives's denomination and because of his religious upbringing: he was raised a Roman Catholic and later converted to Episcopalianism. Reid, in contrast, was a devoted Baptist.

Manly won the August contest by the slimmest of margins, 854 votes out of an entire canvass. One leading Democratic newspaper editor believed that Manly's Episcopalianism—linked with Roman Catholicism in the public mind as a result of tractarianism—lost him the vote in several counties. During a period of widespread anti-Catholicism and intense nativism, those who voted against Manly because of his religious affiliation were responding to the fear of a secret papal conspiracy to subvert democracy; such a fear was common to Jacksonian America. With the gubernatorial election of 1848, the tractarian controversy was placed squarely in front of the laity and, indeed, became a matter affecting state politics. Tractarianism also influenced state politics in mountainous Wilkes County in 1848. Again, according to the same newspaper editorial, General Samuel F. Patterson, a prominent Episcopalian and Whig running for state senate, lost Wilkes County in his three-county district because of his denominational ties. The election definitely occurred against a background of religious controversy arising from the tractarian reforms of the local Episcopal priest, the Rev. W. R. Gries. Gries arrived in Wilkesboro in January 1848 and immediately began to offend local evangelicals with his style.

Although Ives defended Gries, the bishop himself reported to the diocesan convention of 1848 that Wilkesboro Episcopalians "had been made to suffer in their rights as citizens, on the grounds of their religious principles." According to Ives, "political ambition" was behind the persecution of Wilkesboro Episcopalians. Privately, Ives confided that "violent opposition" forced Gries to become more "discreet." If so the change was only temporary. More than three years later, a prominent judge and Chapel Hill Episcopalian described Gries's tractarian innovations and noted that opposition to the young Episcopal priest still existed in Wilkes County. The Episcopal church in Wilkesboro, according to Gries's enemies, was "little else than Roman Catholicism in disguise."

Although it is difficult to believe that educated Episcopalians actually believed that Ives was in league with the pope, the bishop's reforms did nothing to endear him to laypeople, and they helped to revive an older strain of Enlightenment anticlericalism. One wealthy planter from eastern North Carolina declared that tractarian priests were part of a "priestcraft" still intent on swaying the ignorant masses. Gordon S. Wood notes that the nation's founding generation of republicans were Enlightenment thinkers who contrasted their Revolutionary War accomplishments with the "Gothic barbarism" of the past. Although several generations had passed since the Revolution, republicanism was woven into the nation's political fabric, and Episcopalians shared this political inheritance. Tractarian rituals and Gothic architecture certainly must have evoked older republican fears of repressive Catholicism.

During the fall and winter of 1848–49, the bishop created consternation in certain Episcopal quarters as he preached a series of seven sermons around the diocese expounding his tractarian views. At the same time Ives publicly endorsed a previously secret Episcopal clerical order, the Order of the Holy Cross, that he had founded a year earlier at Valle Crucis in the North Carolina mountains. The Order of the Holy Cross, according to its detractors, accentuated ritualistic practices including auricular confession that differed little, if at all, from Roman Catholic analogues. The bishop also established a monastery at Valle Crucis, which he continued to keep secret.

In the last weeks of December 1848, Ives was involved in another state political controversy concerning an attempt to abolish the compulsory chapel attendance policy at the University of North Carolina. Ives precipitated the conflict when he and another prominent Episcopal minister on the University faculty induced a group of Episcopalians on the University Board of Trustees to propose the change. To strengthen his political clout, the bishop had garnered petitions from 130 leading Episcopal laymen in several of the state's largest towns and from nineteen state legislators who backed his plan. Obviously, at least on this particular issue, Ives wielded considerable influence with Episcopal gentlemen. Ives and his allies wanted to alter chapel policy so that Episcopal students at the university might attend the local Episcopal church, not the university chapel, which was nondenominationally Protestant. Supporters of the existing chapel policy, however, believed that compulsory attendance was important in maintaining student discipline, which was a serious, and at times bloody, problem during this period.

Ives's scheme brewed a political storm that spread from the University trustees to the General Assembly. Many state legislators and other members of the state's elite interpreted Ives's plan as a threat to the University Chapel, an institution that they perceived to be an important inculcator of virtue among the rising gene-ration. In the process of the controversy over chapel policy, Ives made powerful enemies. Governor Manly, a trustee of the University, led the opposition. Manly described Ives's plan "as fraught with the most mischievous consequences to the Univ[ersity] and pregnant with still greater evils to the Church of which he was a member." Manly's remarks were especially significant against the background of his recent, close election. Other Episcopal trustees, according to one insider, handled Ives "roughly in familiar conversation." Ultimately, Ives's scheme was amended so that any student who was a communicant of a Christian church could worship locally with his denomination in Chapel Hill. For high church Episcopalians, most of whom were not communicants, it was a partial victory gained at the cost of political controversy.

Almost simultaneously, rumors began to leak out to the laity concerning the monastery at Valle Crucis. Protestant churchmen shuddered as they heard reports that Episcopal priests at Valle Crucis wore black cassocks just as Jesuits did. Nothing could have been better calculated to incite Episcopal lay fears of a tractarian conspiracy than Ives's secretiveness concerning Valle Crucis.

A portion of the Episcopal laity arose in opposition to the bishop and his reforms. United States Senator George E. Badger and George W. Mordecai, both members of Christ's Church, Raleigh, emerged as unusually able leaders. Badger, a fifty-three-year-old lawyer, leader of North Carolina's Whig party, and a skilled church controversialist, kept his hand on the pulse of state politics and diocesan affairs even while in Washington. Mordecai, a Jewish convert to Episcopalianism, president of the state bank, and one of the wealthiest businessmen in the state, was perfectly positioned and connected to direct anti-Ives forces in the state.

By the spring of 1849 Badger and Mordecai were so troubled that they notified Ives of their intention to complain to the annual diocesan convention. A conversation with the bishop, however, satisfied them both so completely that the Raleigh laymen decided to skip the convention altogether. Ives was also able to reassure the delegates at the convention in Salisbury concerning his theological views. Temporarily, Ives had defused the potential for serious conflict in the diocese.

The peace within the diocese did not last. Early in the fall of 1849, Ives made a stunning reversal and published an inflammatory pamphlet, *A Pastoral Letter Addressed to the Clergy and Laity of His Diocese*, that unequivocally reaffirmed his commitment to tractarian reform. According to Ives, his opponents were not theologically motivated by "a fear for Protestantism." Instead, the bishop averred, his enemies were prompted by "deep worldliness, political ambition, overgrown pride, jealousy of restraint, fear of authority, and reckless licentiousness." He was perfectly describing proud, ambitious, and sensual Southern gentlemen of honor.

Hobartian high churchmanship had failed to reform them, but Ives believed that tractarianism was succeeding:

> Churches are beginning to assume a more Church-like appearance—to be more in keeping with their divine and holy purpose. . . . The reverence of both clergy and people is manifestly increasing; the number of surplices is becoming greater; altars are less frequently made the resting places for clerical arms and elbows. . . . Fewer backs are turned towards the Priest at absolution and benediction. The voices are not so loud within the walls of the sanctuary—neither the covered heads quite so numerous, while the rush to escape the Church is not quite so deafening.[11]

Ives's publication reignited the whole diocesan controversy with all its implications for political and domestic culture. The reactions of two prominent evangelical ministers suggests the way in which evangelicals across the state responded to Ives's *Pastoral*. Both the Rev. Peter Doub, one of North Carolina's most respected Methodist ministers, and the Rev. Elisha Mitchell, distinguished scientist, professor at the University of North Carolina, and Presbyterian minister, were upset enough to consider rebutting Ives in print. David L. Outlaw, Episcopalian and United States Congressman, noted in a letter to his wife how harmful the bishop's *Pastoral* was to Episcopal popularity in the state: "Episcopalians had just outlived the prejudice produced by the connection of that church with the colonial government . . . and [were] making considerable progress" before Ives's tractarianism reversed the trend. The bishop's timing was particularly upsetting to the political prospects of North Carolina Whigs with Gov. Manly's reelection bid upcoming in August 1850.[12]

Ives's *Pastoral* stunned and infuriated the old Hobartian high churchmen in the diocese. Only two months after the *Pastoral* was circulated, George E. Badger rushed a lengthy pamphlet into print, *An Examination of the Doctrine Declared and the Powers Claimed by the Right Reverend Bishop Ives*. It was a forceful reply. Badger argued that since the bishop's tractarian beliefs and practices did not conform with either the Book of Common Prayer or the constitution and canons of the church, they were illegal. Badger also bitterly attacked the "Romish" practices at Valle Crucis which he described as "disallowed and forbidden" by the church. Finally, he enjoined the laity to repudiate Ives's teachings as violations of church law.

160

Badger sent word to his publisher to "express" ship the pamphlets to Raleigh so that they could be *"speedily"* circulated in the diocese. Mordecai worked through a sympathetic Episcopal minister and a business associate, who was a layman, to distribute the pamphlets in Piedmont towns.

While Badger and Mordecai were spreading pamphlets across the state, three Raleigh newspapers made the political dimensions of the tractarian controversy a matter of public debate. Since two of these newspapers, the *North Carolina Standard* (Whig) and the *Raleigh Register* (Democrat), were the state's leading newspapers and enjoyed wide circulation, the tractarian controversy achieved a new level of publicity. William W. Holden, editor of the *Standard*, initiated the war of words in an editorial on 5 December 1849.

Holden's editorial accused Badger of writing *An Examination* as a political maneuver to reverse "the tide of unpopularity" with voters. According to Holden, both Governor Manly in the gubernatorial contest and state senator Patterson in his race lost votes because of the connection between Episcopalianism and Roman Catholicism. Badger, according to the Democratic editor, was determined that Ives be "arrested in his course or sacrificed" in order to protect Whig political interests.

The two Whig newspapers in Raleigh wasted no time in answering Holden. Seaton Gales, editor and publisher of the *Register,* who attended Christ's Church, Raleigh, responded first. Gales noted that the *Standard* piece was just another expression of the Democratic newspaper's "bitter and rancorous" feelings toward Badger. As proof of Badger's purely religious, not political, motives, the Register quoted laudatory reviews of Badger's *Examination* from two Episcopal journals, the *Episcopal Recorder* (Philadelphia) and the *Protestant Churchmen* (New York).[13]

Two days later, on December 14, a second Whig newspaper, the *Raleigh Times,* launched its own rejoinder to the *Standard.* The *Times* editorial reproached the *Standard* for drawing "a church difficulty . . . into 'the vortex of partisan strife and political ambition.' " The Whig journal also incisively noted that the *Standard*'s own political purpose was to ensure Governor Manly's defeat by creating the impression among voters that there was "no difference between Romanism and Episcopalianism."

Next, however, the *Times* clumsily praised Badger's *Examination* for accomplishing exactly what Holden accused it of in the first place: gaining a political advantage in the upcoming gubernatorial election. According to the *Times,* Badger's effort had "rolled back" political ill consequences by convincing voters "that Gov. Manly may be an Episcopalian without submitting to the authority of a Bishop who holds to the authority of the Romish church."

In the wake of these sensational articles, the relationship deteriorated between the bishop and Badger, Mordecai, and their allies. According to Ives, this group believed their bishop a "Jesuit" who "must be sent off . . . on some mission to either the North or South Pole." In response to a note from Mordecai, Ives offered to meet with the disgruntled layman. Whatever transpired between the two men, it did nothing to reconcile them. By late March, Mordecai and Badger were corresponding with three powerful laymen from different parts of the diocese to formulate plans to impeach Ives at the upcoming diocesan convention.

The bishop's enemies were considering impeaching him for doctrinal error, or moral delinquency, or both. The doctrinal errors were well known and simply involved a rehearsal of Ives's tractarianism. The basis for the contemplated charge of moral delinquency, however, remains an intriguing mystery. The correspondence indicates that whatever the nature of Ives's moral failure might or might not have been, these laymen genuinely believed him guilty of some transgression. The imputation of immorality also had great symbolic significance since it reinforced Protestant fears of Roman Catholic "corruption."

Francis L. Hawks, a North Carolina native and a nationally prominent Episcopal minister in New York, made the connection between tractarian reform and immorality explicit in another pamphlet, *Auricular Confession in the Protestant Episcopal Church: Considered in a Series of Letters to a Friend in North Carolina.* Hawks leveled the same charges at tractarians that repeatedly had been directed at Catholics: namely, that lascivious tractarian priests used the intimacy of the confessional setting to seduce innocent females. According to Hawks, "It has long been my deliberated conviction that the husband or father who permits his wife or daughter to go to auricular confession, has no one but himself to blame, should he afterwards find the name of his family overwhelmed with shame and disgrace, by a lapse from female virtue."[14]

Another North Carolina high churchman echoed the same fears. After reading a Roman Catholic confessor's manual, Congressman

David Outlaw, from an eastern county, conveyed his dismay and disgust over the book's contents to his wife: "They are filthy abominations unfit for a bawdy house. Questions are put to young girls and married women, which no husband would think of putting to his wife, in relation to matters, which are never spoke of to third persons, but are confined to a man and his wife."[15]

As fantastic as Hawks's contentions and Outlaw's fears seem, several circumstances must have made them quite compelling to other Episcopal husbands and fathers. First, several cases of sexual misconduct by Episcopal ministers lent credence to Episcopal men's fears. Ives had dismissed the Episcopal minister in Warrenton for adultery in 1841. Three years later the General Convention of the Episcopal church suspended Bishop Benjamin Onderdonk of New York, tractarian, from his office after he was charged with taking indecent sexual liberties with females, including uninvited attempts to thrust his hand in their dresses. One prominent Episcopal woman in Chapel Hill wrote her husband about Onderdonk a month before his sensational trial and suspension. Such disclosures must have shocked every Episcopalian in the state.

The persistence of considerable domestic tension within Episcopal marriages also made Episcopal men particularly susceptible to the suggestion of tractarian indiscretions. Hobartian high churchmanship, at its most successful, allowed Episcopal couples to create stable and satisfying marriages. But high churchmanship could also serve as a conservative force that preserved older patriarchal values, which could create emotionally impoverished marriages. The code of honor also allowed men, but not women, considerable extramarital freedom, and some Episcopal men exercised this freedom.

Since tractarian reform was a new movement, most of the tractarian clergy were young, recent graduates of the General Theological Seminary. Episcopal husbands might easily view these deeply committed, passionate young priests as rivals. John F. Burgwyn, a great Episcopal planter in Northampton County, expressed just such jealousy over his wife's fondness for their young Episcopal pastor. When Ellen (Barber) Burgwyn defied her husband and decided to travel to town to hear the young minister's farewell sermon instead of staying home where her husband wished to lead divine service, John sarcastically remarked, "oh but 'he's such a nice *young* Man' say the females—& nice young Men have their advantages—Some may regret his leaving, but I shall not—he is made too much of a spoiled pet." The youthfulness of tractarian ministers may have exacerbated the sexual anxieties of Episcopal husbands and fathers.[16]

Given all the strains of Episcopal domestic life, the possibility that tractarian priests were using the confessional to seduce Episcopal wives and daughters surely struck Episcopal men with considerable force. Episcopal men in North Carolina knew only too well, sometimes from personal experience, that male sexual passion was often expressed outside marriage. Indeed, Episcopal men may well have projected their own anxieties concerning sexual corruption onto Ives and his cohorts. Francis L. Hawks's pamphlet played upon Episcopal men's deepest fears of domestic disorder. Episcopal men must have found it impossible to ignore his warnings.

Episcopalians headed to the diocesan convention in coastal Elizabeth City in the last week of May 1850 with all these issues swirling around them. According to Ives, Mordecai and his accomplices began to lobby for his impeachment immediately. Ever true to their sense of honor, however, Ives's opponents sent him a letter outlining the course of action they intended to pursue the next day. With this information in hand, Ives preempted their design by calling for a committee to investigate his behavior and report to the next annual convention.

The bishop's foes regarded such a course of action as far too slow and lenient. They tried, but were outvoted, in an attempt to call a special session of the convention two months later in Raleigh where they intended to act quickly and definitively on the bishop's case. Obviously, a majority of the laymen and clergymen in the diocese remained either loyal to Ives or, at the very least, wanted to move with great caution in dealing with his case. Under any circumstances discharging an Episcopal bishop was serious business, but, surely, many Episcopal laymen were also reluctant because they appreciated the way in which Ives had led the diocese for the last fifteen years. Others, however, had decided that Ives's current beliefs and behavior were reason enough for removal. The diocese had granted Ives at least another year's reprieve before rendering a final verdict, but the delay ensured another year of conflict.

With a gubernatorial rematch between Manly and Reid scheduled less than a month after the diocesan convention, North Carolina Whigs used the *Raleigh Register* to distance themselves from Ives. Since the *Register*'s standing policy was to avoid all reference to religious controversy, these articles were an exceptional measure taken in response to an urgent political situation. On 3 July 1850, the journal printed an account of the diocesan convention that highlighted the opposition to Ives. Two weeks later, the newspaper reprinted an excerpt from a church periodical that described a clandestine convocation between Ives and his clergy on the eve of the convention. The excerpt depicted Ives as a thoroughgoing tractarian who only recanted before the convention to save himself from an aroused laity.

These newspaper accounts are not the only evidence that Whigs were treating the religious issue seriously in the governor's race. In an attempt to undercut the support of Baptist voters for his opponent, Governor Manly made an issue out of Reid's failure to vote while in the legislature for a state loan to Wake Forest College, a Baptist school.

Once again, the election was extremely close, but this time Reid prevailed and was elected North Carolina's first Democratic governor by a slim margin of three thousand votes. The major issues in the campaign were the abuse of power by the central committee of the Whig party, discussion of the fairness of existing plans for apportioning public school funds among various counties, and debate on whether the basis for legislative representation should be altered. The extent to which Manly's Episcopalianism affected the outcome is impossible to determine, but it certainly won him no votes.

Eight months after Manly's defeat, North Carolina Episcopalians prepared for another fight at the diocesan convention in Fayetteville. George Badger returned from Washington to lead the opposition to Ives. For Badger and others, Ives's immorality and heretical doctrines represented an intolerable source of instability both in their public and private lives. Many of the bishop's supporters remained firm. For them, apparently, Ives remained a respected authority whom they refused to abandon. One of the bishop's most faithful supporters, James W. Bryan, a state leader in the Whig party from Newbern, made remarks that indicate that—despite Ives's tractarianism—he considered the bishop a conservative bulwark against the tide of evangelical culture that threatened to overwhelm the traditional Episcopal way of life.

Ultimately, the bishop's foes overpowered his friends. In a crucial convention vote, Ives's friends failed by one ballot to once again delay immediate action, as they sought to create yet another committee to review the bishop's case. With this final obstacle removed, Badger introduced a resolution calling for Ives's resignation on the grounds that the bishop had "lost the confidence of the people of his charge" and "his usefulness is thereby destroyed or greatly impaired." Another influential layman, Robert Strange, a former Democratic senator, amended Badger's resolution so that it called for the appointment of an assistant bishop rather than Ives's resignation. The convention accepted Badger's proposal as modified by Strange.

Faced with unyielding lay opposition, Ives pathetically recanted rather than accept an assistant bishop who would effectively replace him. He renounced all association with tractarianism and claimed to have returned to his former Hobartian high churchmanship. The Episcopal laity explained Ives's misguided fascination with tractarianism as the result of an earlier illness that, they believed, had impaired his judgment.

Calm returned to the Diocese of North Carolina. Delegates to the diocesan convention of 1852 spoke not a word of criticism of Ives. Ives's flight several months later in the fall to Rome and Catholicism created only a momentary sensation in the diocese before a lasting peace resumed. North Carolina laypeople may well have been relieved that Ives was gone and the issue was buried once and for all. They could also boast that their gravest predictions had been realized.

In reality, however, the Episcopal laity had left Ives with few comfortable choices. The opposition of powerful laymen, not illness, best explains his erratic behavior. Convinced that Episcopalians lacked piety, he had lost confidence in Hobartian high churchmanship and had never been able to embrace low churchmanship as a way of reforming the church. In his mind, tractarianism had offered the only remedy. When the diocesan convention forbade tractarian reform, the Roman Catholic church became the only place to utilize auricular confession and the other practices that Ives believed ensured salvation for even the most hardened sinner.

The Episcopal church in North Carolina was theologically confused after Ives's departure. The new bishop, Thomas Atkinson, was raised in Virginia's low church tradition and shunned tractarian ritualism. According to the Rev. William S. Pettigrew, the grandson of the first bishop-elect of North Carolina, Atkinson followed a "judicious & evangelical course" during his first two years. The bishop's visits to the Pettigrew Chapel near the Albemarle Sound were an assistance "to the Church, and not the cause of hostility without and disaffection within, and what is yet worse the building up of a formalism almost destitute of vitality as was deplorably the case in his predecessor's days."[17]

Atkinson moved the see of the diocese to Wilmington and his leadership may well have contributed to a revival of the low church tradition in the eastern part of the state. The revivals of 1857–58 affected St. James's, Wilmington, and St. John's, Fayetteville, and were unusual in that large numbers of men converted. Similarly, in Christ's Church, Newbern, men were joining the church in record numbers. And at the Church of the Advent, Williamston, the number of Episcopal men attending church was larger than ever. In certain areas in the coastal plain, at least, Episcopal evangelicals were being born again, and not just ladies.

One female member of the distinguished DeRosset family has left a vivid account of the revival's impact on St. James's, Wilmington: "Oh we had a glorious time last night darling Kate—So much enthusiasm and solemnity in the Church—the aisles filled with the candidates for confirmation. To see elderly men kneeling in the aisles—not room for them at the altar—is a sight never before witnessed in our Church—the hearts of all the congregation seemed overflowing."[18]

Eighteen of the thirty-nine confirmants at St. James's were adult males. Among the group was John R. London who had been a lay delegate to the first diocesan convention forty-one years before, but only then came forward to be confirmed. Even in this evangelical outpouring, however, genteel constraints checked religious passions. The resulting religious mood was a synthesis that was simultaneously evangelical yet genteel, full of enthusiasm and solemnity. It was a style of worship that paradoxically revealed Episcopal indebtedness to evangelicalism and the ultimate compromise that Episcopalians had made with older styles of worship.

West of the fall line, however, high churchmanship remained dominant and older patterns persisted. The Rev. Richard Hines, rector of St. John's, Williamsboro, repeated an old refrain as he described his congregation in 1856: "The male portion of my Parishes, though kind friends and good citizens, appear to think that religion is commendable in women, though not at all desirable in

MEN." Although the number of communicants joining the church in the last five years before the Civil War rose, the percentage of new communicants remained about 70 per cent female (see tables 4 and 5). Southern honor still ruled the lives of many, if not most, Episcopal gentlemen.[19]

As the antebellum era came to a close, Episcopalians constituted a powerful and important subculture outside North Carolina's evangelical mainstream. The church had grown to include some twenty-four hundred white communicants and, probably, a slightly greater number of white baptized members. The best estimate is that women made up three-quarters of the communicants. Episcopalians had yoked together gentility and Christianity into an important upper-class faith. Because Episcopalianism had been shorn of so much of its evangelical, antiaristocratic bias, many laypeople could wholeheartedly subscribe to this way of life. High churchmanship allowed others who were less committed to keep one foot in the church and one in the world.

Table 4
Episcopal Communicants, 1860

	Female	Male	Sex Ratio (F/M)
Calvary Episcopal, Wadesboro	26	9	3 : 1
Chapel of the Cross Episcopal, Chapel Hill	47	15	3 : 1
St. Mark's Episcopal, Halifax	9	2	4.5 : 1
Totals	82	26	3.2 : 1

Statistics compiled from the various local Episcopal church records, on microfilm at NCDAH.

Table 5
New Episcopal Communicants
1 January 1855 – 31 December 1859

	Female	Male	Sex Ratio (F/M)
Emmanuel Episcopal, Warrenton	21	8	2.6 : 1
Grace Episcopal, Plymouth	11	2	5.2 : 1
St. James's Episcopal, Wilmington	50	19	2.5 : 1
St. John's Episcopal, Fayetteville	60	28	2 : 1
St. Matthew's Episcopal, Hillsboro	18	1	18 : 1
St. Paul's Episcopal, Beaufort	9	5	1.8 : 1
St. Paul's Episcopal, Edenton	36	20	1.8 : 1
St. Peter's Episcopal, Washington	39	13	3 : 1
St. Stephen's Episcopal, Goldsboro	24	6	4 : 1
Totals	268	92	2.9 : 1

Statistics compiled from the various local Episcopal church records, on microfilm at NCDAH.

Notes

1. Stowe, *Intimacy and Power in the Old South*, 15–23.
2. William Hooper Haigh Dairy, 12 December 1843, SHC.
3. William Hooper Haigh Diary, 14 May 1844, SHC.
4. William Hooper Haigh Diary, 8 September 1844, SHC.
5. Mullin, *Episcopal Vision/American Reality*, 149–52; T. J. Jackson Lears, *No Place of Grace: Antimodernism and the Transformation of American Culture, 1880–1920* (New York: Pantheon Books, 1981), 152, 154–55, 159, 160–62, 177–79, 184–216.
6. Thomas Ruffin to Anne M. Ruffin, 13 March 1826, Thomas Ruffin Papers, SHC; William Norwood to William K. Ruffin, 6 November 1826, Thomas Ruffin Papers, SHC.
7. David Gregg Cantrell, "The Limits of Southern Dissent: The Lives of Kenneth Rayner and John B. Rayner," (Ph.D. diss., Texas A&M University, 1988),1:160–61.
8. L. S. Ives to Richard S. Mason, 11 December 1840, Richard S. Mason Papers, SHC.
9. *NCDJ,* 1841, 18.
10. William Hooper Haigh Diary, 29 January 1844, SHC.
11. L. S. Ives, *A Pastoral Letter Addressed to the Clergy and Laity of His Diocese* (New York: Stanford and Swords, 1849), quoted in Malone, "Ives," 232.
12. David L. Outlaw to his wife [Emily], May 1850, David Outlaw Papers, SHC.
13. *Raleigh Register,* 12 December 1849; Robert Neal Elliot, Jr., *The Raleigh Register, 1799–1863* (Chapel Hill: University of North Carolina Press, 1965) 87, 89.
14. [Francis L. Hawks], *Auricular Confession in the Protestant Episcopal Church; Considered in a Series of Letters Addressed to a Friend in North Carolina* (New York: Putnam, 1850),42–44.

15. David Outlaw to Emily Outlaw, 16 June 1850, David Outlaw Papers, SHC.
16. John Fanning Burgwyn Diary, 17 June [1855], NCDAH. Evangelicals from other denominations exhibited similar patterns of jealousy of the relationship between ministers and wives and daughters. See Mathews, *Religion in the Old South*, 103–4.
17. William S. Pettigrew to [?], 26 April 1855, Pettigrew Family Papers, SHC.
18. Mrs. A. J. DeR[osset] to Katie [Meares], 11 April 1858, DeRosset Family Papers, SHC.
19. *NCDJ*, 1856, 38, quoted in London and Lemmon, *The Episcopal Church in North Carolina*, 227.

Conclusion:
North Carolina Episcopalianism as Cultural Conservator and Creator, 1800–1860

Antebellum Episcopalianism performed an important role as conservator of traditional, non-evangelical culture for a portion of the North Carolina elite. Simultaneously, however, Episcopalianism also functioned as a creative force that fused elements from both traditional and evangelical culture into a new genteel ethos that would be associated with the emerging Victorian sensibility. Episcopalianism's dual role as cultural conservator and creator occurred as a result of the collision between lower-class evangelical culture and traditional genteel culture beginning in the first decade of the nineteenth century.

Before 1805 genteel and evangelical cultures had developed independently. Genteel culture evolved gradually during the colonial era as the Anglican gentry and their descendants inherited several ethical traditions that combined to form a relatively coherent ethos. Either Anglican orthodoxy, its Episcopal successor, or various shades of Enlightenment religion were merged with notions of honor to form a genteel code of conduct. The resulting ethic for men emphasized personal integrity and honesty, charity, physical bravery, risk-taking, and hospitality. The ladies operated on the basis of the same religious beliefs, but an ethic of fashion was substituted for men's honor. As a result, the ladies' code included moral probity and charity as central values, but it substituted beauty, sociability, and polite accomplishment for the other masculine qualities of the ethic of honor.

Traditional culture among the elite remained remarkably intact and unchanged throughout the late eighteenth century despite the virtual disappearance of organized Episcopal religious life. The old Episcopal laity remained unchurched after the Episcopal church vanished in the 1780s, unwilling to connect themselves with one of the evangelical denominations or to accept the cultural norms created by the evangelicals. The laity was divided into an orthodox remnant and an apparently growing number of deists. The rise of religious skepticism among the gentry may be a partial explanation for the inability of Charles Pettigrew and other Episcopal clergy to muster enough lay support to revive the church in the 1790s. Other than the notable absence of organized worship, however, genteel culture remained much the same as always. Genteel ethics still included a moral component that was combined with the ethics of honor and fashion. The upper classes also entertained themselves with the same activities and pursuits as before.

When the Methodists broadened their mission field in the first decade of the nineteenth century to include North Carolina's towns, the evangelical awakening penetrated the upper class for the first time, especially among ladies. These women became the first genteel converts to evangelicalism. By 1815 abundant evidence indicates that upper-class Presbyterian and Methodist women had successfully created an evangelical culture among the elite. The correspondence of these genteel ladies, largely with each other, was filled with copious evangelical sentiments as they reflected on the meaning of their own spiritual rebirths and encouraged unconverted friends and acquaintances to join the new life in Christ. The evangelical ladies also began writing original religious verse and copying the work of leading evangelical romantic poets. Upper-class female converts also began occupying their time differently as they formed religious benevolence societies in most of North Carolina's major towns. These benevolent enterprises afforded a substitute for traditional amusements and diversions, which were no longer acceptable. Before this time, a cultural dichotomy had existed between lower-ranking evangelicals and upper-class traditionalists. The ladies' revival split the upper class into two cultural groups: evangelicals and traditionalists.

Unchurched gentlemen, Episcopalians by heritage, who had heretofore been unable to muster enough support to revive their local Episcopal churches, at last began to do so. Evangelicalism threatened and challenged traditional culture and, in particular, undermined partriarchal control within families. The desire to preserve traditional relationships within families and marriages is central to the restoration of the Episcopal church in North Carolina. Men in Wilmington, Newbern, Edenton, and Fayetteville paid the salaries of Episcopal ministers and controlled the local vestries but refused to join the church as communing members. The percentage of female communicants in the first three churches was 90 percent, 86 percent, and 79 percent respectively. Only in Fayetteville did Episcopal men outnumber women as communicants, and then only temporarily and under unusual circumstances. The other Episcopal churches that would be founded in the state during the remainder of the antebellum period were all made up of a large majority of female communicants.

In an important article that examines the place of religion in Southern slave society, Elizabeth Fox-Genovese and Eugene D. Genovese argue that the "feminization" of religion that historian Ann Douglas describes in northern antebellum society did not occur in the South. If communing membership is the fullest index of church participation, as this study proposes, then the feminization of religion was certainly characteristic of the Episcopal church in North Carolina. On the whole, Episcopal men either remained on the periphery of church life or entered it in a qualified fashion as baptized members. Later, high church theology would serve as a justification for their Christian reservations and continued allegiance to southern honor.

The restoration of the Episcopal church was both a response to and an extension of the ladies' revival as it had begun in evangelical denominations. Unlike the ministers of the old church, the new breed of Episcopal ministers could compete with evangelical counterparts. The Episcopal recovery succeeded because its ministers were able to satisfy the spiritual demands of evangelical ladies, although in the early years of the diocese, Episcopal ladies often attended more than one church. Ministers like Adam Empie, Gregory Bedell, William M. Green, and Bishop John S. Ravenscroft were perhaps more refined and subdued than many "shouting" evangelical preachers, but their preaching nevertheless sought to address the same sorts of evangelical needs.

If Episcopal men reorganized the church in an attempt to contain female evangelicalism, as this study contends, they did not entirely

174

succeed, at least for the first twenty years. Significant differences in religious belief and practice still existed in many Episcopal families. The religious conversation typically involved a pious wife and a traditional husband, but often included adult children as well. Wives worried that husbands were endangering their chances of reaching heaven by refusing to abandon old habits and become communicants. Much about traditional male behavior also disrupted domestic stability and led to emotionally dissatisfying marriages. Often, Episcopalians were chained to the past and waited until late in life—many were actually on their deathbeds—before they finally surrendered themselves fully to Christianity and became communing members in the Episcopal church.

Although the vast majority of Episcopal men did not become communing members of the church until late in life, if at all, a number of prominent and respected exceptions led conspicuously pious lives. By 1840 their examples had brought into being a new masculine genteel pious ideal that existed alongside the traditional ethic of male behavior. The Episcopal "Christian gentleman" had been born. High churchmanship allowed sincere Episcopal men to reclaim their role as Christian patriarchs within their families. The most sensitive were able to create stable and caring marriages that combined elements of both older patriarchal and newer companionate conjugal styles.

The gradual disappearance of religious discussion from Episcopal families after 1840 reflected one of the most important changes within antebellum Episcopalianism in North Carolina. Beginning a decade earlier, Episcopal women began to accept the high churchmanship of Episcopal men. What was the reason for this enormously important change with all its implications for genteel culture? Lacking direct evidence, any answer must be tentative. Clement Eaton's time-honored interpretations concerning the suppression of freedom of thought and expression during the defensive 1830s offer, by extension, the best explanation. The same conservative forces that were forcing southerners to squelch dissent may also have fostered a social climate in which Episcopal women abandoned Episcopal evangelicalism for the safety and security of more culturally and socially conservative high churchmanship.

The triumph of Hobartian high churchmanship had important consequences for church morals and ethics. So did the growth of southern sectionalism. Although Episcopalians originally

175

cooperated with other evangelicals in organized benevolence, pressure from high church clergymen convinced most to abandon such reform in the late 1820s. The rise of radical reform in the North completely alienated southern Episcopalians from interdenominational, national reform. In 1836 the church delineated its proslavery position when it published George W. Freeman's two sermons defending that peculiar institution.

Four years later the conclusion of the amusements controversy at Christ's Church, Raleigh, signaled that a high church moral code, one that tolerated traditional genteel amusements, had supplanted evangelical morality as the church's official standard. As a result, Episcopal ladies who had once been stricter evangelicals gave their approval to the change and resumed participation in fashionable amusements. Episcopal evangelicalism survived in the North Carolina church only as an optional lifestyle embraced by a minority.

The triumph of high churchmanship after 1840 was a milestone in the development of genteel piety in North Carolina. It determined that the dominant Episcopal form of genteel piety for the remainder of the antebellum period would be one that was far less critical of traditional genteel culture than earlier evangelicalism. Henceforth, Episcopal faith combined elements of traditional culture and evangelicalism to form a new religious synthesis that accentuated propriety, moderation, and domesticity: three hallmarks of emerging Victorian values. As a result of these changes, religious conversation in Episcopal families began to disappear, and the Episcopal church became more staid and tranquil.

The Episcopal church's ability to reconcile old differences between evangelical and high church belief and practice should have inaugurated and sustained an era of harmony and prosperity in the last years before the Civil War. Hobartian high churchmanship, however, became increasingly antiquated and internal tensions grew within the system. Bishop Ives's tractarian reform movement in the late 1840s reflected one attempt to address these problems. Unfortunately, since Ives's reforms were similar to Roman Catholicism, they antagonized both Hobartian high churchmen and evangelicals from other denominations, damaged the political prospects of several prominent Episcopal state politicians, and aggravated Episcopal fears of corruption, particularly as those fears related to female virtue. The tractarian controversy split the diocese almost evenly into those who remained faithful to Ives and those who

176

wanted him removed. In 1851 Ives's opponents forced the bishop to recant under the threat of effectively replacing him with an assistant bishop. Ives defected to the Church of Rome soon after.

The Episcopal church became placid after Ives's departure, but deep division remained. A series of local revivals awakened dormant low churchmanship in the eastern part of the diocese. Away from the coast, honor and fashion still wrestled with high church orthodoxy for Episcopal allegiances.

The state of the Episcopal church in North Carolina at the end of the antebellum period was powerful testimony not only to the profound impact that the evangelical awakening had on traditional genteel culture, but also to the remarkable ability of traditional genteel culture to transform the evangelical impulse into a less threatening form. In 1800 North Carolina had no organized Episcopal church to speak of. Episcopal orthodoxy was on the decline; deism appears to have been on the increase. Sixty years later Episcopal churches were in almost every town in central and eastern North Carolina. In that year there were also twenty-four hundred white communicants and probably that many white baptized adult members as well. An additional eleven hundred individuals were catechumens, mostly young people being prepared for membership in the church. All this resulted from an evangelical awakening that scared traditional men enough to restore the Episcopal church for their wives. In the process, orthodoxy was resuscitated, evangelicalism contained, and religious skepticism officially proscribed.

Episcopalianism in the late antebellum era represented a new religious culture that replaced old norms with new ideals of behavior and belief. Uncommitted Episcopalians could still evade Christian responsibility, however. Baptized membership remained a back door within the Episcopal church that allowed less serious men to slip between traditional and pious culture. Although high churchmanship placed fewer ethical demands on a communicant, the majority of Episcopal men still refused to abandon the traditional code of honor, not becoming Episcopal communicants until late in life. The church remained 75 percent female as North Carolina seceded from the Union.

The evangelical awakening had released a flood of religious passions early in the century. By 1860 North Carolina Episcopalians had transformed genteel piety to a point that it bore only faint resemblance to the fervent, antiaristocratic piety of the first female

Selected Bibliography

I. Primary Sources

A. Manuscript Collections

Duke University Library, Durham, North Carolina
John Bullock Papers.
William Lord DeRosset Papers.
Devereux Family Papers.
William C. Doub Papers.
James Iredell Papers.
Charles E. Johnson Papers.
Adelaide Savage Meares Papers.
Joseph H. Saunders Papers.
William L. Saunders Papers.
Josiah Townsend Smith Papers.
Tillinghast Family Papers.
Lower Cape Fear Historical Society, Wilmington, North Carolina
The Rev. Thomas Wright Papers.
North Carolina Division of Archives and History, Raleigh, North Carolina
John H. Bryan Papers.
John Fanning Burgwyn Diary.
Joseph Blount Cheshire, Jr., Memoirs.
Josiah Collins III Letterbook.
Gales Family Papers.
Hillsborough Academy Papers.
Charles E. Johnson Papers.
Frederick Nash Papers.
James Norcom Papers.
Benjamin H. Rice and John Holt Rice Papers.

179

Protestant Episcopal Church Archives, Austin, Texas
  Francis Lister Hawks Historical Papers.
  John Stark Ravenscroft Papers.
Southern Historical Collection, University of North Carolina Library,
  Chapel Hill, North Carolina.
  John L. Bailey Papers.
  Battle Family Papers.
  Edmund Ruffin Beckwith Papers.
  Bryan Family Papers.
  Mary Norcott Bryan Scrapbook.
  Burgwyn Family Papers.
  Charles Wetmore Broadfeet Papers.
  Cameron Family Papers.
  Eliza Clitherall Diary.
  Moses Ashley Curtis Diary.
  Moses Ashley Curtis Papers.
  Davis and Walker Family Papers.
  DeRosset Family Papers.
  Robert Brent Drane Papers.
  William Hooper Haigh Diary.
  Francis Lister Hawks Historical Papers.
  Hayes Collection.
  Ernest Haywood Papers.
  John Haywood Papers.
  Rebecca Hill Papers.
  Thomas D. Hogg Papers.
  John DeBerniere Hooper Papers.
  Caroline Mallett Hooper Papers.
  Benjamin R. Huske Papers.
  Jones and Patterson Family Papers.
  London Family Papers.
  Archibald MacLaine Papers.
  Richard S. Mason Papers.
  George W. Mordecai Papers.
  Mordecai Family Papers.
  Murdock-Wright Papers.
  James H. Otey Papers.
  David Outlaw Papers.
  Pettigrew Family Papers.
  Polk-Badger-McGehee Papers.
  Leonidas Polk Papers.
  Thomas Ruffin Papers.
  Ruffin-Roulhac-Hamilton Papers.
  Wheat-Shober Papers.

180

Wright and Green Family Papers.
University of North Carolina Archives, University of North Carolina Library, Chapel Hill, North Carolina.
Dialectic Society. Papers, Addresses, and Debates.
University of North Carolina Papers.
Minutes of the Board of Trustees of the University of North Carolina at Chapel Hill.
University of the South Archives, Sewanee, Tennessee.
Leonidas Polk Papers.

B. Church Records
Calvary Episcopal, Wadesboro, Parish Register.
Chapel of the Cross Episcopal, Chapel Hill, Parish Register.
Christ Church Episcopal, Elizabeth City, Parish Register.
Christ's Church Episcopal, Newbern, Parish Register.
Church of the Saviour Episcopal, Jackson, Parish Register.
Edenton Methodist Church Record Book.
Emmanuel Episcopal, Warrenton, Parish Register.
First Presbyterian Church of Fayetteville, Session Records.
Grace Episcopal, Plymouth, Parish Register.
Hillsborough Presbyterian, Church Register and Session Records.
Journals of the Proceedings of the Annual Conventions of the Protestant Episcopal Church in the State of North Carolina, 1817–1860.
Minutes of the Synod of the Carolinas, Presbyterian Church, 1794.
St. James's Episcopal, Wilmington, Parish Register.
St. John's Episcopal, Fayetteville, Parish Register.
St. Mark's Episcopal, Halifax, Parish Register.
St. Matthew's Episcopal, Hillsboro, Parish Register.
St. Paul's Episcopal, Beaufort, Parish Register.
St. Paul's Episcopal, Edenton, Parish Register, Vestry Book, and Restoration Documents.
St. Paul's Episcopal, Greenville, Parish Register.
St. Peter's Episcopal, Washington, Parish Register.
St. Stephen's Episcopal, Goldsboro, Parish Register.
Trinity Episcopal, Scotland Neck, Parish Register.

C. Public Records
North Carolina General Assembly. Session Records, 1785–1825. Petitions, bills, and acts dealing with local churches and academies.
North Carolina wills, miscellaneous.

D. Newspapers
Church Intelligencer (Raleigh, North Carolina, Episcopal).
Edenton Gazette.

Raleigh Minerva.

Raleigh Register.

Southern Churchman (Alexandria, Virginia, Episcopal).

Wilmington Gazette.

E. Published Materials

American Colonizátíòn Society. *Fifth Annual Report of the American Society for Colonizing the Free People of Colour of the United States, With an Appendix.* Washington, D.C.: James C. Dunn, 1822.

American Colonization Society. *Third Annual Report of the American Society for Colonizing the Free People of Colour of the United States, With an Appendix.* Washington, D.C.: Davis and Force, 1820.

Asbury, Francis. *Francis Asbury in North Carolina: The North Carolina Portions of "The Journal of Francis Asbury."* Nashville: Parthenon Press, 1964.

Atkinson, Thomas. *Confirmation: A Sermon, Preached in Christ Church, Newbern, N.C. in 1869.* n.p.: n.d.

————. *Primary Charge of the Rt. Rev. Thomas Atkinson, Bishop of North Carolina, To the Clergy, Delivered at the Convention at Warrenton, May, 1855.* Fayetteville, N.C.: Edward J. Hale & Son, 1855.

[Badger, George E.] *An Examination of the Doctrine Declared and the Powers Claimed by the Right Reverend Bishop Ives, in a Pastoral Letter to the Clergy and Laity of His Diocese. By a Lay Member of the Protestant Episcopal Church in North Carolina.* Philadelphia: H. Hooker, 1849.

[Badger, George E.] *Notes Upon Dr. Freeman's Appendix To The Documents Connected With His Resignation as Rector of Christ's Church Raleigh, By One of the Vestry.* n.p.: n.d.

Bain, William T. *Letters and Meditations on Religious and Other Subjects.* Raleigh: Office of the Raleigh Register, 1839.

Battle, Kemp P., ed. *James Sprunt Historical Monograph No. 4: Letters and Documents Relating to the Early History of the Lower Cape Fear.* Chapel Hill: University of North Carolina, 1903.

————. *Memories of an Old-Time Tar Heel.* Chapel Hill: University of North Carolina Press, 1945.

Bryan, John H. *An Oration Delivered at Chapel Hill, on Wednesday, the 23d June, 1830; The day preceding Commencement, at the University of North Carolina; According to the Annual Appointment of the Two Literary Societies Belonging to the University.* Newbern, N.C.: John I. Pasteur, 1830.

Bryan, Mary Norcott, *Echoes from the Past.* Newbern, 1921.

————. *A Grandmother's Recollection of Dixie.* Newbern, N.C.: n.d.

Selected Bibliography

Cheshire, Joseph Blount, Jr., comp. *The Early Conventions: Held at Tarborough, Anno Domini, 1790, 1793, and 1794: The First Effort to Organize the Church in North Carolina.* Raleigh: Spirit of the Age Press, 1882.

————. *Nonnulla: Memories, Stories, Traditions, More or Less Authentic.* Chapel Hill: University of North Carolina Press, 1930.

Christ's Church Episcopal, Newbern, Sunday School. *Constitution and By-Laws of the Prot. Episcopal Sunday School, of Christ Church, Newbern: Established January 16th, 1829.* n.p.: [ca.1829].

Christ's Church Episcopal, Raleigh, Vestry. *At a special meeting of the Vestry of Christ's Church Raleigh, held on the 18th day of June 1840.* n.p.: n.d.

Clark, Walter, ed. *The State Records of North Carolina.* 16 vols. numbered 11–26. Winston: State of North Carolina, 1895–1907.

The Communicant's Manual; Containing The Order For The Administration of The Holy Communion With Suitable Prayers and Ejaculations Taken From A Companion For The Alter By The Late Bishop Hobart, of New York. New York: Swords, Stanford and Co., 1839.

Connor, R. D. W., comp. *A Documentary History of the University of North Carolina.* 2 vols. Chapel Hill: University of North Carolina Press, 1953.

Controversy between Gen. Richard D. Spaight and John Stanley, esq., to which is annexed an abstract from a funeral discourse, intended to have been delivered by the Rev. Thomas P. Irving on the death of the former. Newbern, N.C.: John S. Pasteur, 1802.

Coon, Charles L., comp. *North Carolina Schools and Academies, 1790–1840.* Raleigh: State of North Carolina, 1915.

Empie, Adam, D. D. *Sermons on Various Subjects, Written and Preached at Different Places and Times During His Public Ministry of Forty-Four Years.* New York: Dana and Company, Publishers, 1856.

Episcopal School of North Carolina. *An Address of the Trustees of the Episcopal School of North Carolina to the Public.* Raleigh: Thomas J. Lemay, 1836.

Raleigh. Raleigh: Joseph Gales & Son, 1834.

————. *Report on the State of the Episcopal School of North Carolina, November 1835.* Raleigh: J. Gales & Son, 1835.

[Freeman, George W.] *An Appendix To the Documents Printed By the Vestry, Connected with the Resignation of the Rector of Christ Church, Raleigh, Aug. 22, 1840.* n.p.: n.d.

————. *The Rights and Duties of Slaveholders: Two Discourses Delivered on Sunday, November 27, 1836, in Christ Church, Raleigh, North Carolina.* Raleigh: J. Gales & Son, 1836.

183

[Freeman, George W. and Ives, Levi S.] *Prospectus of the Episcopal School of North-Carolina Near the City of Raleigh.* Raleigh: Joseph Gales & Son, 1834.

General Protestant Episcopal Sunday School Union. *Twenty-first Annual Report of the Executive Committee; Read at a Meeting of the Board of Managers, Held June 23, 1847.* New York: Daniel Dana, Jr., Agent, 1847.

Hamilton, J. G. de Roulhac. *The Papers of Thomas Ruffin.* 4 vols. Raleigh: North Carolina Historical Commission, 1918.

[Hawks, Francis L.] *Auricular Confession in the Protestant Episcopal Church; Considered in a Series of Letters Addressed to a Friend in North Carolina.* New York: Putnam, 1850.

Higginbotham, Don, ed. *The Papers of James Iredell, 1767–1777.* 2 vols. Raleigh: Division of Archives and History, Department of Cultural Resources, 1976.

Hooper, Rev. William, *The Happy Choice: A Sermon Occasioned by the Death of Mrs. Mallett, Wife of Peter Mallett, Esq. of Fayetteville, N.C.; Who Died March 1st, 1824.* Philadelphia: W. W. Woodward, 1824.

Ives, L. S. *The Duties Now Especially Called For, to Preserve the Truth of the Church: A Charge to the Clergy of the Diocese of North Carolina, Delivered in Christ Church, New Bern, on the Fifth Sunday after Easter, May 8, 1836.* Raleigh: J. Gales and Son, 1836.

———. *Humility, a Ministerial Qualification: An Address to the Students of the General Theological Seminary of the Protestant Episcopal Church in the United States. Delivered at the Seventeenth Annual Commencement, in St. Peter's Church, New York, June 28, 1840.* New York: Swords, Stanford, and Co., 1840.

———. *A Pastoral Letter Addressed to the Clergy and Laity of His Diocese.* New York: Stanford and Swords, 1849.

Jacobs, Harriet A. *Incidents in the Life of a Slave Girl.* Edited by Jean Fagan Yellin. Cambridge: Harvard University Press, 1987.

Jenkins, James. *Experiences, Labours, and Sufferings of Rev. James Jenkins, of the South Carolina Conference.* n.p.: 1842.

Kellam, Ida Brooks, and McKoy, Elizabeth Francenia, eds. *St. James Church, Wilmington, North Carolina: Historical Records, 1737–1852.* Wilmington, N.C.: Mimeographed by Ida B. Kellam, 1965.

Lemmon, Sarah McCulloh, ed. *The Pettigrew Papers*, vol. 1. Raleigh: State Department of Archives and History, 1971.

Mallett, Edward Jones. *Memoirs of Edward Jones Mallett.* n.p.: [ca.1885].

[Mason, Mary.] *Her Church and Her Mother: A Story of Filial Piety.* New York: General Protestant Episcopal Sunday School Union and Church Book Society, 1860.

184

————. *A Wreath from the Woods of Carolina*. New York: General Protestant Episcopal Sunday School Union and Church Book Society, 1859.

[Mason, Richard Sharpe.] *A Letter to the Bishop of North Carolina on the Subject of His Late Pastoral on the Salisbury Convention: By the Chairman of the Committee on the State of the Church*. New York: Stanford and Swords, 1850.

McCorkle, Samuel E. *Four Discourses on the general first Principles of Deism and Revelation contrasted; delivered in Salisbury, and Thyatira, on different days in April & May, 1797*. Salisbury, N.C.: Francis Coupee, & John M. Slump, 1798.

McRee, Griffith J., ed. *Life and Correspondences of James Iredell, One of the Associate Justices of the Supreme Court of the United States*. 2 vols. New York: D. Appleton and Co., 1858.

Meares, Catherine DeRosset. *Annals of the DeRosset Family: Hugenot Immigrants to the Province of North Carolina Early in the Eighteenth Century*. Columbia, S.C.: The R. L. Bryan Company, n.d.

Miller, Robert Johnston. "The Robert J. Miller Letters, 1813–1831." Edited by D. L. Corbitt. *North Carolina Historical Review* 25 (October 1948): 483–521.

More, Hannah, *The Complete Works of Hannah More*. New York: Harper & Brothers, 1835.

Morgan, David T., ed. *The John Gray Blount Papers*, vol. 4. Raleigh: North Carolina Department of Cultural Resources, Division of Archives and History, 1982.

Newsome, A. R. "Twelve Counties in 1810–1811." *North Carolina Historical Review* 6 (January 1929): 67–99.

North Carolina Bible Society. *Report of the North-Carolina Bible Society, December 1815*. n.p.: n.d.

North Carolina Tract Society. *The Organization of the North-Carolina Branch of the American Tract Society at Raleigh, March, 6, 1828, with a Circular Address and List of Publications of the Society*. Raleigh: Joseph Gales, 1828.

Orme, William, *Memoirs, Including Letters, and Select Remains of John Urquart, Late of the University of St. Andrew's. With a Prefatory Notice and Recommendation, By Alexander Duff, D.D., LL.D.* Philadelphia: Presbyterian Board of Education, 1855.

Patillo, Henry. *Sermons, &c.* Wilmington, N.C.: James Adams, 1788.

Quincy, Josiah. *Memoir of the Life of Josiah Quincy Jun. of Massachusetts*. Boston: Cummings, Hilliard, & Co., 1825.

Raleigh Female Religious Tract Society. *The Fourth Annual Report of the Raleigh Female Religious Tract Society*. Raleigh, N.C.: Joseph Gales, 1820.

185

——— . *The Second Annual Report of the Raleigh Female Religious Tract Society. Anno Domini, 1818, Etc.* Raleigh: Joseph Gales, 1818.

Ravenscroft, John Stark. *The Doctrine of the Church Vindicated from the Misrepresentations of Dr. John Rice; and the Integrity of Revealed Religion Defended Against the "No Comment Principle" of Promiscuous Bible Societies.* Raleigh: Joseph Gales and Sons, 1826.

——— . *A Sermon Delivered on the Anniversary of the Female Benevolent Society, Raleigh, On Sunday the 25th of July, 1824.* Raleigh: J. Gales & Son, 1824.

——— . *The Works of the Right Reverend John Stark Ravenscroft, D.D.* 2 Vols. Edited by Jonathan M. Wainright. New York: Protestant Episcopal Press, 1830.

Saunders, William L., ed., *The Colonial Records of North Carolina.* 10 vols. Raleigh: State of North Carolina, 1886–90.

Schaw, Janet, *Journal of a Lady of Quality: Being the Narrative of a Journey from Scotland to the West Indies, North Carolina, and Portugal, in the Years 1774–1776.* Edited by Evangeline Walker Andrews with the collaboration of Charles McLean Andrews. New Haven: Yale University Press, 1921.

[Smedes, Albert.] *Hints on the Rite of Confirmation Addressed To the Pupils of St. Mary's School.* Raleigh: n.p., 1857.

——— . *Manual of St. Mary's School, Raleigh, N.C.* Raleigh: Carolina Cultivator Office, 1857.

Sprunt, James. *Windows on the Word.* Raleigh: n.p., 1958.

[Strange, Robert.] *Eoneguski, or, the Cherokee Chief: A Tale of Past Wars. By an American.* Washington: Franck Taylor, 1839.

Swift, Joseph Gardner. *The Memoirs of Gen. Joseph Gardner Swift, LL.D., U.S.A., First Graduate of the United States Military Academy, West Point, Chief Engineer, U.S.A. From 1812 to 1818.* n.p.: Privately Printed, 1890.

Travis, Joseph. *Autobiography of the Rev. Joseph Travis, A.M.* Nashville: E. Stevenson & F. A. Owens, Agents, 1855.

Turner, Jesse. *Women Ought to Labour in the Church of God; and Men Ought to Help Them; A Sermon Preached for the Benefit of the Female Tract Society, in Fayetteville, on Sabbath, 28th December, 1817.* Fayetteville, N.C.: Duncan Black, 1818.

Wagstaff, H. M., ed. *The Harrington Letters.* Chapel Hill: n.p., 1914.

White, William, D. D. *Memoirs of the Protestant Episcopal Church in the United States of America.* 3d ed. Philadelphia: S. Potter, 1820. New York: Swords, Stanford, and Co., 1836.

Wightman, William M., D. D. *Life of William Capers, D. D., One of the Bishops of the Methodist Episcopal Church, South; Including an Autobiography.* Nashville: Southern Methodist Publishing House, 1859.

Wilmington Bible Society. *Constitution of the Bible Society of Wilmington, North Carolina.* n.p.: [ca.1817].

II. Secondary Sources

Addison, James Thayer. *The Episcopal Church in the United States: 1789–1931.* New York: Charles Scribner's Sons, 1951.

Addleshaw, G. W. O., and Etchells, Frederick. *The Architectural Setting of Anglican Worship.* 2d ed. London: Faber and Faber, 1950.

Ahlstrom, Sydney E. *A Religious History of the American People.* New Haven: Yale University Press, 1972.

Albright, Raymond W. *A History of the Protestant Episcopal Church.* New York: Macmillan, 1964.

Balda, Wesley. "Ecclesiastics and Enthusiasts: The Evangelical Emergence in England, 1760–1800." *Historical Magazine of the Protestant Episcopal Church* 49 (September 1980): 221–32.

Banner, Lois W. "Religious Benevolence as Social Control: A Critique of An Interpretation." *Journal of American History* 60 (June 1973): 23–41.

Battle, Kemp P. *History of the University of North Carolina.* 2 vols. Raleigh: for the Author by Edwards & Broughton Printing Company, 1907.

Berger, Peter L. *The Sacred Canopy: Elements of a Sociological Theory of Religion.* Garden City: Doubleday and Company, Anchor Books, 1969.

Billington, Ray A. *The Protestant Crusade, 1800–1860: A Study of the Origins of American Nativism.* New York: Macmillan, 1938.

Blanks, William Davidson. "Corrective Church Discipline in the Presbyterian Churches of the Nineteenth-Century South." *Journal of Presbyterian History* 44 (June 1966): 89–105.

———. "Ideal and Practice; A Study of the Conception of the Christian Life Prevailing in the Presbyterian Churches of the South during the Nineteenth Century." Th.D. diss., Union Theological Seminary in Virginia, 1960.

Bleser, Carol, ed. *In Joy and in Sorrow: Women, Family, and Marriage in the Victorian South.* New York: Oxford University Press, 1991.

Bodo, John R. *The Protestant Clergy and Public Issues, 1812–1848.* Princeton: Princeton University Press, 1954.

Boles, John B. *The Great Revival, 1787–1805: The Origins of the Southern Evangelical Mind.* Lexington: University of Kentucky Press, 1972.

Boylan, Anne M. *Sunday School: The Formation of an American Institution.* New Haven: Yale University Press, 1988.

Branca, Patricia. *Silent Sisterhood. Middle Class Women in the Victorian Home.* Pittsburg: Carnegie-Mellon University Press, 1975.

187

Breen, T. H. "Horses and Gentlemen: The Cultural Significance of Gambling Among the Gentry of Virginia." *William and Mary Quarterly*, 3d ser., 34 (April 1977): 239–57.

Brewer, Clifton Hartwell. *A History of Religious Education in the Episcopal Church to 1835*. New York: Arno Press & the New York Times, 1969.

Brown, Lawrence L. "Richard Channing Moore and the Revival of the Southern Church. *Historical Magazine of the Protestant Episcopal Church* 35 (March 1966): 3–64.

Bruce, Dickson D., Jr. *And They All Sang Hallelujah: Plain-Folk Camp-Meeting Religion, 1800–1845*. Knoxville: University of Tennessee Press, 1974.

———. *Violence and Culture in the Antebellum South*. Austin: University of Texas Press, 1979.

Burr, Nelson R. *A Critical Bibliography of Religion in America*. Princeton: Princeton University Press, 1961.

———. "New Eden and New Babylon: Religious Thought of American Authors: An Annotated Bibliography, VII: Southern Religious Literature." *Historical Magazine of the Protestant Episcopal Church* 55 (September 1986): 213–48.

Butts, R. Freeman, and Cremin, Lawrence A. *A History of Education in American Culture*. New York: Holt, Rinehart and Winston, 1953.

Calhoon, Robert M., *Evangelicals and Conservatives in the Early South*. Columbia: University of South Carolina Press, 1988.

———. *Religion and the American Revolution in North Carolina*. Raleigh: North Carolina Department of Cultural Resources, Division of Archives and History, 1976.

Cantrell, David Gregg. "The Limits of Southern Dissent: The Lives of Kenneth Rayner and John B. Rayner." 2 vols. Ph.D. diss., Texas A&M University, 1988.

Cardwell, Guy A. "The Duel in the Old South: Crux of a Concept." *South Atlantic Quarterly* 66 (1967): 50–69.

Carraway, Gertrude S. *Crown of Life: History of Christ Church, New Bern, N.C. 1715–1940*. New Bern: Owen G. Dunn, 1940.

Carwardine, Richard. "The Second Great Awakening in the Urban Centers: An Examination of Methodism and the 'New Measures'." *Journal of American History* 59 (September 1972): 327–40.

Censor, Jane Turner. *North Carolina Planters and Their Children, 1800–1860*. Baton Rouge: Louisiana State University Press, 1984.

Cheshire, Joseph Blount, ed. *Sketches of Church History in North Carolina: Addresses and Papers by Clergymen and Laymen of the Diocese of North and East Carolina: Prepared for the Joint Centennial*

Convention at Tarborough, May 1890. Wilmington, N.C.: William L. DeRosset Pub., 1892.

Chorley, Edward Clowes. *Men and Movements in the American Episcopal Church.* New York: Charles Scribner's Sons, 1950.

Clinton, Catherine. *The Plantation Mistress: Woman's World in the Old South.* New York: Pantheon Books, 1982.

Conkin, Paul. "The Church Establishment in North Carolina, 1765–1776." *North Carolina Historical Review* 32 (January 1955): 1–30.

Cooper, William J., and Terrell, Thomas E. *The American South,* 2 vols. New York: McGraw-Hill, 1991.

Cott, Nancy F. *The Bonds of Womanhood: "Woman's Sphere" in New England, 1780–1835.* New Haven: Yale University Press, 1977.

Coulter, E. Merton. *College Life in the Old South.* Athens: University of Georgia Press, 1951, 1979.

Cyclopedia of Eminent and Representative of the Carolinas of the Nineteenth Century. 2 vols. Madison, Wis.: Brant and Fuller, 1892.

Davis, Richard Beale. *A Colonial Southern Bookshelf: Reading in the Eighteenth Century.* Athens: University of Georgia Press, 1979.

──── . *Intellectual Life in the Colonial South, 1585–1763.* 3 vols. Knoxville: University of Tennessee Press, 1978.

──── . *Intellectual Life in Jefferson's Virginia, 1790–1830.* Chapel Hill: University of North Carolina Press, 1964.

Degler, Carl N. *At Odds: Women and the Family in America from the Revolution to the Present.* New York: Oxford University Press, 1980.

De Mille, George E. *The Catholic Movement in the American Episcopal Church.* Philadelphia: Church Historical Society, 1941.

Dill, Alonzo Thomas, Jr., "Eighteenth Century New Bern. A History of the Town and Craven County, 1700–1800, Part 8, New Bern as Colonial Capital." *North Carolina Historical Review* 23 (April 1946): 495–535.

Douglas, Ann. *The Feminization of American Culture.* New York: Knopf, 1977.

Eaton, Clement. *Freedom of Thought in the Old South.* New York: Peter Smith, 1951.

──── . *The Growth of Southern Civilization.* New York: Harper Brothers, 1961.

──── . *A History of the Old South.* New York: Macmillan, 1949.

Elliot, Robert Neal, Jr. *The Raleigh Register, 1799–1863.* Chapel Hill: University of North Carolina Press, 1965.

Faust, Drew Gilpin. *A Sacred Circle: The Dilemma of the Intellectual in the Old South, 1840–1860.* Baltimore: Johns Hopkins University Press, 1977.

Faust, Drew Gilpin. *A Sacred Circle: The Dilemma of the Intellectual in the Old South, 1840–1860.* Baltimore: Johns Hopkins University Press, 1977.

Foster, Charles I. *An Errand of Mercy: The Evangelical United Front, 1790–1837.* Chapel Hill: University of North Carolina Press, 1954.

Fox-Genovese, Elizabeth. *Within the Plantation Household: Black and White Women of the Old South.* Chapel Hill: University of North Carolina Press, 1988.

Fox-Genovese, Elizabeth, and Genovese, Eugene D. "The Divine Sanction of Social Order: Religious Foundations of the Southern Slaveholders' World View." *Journal of the American Academy of Religion* 55 (Summer 1987): 211–26.

Franklin, John Hope. "Negro Episcopalians in Ante-Bellum North Carolina." *Historical Magazine of the Protestant Episcopal Church* (September 1944): 216–34.

Freeze, Gary, "Like a House Built Upon Sand: The Anglican Church and Establishment in North Carolina, 1765–1776." *Historical Magazine of the Protestant Episcopal Church* 48 (December 1979): 405–32.

Friedman, Jean. *The Enclosed Garden: Women and Community in the Evangelical South, 1830–1900.* Chapel Hill: University of North Carolina Press, 1985.

Gamble, Thomas. *Savannah Duels and Duellists, 1733–1877.* Savannah, Ga.: Review Publishing and Printing Company, 1972.

Gass, W. Conrad. "A Felicitous Life: Lucy Martin Battle, 1805–1874." *North Carolina Historical Review* 52 (1975): 367–93.

Genovese, Eugene D. *Roll, Jordan, Roll: The World the Slaves Made.* New York: Pantheon Books, 1972.

———. *The World the Slaveholders Made: Two Essays in Interpretation.* New York: Pantheon Books, 1969.

Genovese, Eugene D., and Fox-Genovese, Elizabeth. "The Religious Ideals of Southern Slave Society." *Georgia Historical Review* 70 (Spring 1986): 1–16.

Gill, Frederick C. *The Romantic Movement and Methodism: A Study of English Romanticism and the Evangelical Revival.* London: Epworth, 1937.

Grant, Daniel Lindsay, ed. *Alumni History of the University of North Carolina.* 2d ed. Durham: General Alumni Association of the University of North Carolina, 1924.

Grant, Minnie Spencer. "The American Colonization Society in North Carolina." Master's thesis, Duke University, 1930.

Green, Elna C. "Those Opposed: The Antisuffragists in North Carolina, 1900–1920 "*North Carolina Historical Review* 67 (July 1990): 315–330.

Green, The Rt. Rev. William Mercer. *Memoir of Rt. Rev. James Hervey Otey D.D., LL.D., The First Bishop of Tennessee.* New York: James Pott and Company, 1885.

Greven, Philip J., Jr. *The Protestant Temperament: Patterns of Child-Rearing, Religious Experience, and the Self in Early America.* New York: Knopf, 1977.

Gundersen, Joan R. "The Non-Institutional Church: The Religious Role of Women in Eighteenth-Century Virginia." *Historical Magazine of the Protestant Episcopal Church* 51 (December 1982): 347–58.

Hall, Bennett H. "Charles Pettigrew, First Bishop-Elect of the North Carolina Episcopal Church." *North Carolina Historical Review* 28 (January 1951): 15–46.

Handlin, Oscar, and Handlin, Mary. *Facing Life: Youth and the Family in American History.* Boston: Little, Brown, 1971.

Hartman, Mary S., and Banner, Lois, eds. *Clio's Consciousness Raised: New Perspectives on the History of Women.* New York: Octagon Books, 1976.

Hassler, William W. "The Religious Conversion of Gen. W. Dorsey Pender, C.S.A." *Historical Magazine of the Protestant Episcopal Church* 33 (June 1964): 171–78.

Hayden, J. Carleton. "Conversion and Control: Dilemma of Episcopalians in Providing for the Religious Instruction of Slaves, Charleston, South Carolina, 1845–1860." *Historical Magazine of the Protestant Episcopal Church* 40 (June 1971): 143–72.

Henshaw, J. P. K. *Memoir of the Life of the Rt. Rev. Richard Channing Moore, D.D., Bishop of the Protestant Episcopal Church in the Diocese of Virginia.* Philadelphia: W. Stavely, 1843.

Hill, Samuel S., ed. *Varieties of Southern Religious Experience.* Baton Rouge: Louisiana State University Press, 1988.

Himmelfarb, Gertrude. *Victorian Minds.* New York: Knopf, 1968.

Holifield, E. Brooks, *The Gentlemen Theologians: American Theology in Southern Culture, 1795–1860.* Durham, N.C.: Duke University Press, 1978.

Hood, R. E. "From Headstart to Deadstart: The Historical Basis for Black Indifference toward the Episcopal Church, 1800–1860." *Historical Magazine of the Protestant Episcopal Church* 51 (September 1982): 269–96.

Houghton, Walter E. *The Victorian Frame of Mind, 1830–1870.* New Haven: Published for Wesley College by Yale University Press, 1957.

Howe, Daniel Walker, *The Political Culture of the American Whigs.* Chicago: University of Chicago Press, 1979.

——, ed. *Victorian America.* Philadelphia: University of Pennsylvania Press, 1976.

Isaac, Rhys. *The Transformation of Virginia, 1740–1790.* Chapel Hill: University of North Carolina Press for the Institute of Early American History and Culture, 1982.

Jeffrey, Thomas E. *State Parties and National Politics: North Carolina, 1815–1861.* Athens: University of Georgia Press, 1989.

Jenkins, William Sumner. *Pro-Slavery Thought in the Old South.* Chapel Hill: University of North Carolina Press, 1935.

Johnson, Charles A. *The Frontier Camp Meeting: Religion's Harvest Time.* Dallas: Southern Methodist University Press, 1955.

Johnson, Guion Griffis. *Ante-Bellum North Carolina: A Social History.* Chapel Hill: University of North Carolina Press, 1937.

———. "The Camp Meeting in Ante-Bellum North Carolina." *North Carolina Historical Review* 10 (April 1933): 95–110.

———. "Recreational and Cultural Activities in the Ante-Bellum Town of North Carolina." *North Carolina Historical Review* 6 (January 1929): 17–37.

———. "Revival Movements in Ante-Bellum North Carolina." *North Carolina Historical Reivew* 10 (January 1933): 21–43.

Johnson, Paul E. *A Shopkeeper's Millenium: Society and Revivals in Rochester, New York, 1815–1837.* New York: Hill and Wang, 1978.

Jones, M. G. *Hannah More.* Cambridge: Cambridge University Press, 1952.

Kulikoff, Allan, *Tobacco and Slaves.* Chapel Hill: University of North Carolina Press, 1986.

Lane, Mills. *Architecture of the Old South: North Carolina.* Savannah, Ga.: Beehive Press, 1985.

Lears, T. J. Jackson, *No Place of Grace: Antimodernism and the Transformation of American Culture, 1880–1920.* New York: Pantheon Books, 1981.

Lee, Lawrence, *The Lower Cape Fear in Colonial Days.* Chapel Hill: University of North Carolina Press, 1965.

———. *The History of Brunswick County, North Carolina.* n.p.: Brunswick County American Revolution Bicentennial Committee, 1978.

Lefler, Hugh Talmadge. "Thomas Atkinson, Third Bishop of North Carolina." *Historical Magazine of the Protestant Episcopal Church* 17 (December 1948): 422–34.

Lefler, Hugh T., and Newsome, Albert. *North Carolina: The History of a Southern State.* 3d ed. Chapel Hill: University of North Carolina Press, 1973.

LeMahieu, D. L. *The Mind of William Paley: A Philosopher and His Age.* Lincoln: University of Nebraska Press, 1976.

192

Lemmon, Sarah McCulloh. "The Genesis of the Protestant Episcopal Diocese of North Carolina, 1701–1823." *North Carolina Historical Review* 28 (October 1951): 426–62.

———. *Parson Pettigrew of the "Old Church."* Chapel Hill: University of North Carolina Press, 1970.

Lewis, Henry W. "Horses and Horsemen in Northampton Before 1900." *North Carolina Historical Review* 51 (April 1974): 126–48.

Lewis, Jan. *The Pursuit of Happiness: Family and Values in Jefferson's Virginia.* Cambridge: Cambridge University Press, 1983.

Lines, Stiles Bailey. "Slaves and Churchmen: The Work of the Episcopal Church among Southern Negroes, 1830–1860." Ph.D. diss., Columbia University, 1960.

Lloyd, Pauline O., and Lloyd, Allen A. *History of the Churches of Hillsborough, N.C., ca. 1766–1962.* n.p.: n.d.

London, Lawrence Foushee, and Lemmon, Sarah McCulloh, eds. *The Episcopal Church in North Carolina, 1701–1959.* Raleigh: Episcopal Diocese of North Carolina, 1987.

Long, Ronald Wilson. "Religious Revivalism in the Carolinas and Georgia, 1740–1805." Ph.D. diss., University of Georgia, 1968.

Loveland, Anne C. *Southern Evangelicals and the Social Order, 1800–1860.* Baton Rouge: Louisiana State University Press, 1980.

Luraghi, Raimondo. *The Rise and Fall of the Plantation South.* New York: New Viewpoints, 1978.

Malone, Michael T. "The Episcopal School of North Carolina, 1832–1842." *North Carolina Historical Review* 49 (1972): 178–94.

———. "Levi Silliman Ives: Priest, Bishop, Tractarian, and Roman Catholic Convert." Ph.D. diss., Duke University, 1970.

Manross, William Wilson. "Episcopal Church and Reform." *Historical Magazine of the Protestant Episcopal Church* 12 (December 1943): 339–66.

———. *A History of the American Episcopal Church.* 2d ed. New York: Morehouse-Gorham, 1950.

Martin, Bernard. *John Newton: A Biography.* London: William Heinemann, 1950.

Mathews, Alice. *Society in Colonial North Carolina.* Zebulon, N.C.: Theo Davis Sons, Inc., 1976.

Mathews, Donald G. *Religion in the Old South.* Chicago: University of Chicago Press, 1977.

———. *Slavery and Methodism: A Chapter in American Morality, 1787–1845.* Princeton: Princeton University Press, 1965.

May, Henry F. *The Divided Heart: Essays on Protestantism and Enlightenment in America.* New York: Oxford University Press, 1991.

————. *The Enlightenment in America*. New York: Oxford University Press, 1976.

————. *Ideas, Faiths, and Feelings: Essays on American Intellectual and Religious History, 1952–1982*. New York: Oxford University Press, 1983.

————. *Religion and the Enlightenment in America*. New York: Oxford University Press, 1991.

McAllister, James L. "Architecture and Change in the Diocese of Virginia." *Historical Magazine of the Protestant Episcopal Church* 45 (September 1976): 297–324.

McClain, Frank M. "The Theology of Bishops Ravenscroft, Otey, and Green Concerning the Church, the Ministry, and the Sacraments." *Historical Magazine of the Protestant Episcopal Church* 33 (June 1964): 103–36.

McEachern, Leora Hiatt. *History of St. James Parish, 1729–1979*. Assisted by Bill Reaves. Wilmington, N.C.: n.p., 1985.

McMillen, Sally G. *Southern Women: Black and White in the Old South*. Arlington Heights, Ill.: Harlan Davidson, Inc., 1992.

Mead, Sidney E. *The Lively Experiment: The Shaping of Christianity in America*. New York: Harper and Row, Publishers, 1965.

Miller, Perry. *The Life of the Mind in America: From the Revolution to the Civil War*. New York: Harcourt, Brace & World, 1965.

Miyakawa, T. Scott. *Protestants and Pioneers: Individualism and Conformity on the American Frontier*. Chicago: University of Chicago Press, 1964.

Morais, Herbert. *Deism in Eighteenth Century America*. New York: Russell & Russell, 1934, 1960.

Morehouse, Clifford P. "Origins of the Episcopal Church Press From Colonial Days to 1840." *Historical Magazine of the Protestant Episcopal Church* (September 1942): 201–316.

Morgan, David T., Jr. "The Great Awakening in North Carolina, 1740–1775: The Baptist Phase." *North Carolina Historical Review* 45 (Summer 1968): 264–83.

Morgan, Edmund S. *Virginians at Home: Family Life in the Eighteenth Century*. Williamsburg: Colonial Williamsburg, 1952.

Mullin, Robert Bruce. *Episcopal Vision/American Reality: High Church Theology and Social Thought in Evangelical America*. New Haven: Yale University Press, 1986.

Murray, Elizabeth Reid. *Wake: Capitol County of North Carolina*. Raleigh: Capitol County Publishing Co., 1983.

Nash, Gary B. "The American Clergy and the French Revolution." *William and Mary Quarterly*, 3d ser., 22 (July 1965): 392–412.

Noll, Mark A., ed. *Religion and American Politics: From the Colonial Period to the 1980s.* New York: Oxford University Press, 1990.

Oakes, James. *The Ruling Race: A History of American Slaveholders.* New York: Knopf, 1982. *Slaveholders.* New York: Alfred A Knopf, 1982.

———. *Slavery and Freedom: An Interpretation of the Old South.* New York: Knopf, 1990.

Ownby, Ted. *Subduing Satan: Religion, Recreation, and Manhood in the Rural South, 1865–1920.* Chapel Hill: University of North Carolina Press, 1990.

Padgett, James A., ed. "The Life of Alfred Mordecai." *North Carolina Historical Review* 22 (January 1945): 58–108.

Page, Jesse. *Henry Martyn His Life and Labours: Cambridge-India-Persia.* London: S. W. Partridge & Co., n.d.

Parks, Joseph H. *General Leonidas Polk, C.S.A.: The Fighting Bishop.* Baton Rouge: Louisiana State University Press, 1962.

Pope, Christie Farnum. "Preparation for Pedestals: North Carolina Antebellum Female Seminaries." Ph.D. diss., University of Chicago, 1977.

Powell, William S., ed., *Dictionary of North Carolina Biography.* Multi-volume series. Chapel Hill: The University of North Carolina Press, 1979–.

Price, William S., Jr. " 'Men of Good Estates': Wealth Among North Carolina's Royal Councillors." *North Carolina Historical Review* 49 (January 1972): 72–82.

Rankin, Richard. "Benevolence and Progress: Motives for Leadership of North Carolina's Evangelical United Front, 1814–1837." Master's thesis, University of North Carolina at Chapel Hill, 1985.

———. "Bishop Levi S. Ives and High Church Reform in North Carolina: Tractarianism as an Instrument to Elevate Clerical and Lay Piety." *Anglican and Episcopal History* 57 (September 1988): 298–319.

———. " 'Musquetoe' Bites: Caricatures of Lower Cape Fear Whigs and Tories on the Eve of the American Revolution." *North Carolina Historical Review* 65 (April 1988): 173–207.

Reily, Timothy. "Genteel Reform Versus Southern Allegiance: Episcopalian Dilemma in Old New Orleans." *Historical Magazine of the Protestant Episcopal Church* 44 (December 1975): 437–50.

Robinson, Blackwell P. *William R. Davie.* Chapel Hill: University of North Carolina Press, 1957.

———. "Willie Jones of Halifax." *North Carolina Historical Review* 18 (January 1941): 1–26.

Rumple, Jethro. *The History of Presbyterianism in North Carolina. Reprinted from the North Carolina Presbyterian, 1878–1887.* Richmond: The Library of Union Theological Seminary in Virginia, 1966.

Ryan, Mary P. *Cradle of the Middle Class: The Family in Oneida County, New York, 1790–1815.* New York: Cambridge University Press, 1981.

Salley, Katherine Batts, ed. *Life at St. Mary's.* Chapel Hill: University of North Carolina Press, 1942.

Seitz, Don C. *Famous American Duels: With Some Account of the Causes that Led up to Them and the Men Engaged.* Freeport, N.Y.: Book for Libraries Press, Inc., 1929, 1961.

Scott, Anne Firor. *The Southern Lady: From Pedastal to Politics, 1830–1890.* Chicago: University of Chicago Press, 1970.

Simkins, Francis Butler. *A History of the South.* New York: Knopf, 1963.

Smith, Cortland, Victor. "Church Organization as an Agency of Social Control: Church Discipline in North Carolina, 1800–1860." Ph.D. diss., University of North Carolina at Chapel Hill, 1966.

Smith, Daniel Blake. *Inside the Great House: Planter Life in Eighteenth-Century Chesapeake Society.* Ithaca: Cornell University Press, 1980.

Smith, H. Shelton. *In His Image, But . . . Racism in Southern Religion, 1780–1910.* Durham, N.C.: Duke University Press, 1972.

Smith, Timothy L. *Revivalism and Social Reform: American Protestantism on the Eve of the Civil War.* New York: Harper and Row, 1957.

Sonne, Niels Henry. *Liberal Kentucky, 1780–1828.* New York: Columbia University Press, 1939.

Spruill, Julia Cherry. *Women's Life and Work in the Southern Colonies.* Chapel Hill: University of North Carolina Press, 1938.

Stoops, Martha. *The Heritage: The Education of Women at St. Mary's College, Raleigh, North Carolina, 1842–1982.* Raleigh: St. Mary's College, 1984.

Stowe, Steven M. *Intimacy and Power in the Old South: Ritual in the Lives of the Planters.* Baltimore: Johns Hopkins University Press, 1987.

Stroupe, Henry. *The Religious Press in the South Atlantic States, 1802–1865: An Annotated Bibliography with Historical Introduction and Notes.* Durham, N.C.: Duke University Press, 1956.

Sykes, Norman. "The Theology of Divine Benevolence." *Historical Magazine of the Protestant Episcopal Church* 16 (September 1947): 422–34.

Thomas, John L. "Romantic Reform in America, 1815–1865." *American Quarterly* 17 (Winter 1965): 656–81.

Tise, Larry E. *Proslavery: A History of the Defense of Slavery in America, 1701–1840.* Athens: University of Georgia Press, 1987.

Tyler, Lyon G. "God and Mr. Petigru: Episcopal Attitudes Toward Faith and Doctrine in Antebellum South Carolina." *Historical Magazine of the Protestant Episcopal Church* 52 (September 1983): 229–43.

Tyng, Stephen H. *Memoir of the Rev. Gregory T. Bedell.* Philadelphia: Henry Perkins, 1836.

Up From Independence: The Episcopal Church in Virginia. Orange, Va.: Interdiocesan Bicentennial Committee of the Virginias, 1976.

Vass, Rev. L. C. *History of the Presbyterian Church in New Bern, N.C.* Richmond: Whittet & Shepperson, 1886.

Walser, Richard. "Senator Strange's Indian Novel." *North Carolina Historical Review* 26 (January 1949): 1–27.

——— . *Literary North Carolina: A Historical Survey, Revised and Enlarged.* Assisted by E. T. Malone, Jr. Raleigh: Division of Archives and History, North Carolina Department of Cultural Resources, 1986.

Wand, J. W. C. *Anglicanism in History and Today.* New York: Thomas Nelson and Sons, 1962.

Waterman, Thomas Tileston. *The Early Architecture of North Carolina.* Chapel Hill: University of North Carolina Press, 1941.

Wheeler, John H. *Reminiscences and Memoirs of North Carolina and Eminent North Carolinians.* Columbus, Ohio: Columbus Print Works, 1884; Baltimore: Genealogical Publishing Company, 1966.

Whitener, Daniel Jay. *Prohibition in North Carolina, 1715–1945.* Chapel Hill: University of North Carolina Press, 1945.

Williams, Jack Kenny. "The Code of Honor in Ante-Bellum South Carolina." *South Carolina Historical Magazine* 54 (July 1953): 113–28.

Woodmason, Charles. *The Carolina Backcountry on the Eve of the American Revolution.* Edited and with an Introduction by Richard J. Hooker. Chapel Hill: University of North Carolina Press, 1953.

Wyatt-Brown, Bertram. "The Ideal Typology and Antebellum Southern History: A Testing of a New Approach." *Societas* 5 (Winter 1975): 1–29.

——— . *Southern Honor: Ethics and Behavior in the Old South.* New York: Oxford University Press, 1982.

Zabrinskie, Alexander C., ed. *Anglican Evangelicalism.* Philadelphia: Church Historical Society, 1943.

Index